Michigan Trees

**A HANDBOOK
OF THE NATIVE AND MOST IMPORTANT
INTRODUCED SPECIES**

By

CHARLES HERBERT OTIS

with an introduction by

GEORGE PLUMER BURNS

THE UNIVERSITY OF MICHIGAN PRESS
ANN ARBOR

Nineteenth printing 1972
Copyright © by The University of Michigan 1931
All rights reserved
Revised edition.
ISBN 0-472-08708-8
Published in the United States of America by
The University of Michigan Press
in Don Mills, Canada, by Longmans Canada Limited
Manufactured in the United States of America

CONTENTS

MICHIGAN

Showing Only Locations Mentioned in the Manual

PREFACE

Since the original appearance of "Michigan Trees" in 1915, many editions have been printed and distributed. These have been edited with much care, but aside from some small revisions of the text from time to time, no extensive changes have been made.

In the preparation of the present edition the author has departed somewhat from previous policy and has made the first radical revision of the handbook. With the increasing interest in planting for ornamental and practical purposes and the more extensive use of introduced species, a manual devoted largely to the native trees is too narrow in scope to be of the greatest use. To meet the situation, the index has been greatly enlarged to include briefer descriptions and notes on the important exotics and less familiar species. The arbitrary definition of a tree automatically excludes many kinds of woody plants which are large shrubs with us, but which may become small trees in more favorable situations. Some of these common borderline species are here introduced for the first time, accompanied by a simple key, under the title "Additional Notes on the Species." The most important change, and one which it is hoped will extend the usefulness of the handbook, is the addition of a section devoted to the structure and identification of our common woods. Finally, numerous lesser changes have been made throughout the text.

In the preparation of the first edition, grateful acknowledgment has been made to Miss Sarah Phelps, who did most of the inking in and gave life to the author's pencil-drawings; to Dr. J. H. Ehlers for assistance in the preparation of many of the drawings; to Dr. Henri Hus for assistance in reading the proof; to Professor Frederick C. Newcombe and to Professor Ernst Bessey for the loan of sheets from the herbariums of the University of Michigan and of Michigan State University; and especially to Professor George P. Burns, from whose inspiration the book had its inception and under whose direction the work progressed to completion. In the preparation of this edition, further acknowledgment is made to the University of Vermont and

Agricultural Experiment Station for permission to make liberal use of the illustrations and text from Bulletin 194: The Trees of Vermont, by G. P. Burns and C. H. Otis, especially the section dealing with the structure and identification of woods, and in a few instances from other parts of this bulletin. Not only has the original "Key to the Woods of Vermont" been revised, but it has been amplified by the incorporation of additional woods. The author is grateful also to the Forest Products Laboratory, Madison, Wisconsin, for the loan of a number of slides of wood sections, used in the preparation of some of the drawings.

CHARLES H. OTIS

INTRODUCTION

The idea of a handbook on Michigan trees was first suggested by Professor Volney M. Spalding. It was thought that a work devoted entirely to the study of certain phases of tree life in Michigan would stimulate interest in the study of our trees, and influence many more people to associate themselves with the growing number of tree lovers and with the supporters of the movement for better forest conditions in the state.

The distinctive feature of the handbook lies in its keys. The keys commonly published are based upon characters which are present but a short time during the year, or which can be used only by advanced students of botany. The present work has two keys. One is based upon characters which are present all summer; the other uses the winter characters as a basis for identification. By the use of the keys any person should be able to name and learn the characteristics of the trees of Michigan at any time of the year. These keys should prove of special value to our students in the high schools, to members of nature study clubs, and to the students in forestry schools.

The drawings have been made from living or herbarium material and are original. They are accurately drawn to a scale, which is given in each case. In their preparation the author has endeavored to call attention to the salient characters. In the drawings of buds and twigs certain points, bundle-scars, etc., have been emphasized more than is natural. In the descriptions the attempt has been made to bring out those points of similarity and contrast which are most useful for identification.

As this work was not prepared especially for technical students of botany, the author thought best to use as few technical terms as possible in the descriptions. In some cases it was impossible to avoid such terms, but with the help of the glossary the meaning can be easily understood. Any person desiring to get a more complete knowledge of trees should consult one of the larger manuals. The arrangement used for the illustration and discussion of each single tree makes it possible for the student to compare the drawings with the description without turning a page.

George Plumer Burns

HOW TO STUDY THE TREES

People are everywhere associated with trees. Trees give cooling shade in our parks and dooryards and along our highways; they lend their beauty to the landscape and relieve it of monotony; they yield many kinds of fruits, some of which furnish man and the animals of the forest with food; and they produce vast quantities of lumber for a multitude of uses. It is important, then, that every person, whether in the schools or beyond school age, should become acquainted with our trees. Most people know a few of our commonest trees, but are ignorant of the great number of various kinds about them. Some persons who may have wished to learn more have been hindered for lack of a teacher, and others have been dismayed by the very multitude of manuals to which they have had access.

In beginning a study of the trees the student should be careful to confine himself to well-established facts. Once started he should proceed slowly, assimilating each new discovery before seeking another. He should begin with the trees nearest home, and, as he gradually grows to know these in all their aspects, should extend his trips afield. Not only should he be able to name the trees when they are fully clothed in their summer dress, but he should know as readily these same trees when the leaves have fallen and only the bare branches stand silhouetted against the sky. Then, and only then, will he derive the utmost satisfaction from his efforts.

The characters which are used in studying the trees are habit, leaves, flowers, fruit, buds, bark, distribution and habitat. These will be discussed briefly in the next few pages, the same order that is used in the detailed descriptions of species being maintained in the present discussion. A few drawings also will be added to make certain points clear and to show comparative forms.

NAME.—Every tree has one or several common names and a scientific or Latin name. Some of these common names are merely local, while others have a more extended use. Some few names apply to totally different species. Thus, Cottonwood in Michigan is *Populus deltoides,* in Idaho and Colorado *Populus angustifolia,* in California *Populus fremontii* and in Kentucky *Tilia heterophylla.* While it should not be forgotten that in common speech it is proper as well as convenient to call trees by their common names, yet, in view of the many uncertainties pertaining to their use, a scientific name at times is absolutely essential to the clear understanding of what is meant. Latin is the language in universal use by all scientists. No longer used by any civilized nation, it has become a dead language and consequently never changes. Its vocabulary and its constructions a thousand years hence will probably be the same as they are today. Being in universal use among scientists of all nationalities no confusion arises from the use of a Latin word. The Oak in Germany is known as *Eiche*, in France as *chêne* and in Spain as *roble*, but the Latin word *Quercus* is the same in all these countries.

A scientific name as applied to trees consists of at least two parts, as *Quercus alba*; the first is the genus and always is written with a capital letter, the second is the species and is written with a small letter, the two names constituting the briefest possible description of the particular tree. It is customary to add to these the name or an abbreviation of the name of the person who first gave the name to the tree, as *Quercus alba* L., the abbreviation standing for Linnaeus. Sometimes a third name is used, as *Acer saccharum nigrum*, referring in this instance to a variety of the ordinary Sugar Maple. In some cases trees have more than one Latin name. When this is true the synonym or synonyms are placed in brackets after the accepted name.

Genera which bear a relationship to each other are placed in the same family, the family name always having the characteristic ending—*aceae*. Related families again are grouped into orders, with the characteristic ending—*ales*. Orders in like manner are arranged into larger groups, called classes, and the latter into still larger groups, divisions, etc., each with its characteristic ending. Thus, *Acer saccharum nigrum* (Michx. f.) Britt. is classified as follows:

Division—Spermatophyta
Subdivision—Angiospermae
Class—Dicotyledoneae
Order—Sapindales
Family—Aceraceae
Genus—Acer
Species—saccharum
Variety—nigrum.

HABIT.—Habit, or the general appearance of a plant, is an important character of identification, especially as we become more and more familiar with the trees. Two main types are recognized, based on the manner of branching of the trunk, the upright and the spreading. In the one the trunk extends straight upwards without dividing, as is typical in most of the conifers; in the other the trunk divides to form several large branches and the broad, spreading crown of most of our broad-leaf trees. In either case the crown may be regular in outline or very irregular, straggling or straight-limbed. Moreover, the tree growing in the open, where there is no crowding and there is plenty of light, may differ greatly from the tree in the forest, where the struggle for existence becomes very keen. A short, thick trunk and a low, spreading, many-branched crown character-ize the tree in the open, whereas the forest tree has a long, slender, clean trunk and a narrow crown of few branches. In the descriptions of trees in this bulletin, unless otherwise stated, the habit in the open is the one given. Again, the tree may have been injured by storm or insect at some period of its growth and its natural symmetry destroyed. Moreover, the age of a tree has a great influence on its outline, young trees generally being narrow and more or less conical, broadening out as they become older. We may say, then, that each tree has an individuality of its own, little eccentricities similar to those that make people different from one another. And just as we have little difficulty in recognizing our friends at a distance by some peculiarity of walk or action, so we are able to recognize a great many trees at a distance by some peculiarity of form or habit.

LEAVES.—With the advent of spring the buds of our broad-leaf trees swell and burst and the leaves come forth and clothe the trees with mantles of green, hiding the branches which have been bare through the cold winter months. The evergreens, too, take on fresh color and commence a new period of growth. The beginner in botanical study finds the leaves the most interesting portion of a tree and one which affords him a ready means of identification. It must be remembered, however, that leaves vary greatly in size, shape and general appearance. For example, the leaves on a flourishing sprout are usually relatively large, whereas they may be much smaller on a stunted tree of the same species

I. LEAF OUTLINES

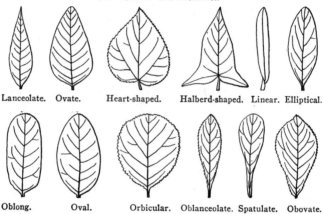

Lanceolate. Ovate. Heart-shaped. Halberd-shaped. Linear. Elliptical.

Oblong. Oval. Orbicular. Oblanceolate. Spatulate. Obovate.

growing nearby and subjected to adverse circumstances. The leaves of a big white oak standing in the yard may be hardly lobed on the lowermost branches, while higher up they are deeply cut.

II. LEAF TIPS

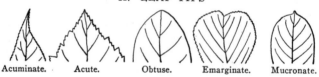

Acuminate. Acute. Obtuse. Emarginate. Mucronate.

However, in spite of the many modifications they undergo, the leaves of any one species have certain rather constant characteristics which are found in all forms, and the student who has once learned what these are will have little difficulty in selecting and recognizing typical specimens.

Leaves are either persistent, as in most of our conifers, which remain green all winter, or they assume various colors with the coming of the frost, and drop to the ground early in autumn, although often they hang dead and lifeless far into the winter. The characteristics of leaves which we are accustomed to consider in determining their relationships are their position or arrangement

III. LEAF MARGINS

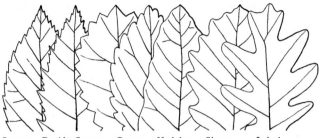

Serrate. Doubly Serrate. Crenate. Undulate. Sinuate. Lobed.
Dentate.

on the branch, whether simple or compound, size, shape, texture, color, the amount and character of pubescence, the character of the margin, venation, etc. The accompanying diagrams will serve to illustrate some of the ordinary forms and shapes of leaves, their margins, etc.

FLOWERS.—Every tree when old enough bears flowers in its proper season. Some of these, as the Catalpas, Locusts and Horse-chestnuts, are very showy; others, like the Oaks and Hickories, are comparatively inconspicuous. Some are brilliantly colored, while others are of the same color as the leaves. Nevertheless, the flowers are very accurate means of classification, and the only drawback to their use for this purpose is the fact that they last for such a little while each year.

IV. PARTS OF A FLOWER

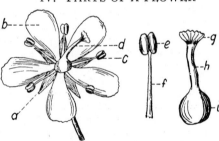

Perfect Flower.

a. Sepal (Calyx).
b. Petal (Corolla).
c. Stamen.
d. Pistil.
e. Anther.

Stamen.   Pistil.

f. Filament.
g. Stigma.
h. Style.
i. Ovary.

Just as there are male and female in the animal world, so the male and female are found in the plant world. A few of our trees, as the Locust, Basswood and Cherries, have perfect flowers, bearing both stamens and pistils. The great majority, however, have unisexual flowers, bearing either stamens or pistils, but not both. When both male and female flowers are found on the same tree, the plant is said to be monoecious, and when male flowers occur on one tree and the female on a different tree, the plant is said to be dioecious. The Cottonwood is dioecious. Each of its little seeds is surrounded by "cotton," a tuft of long, white hairs. Multitudes of seeds may be produced by a single tree and these may be carried by the wind to a considerable distance, much to the disgust of the people living in the vicinity. Because of this objectionable characteristic, many cities forbid the planting

V. TYPES OF INFLORESCENCES

Spike. Raceme.   Panicle.   Corymb.   Umbel.   Cyme.

of Cottonwood. Since in some cases it is desirable to plant this rapid-growing tree, as in cities burning large amounts of soft coal, it is a distinct advantage to know that the male trees may be planted safely, since they bear no seed and shed no "cotton."

Before trees can produce fruit their flowers must be pollinated, i.e., pollen from the anther of a stamen must come in contact with the stigma of a pistil. Some flowers are self-pollinated, others are cross-pollinated. For a long time it was not understood how pollination was accomplished, but now we know that many insects, like the nectar-loving bees and butterflies, and in other instances the wind, transport the pollen from one flower to another, often miles being traversed before the right kind of flower or a flower in the right stage of development is found. And many are the modifications of flowers to insure this transference of pollen.

FRUIT.—So numerous and so varied are the forms of tree fruits that it would be only confusing to enumerate their various characters. Some fruits, such as the achenes of the Poplars and Willows, are so small and light that they are carried long distances by the wind; others, like the hickory nuts and walnuts, are too heavy to be wind-blown. Many fruits are of considerable economic and commercial importance and are gathered and marketed on a large scale. Among these are the hickory nuts, walnuts, chestnuts, etc. Some, not esteemed by man, form an important article of diet for the birds and small animals of the forest. Unfortunately, there are a number of limitations to the usefulness of fruit for identification purposes. Some trees require years to mature their fruit. Many trees, while producing an abundance of fruit at certain intervals, bear none at all or only very small and uncertain quantities between the years of abundance. Again, in the case of dioecious trees, only the female or pistillate bear fruit. Notwithstanding these limitations tree fruits are a very valuable aid to the student, and he should always search closely for evidences of their presence and character.

VI. WINTER TWIG OF RED MULBERRY

a. Tip-scar.
b. Lateral bud.
c. Leaf-scar.
d. Stipule-scars.

WINTER-BUDS.—Buds, with their accompanying leaf- and stipule-scars, form the basis of tree identification in winter. The size, color, position with reference to the twig, number and arrangement and character of bud-scales, etc., are all characters of the greatest value in winter determinations. Buds are either terminal or lateral, depending on their position on the twig. A lateral bud is one situated on the side of a twig in the axil of a leaf-scar. A terminal bud is one situated at the end of a twig, where it is ready to continue the growth of the twig the following spring. In the winter keys much importance is attached to the presence or absence of the terminal bud. Inasmuch as the determination of this point gives the beginner some trouble at first, it is hoped that the accompanying diagrams and explanatory remarks will serve to make the distinction clear.

In the Elms, Willows, Basswood and many other species the terminal bud and a small portion of the tip of the twig dies and drops off in late autumn, leaving a small scar at the end of the twig (*a*, fig. VI). The presence of this tip-scar indicates that the terminal bud is absent. Often a lateral bud will be found very close to the tip-scar (*b*, fig. VI), which, bending into line with the twig, makes it appear to be a terminal rather than a lateral bud. However, the presence of a leaf-scar immediately below it shows it to be a lateral bud (*c*, fig. VI). In some large twigs the unaided eye will serve to find the tip-scar, but with the smaller twigs a magnifier is necessary.

VII. WINTER TWIG OF BLACK WALNUT

a. Terminal bud.
b. Lateral bud.
c. Leaf-scar.
d. Bundle-scars.
e. Pith.

The arrangement, size and shape of the leaf-scars (*c*, fig. VII) are important characters in identification in winter. Within the leaf-scars are one or more dots (*d*, fig. VII), sometimes quite inconspicuous, often very prominent. These are the scars left by the vascular bundles which run through the petiole into the blade of the leaf, and are designated as bundle-scars. There may be only one as in Sassafras and Hackberry, two as in Ginkgo, three as in the Poplars and Cherries, or many; and they may be arranged in a U- or V-shaped line, or they may be without definite order. Often stipule-scars (*d*, fig. VI) occur on either side of the leaf-scar; these are scars left by the shedding of a pair of small leaflets called stipules, located at the base of the leaves, and their form varies according to the form of the stipules which made them.

BARK.—The woodsman uses the bark more than any other feature in identifying trees, and often he is able in this manner to distinguish trees with much accuracy at great distances. However, the appearance of bark differs so greatly with the age of the tree and with its environment that it is difficult to describe it accurately. Some characters are distinctive, however, and serve as a ready means of identification, as, for example, the peeling of the Sycamore and Paper Birch, the "shagging" of the Shagbark Hickory, the spicy taste of Sassafras bark and the mucilaginous inner bark of the Slippery Elm.

WOOD.—Under this heading are given some of the general characteristics of wood. While it is not expected that this information will be of any particular value to the student of tree botany in identifying living trees, it happens often that such a one finds himself in the midst of felling operations or in the lumberyards; and under such circumstances a knowledge of the wood characters may be of considerable value. Few, if any, manuals or bulletins have been published dealing in a simple but comprehensive manner with the structure of wood. Especially is this true of the photographs or drawings accompanying such works. It hardly comes within the scope of this bulletin to discuss in detail all the woods of all the tree species growing in Michigan, although such a study doubtless would be worth while. Yet there does seem to be an urgent demand for information dealing with our more common trees; and hence a detailed study has been made of such of our woods as are of importance from a lumbering standpoint. Illustrations, showing cross-, radial- and tangential-sections, accompanied by descriptions and a key, have been brought together in a section at the end of the manual proper, to which are referred persons desirous of a more thorough acquaintance with our commercial woods.

DISTRIBUTION AND HABITAT.—To a lesser extent do distribution and habitat of a species aid in the identification of a tree. It is of distinct advantage to know that the Chestnut is native in south-eastern Michigan only and that the Mountain Ash does not extend south of Ludington. So, too, knowing the water-loving habit of the Swamp White Oak, we would not expect to find it flourishing on the top of a hard, dry hill.

The characteristics, then, which are used to identify the trees about us are many. Not all will be available at any one time, and not all have been mentioned in the foregoing pages nor in the manual. It is our opinion, however, that the student will not be handicapped greatly by this lack of detail, but rather that he will take great interest and genuine pleasure in discovering these things for himself.

ARTIFICIAL KEYS, HOW MADE AND USED

An artificial key is a scheme for identifying any unknown object under consideration easily and quickly. This bulletin being devoted to the trees of Michigan, its keys are intended to make it possible for any person, even if his botanical training be meager, to determine what native or introduced trees grow about his home or farm or in any Michigan city park or woodlot. With certain modifications and within limitations they may prove useful in other localities as well.

Since many people are unfamiliar with the construction and use of keys for identification, it is the purpose of the following paragraphs briefly to outline the principles upon which they are built and the manner in which they are used.

The keys are based on the most striking similarities and differences manifested by the various parts of trees—twigs, buds, leaves, etc.—that is to say, those characters which stand out in bold relief, which catch the eye at first sight. Two alternatives are presented, either a character *is* or *is not* presented; these are the only choices possible. Indeed, further divisions are unnecessary and lead only to confusion and possible oversight. The two diametrically opposed characters are said to be coördinate in rank. In the keys they are preceded by the same letter or letters (*a* and *aa* or *b* and *bb,* etc.) and are set at the same distance from the left margin of the page. Often *a* and *aa,* or *b* and *bb,* are divisible further into other groups; in every case the characters are opposed (a positive and a negative) and are given coördinate rank. It is desirable for mechanical reasons to divide the main divisions of the key more or less evenly, but this is not always feasible, nor should it be adhered to strictly.

The nature and use of a key may be made the more clear by a homely but concrete example. Let us suppose that it is desired to construct a key in order to distinguish from one another five houses in a city block. Three of these houses are built of wood, two of brick, and of the three wooden houses two are painted white and one brown. We may classify them as follows:

a. Houses wood.
    b. Body paint brown ....*Smith's house*
    bb. Body paint white.
        c. Trimmings green color ....*Jones' house*
        cc. Trimmings slate color ....*Brown's house*
aa. Houses brick.
    b. Roof gray slate ....*Johnson's house*
    bb. Roof red tile ....*Public library*

It is desirable in many instances to add other characters to lessen the likelihood of confusion, in cases where the characters chosen are not distinct, and in order to show the user that he is on the right track. Thus, in the example just given, green color and slate color might be confused owing to certain defects of the eye, to a coating of dust or deficiencies of the light. Hence, we would be justified in adding to the above statements additional distinguishing characteristics. Thus:
    bb.
        c. Trimmings green color; gable roof .....*Jones' house*
        cc. Trimmings slate color; mansard roof..*Brown's house*

The keys in this bulletin are constructed on these principles. They are not always as simple as the illustration just used, but if the reader has mastered the house illustration he will have little or no trouble with the larger keys. In order that the usage of the keys may be made the more clear, the following example, couched in language using the personal pronoun, is set forth at some length. The reader is advised to trace it from beginning to end as a ready means of familiarizing himself with the use of and possibilities of the key system.

Suppose that during a summer stroll you come across a large tree with rough, flaky bark and thin, lobed leaves which you do not know. Turning to the *Summer Key to the Genera* on page 22, you find first *a. Leaves simple,* and contrasted with this *aa. Leaves compound.* Obviously the leaf is simple and the genus sought lies in that portion of the key preceding *aa,* i.e., under *a.* The subdivisions, *b* and *bb,* under *a* afford you a choice between *Leaves needle-shaped, awl-shaped, strap-shaped or scale-like* and *Leaves broad and flat.* The leaf being broad and flat you pass onwards in the key to *c* and *cc* under *bb.* Here you have a choice between *Leaves alternate or clustered* and *Leaves opposite or whorled.* Inspection shows the arrangement to be alternate, and you know that the genus sought is in that portion of the key which lies between *c* and *cc*. Passing to *d* and *dd* under *c* you are offered the choice between *Margin of leaves entire or only slightly undulate* and *Margin of leaves serrate, toothed or lobed* and your observation clearly indicates that the leaf is neither entire nor undulate, hence the genus is under *dd*. Under *dd* you may choose between *e. Margin of leaves serrate to toothed* and *ee. Margin of leaves distinctly lobed.* The leaf being deeply lobed, you know that the genus sought is one of seven lying between *ee* and *cc*, all of which have lobed leaves. To make the determination, you must look for the fruit, since *f* and *ff* under *ee* give a choice between *Fruit an acorn* and *Fruit not an acorn.* You poke about in the grass beneath the tree with your foot, finding an acorn, water-soaked and worm-eaten, and then another. But these may have been carried hither by an industrious squirrel or washed here by the rain or blown by the wind and deposited for the entrapment of the unwary. Hence you look up into the tree for affirmation, and, observing more closely than heretofore, you note that the young, green acorns are quite apparent. The genus, then, is *Quercus.*

Before going further in your pursuit it will be well for you to go back over the key to make careful note of the particular characters which were used to separate this genus from the other genera and to try to fix these in mind. This being done, you should turn to the page indicated, where you will find a *Summer Key to the Species of Quercus.* You may then run through this key in the same manner that you did the genus key. If you have been careful in your search you will stop finally at *Quercus alba.* At this point you will do well once more to pause and go back over this key and try to fix in mind the characters which were used to separate the various species, especially the difference between your tree and *Quercus macrocarpa,* which it resembles so closely. This done, you will turn to the page indicated and compare the characters of your tree with the drawings and descriptions. If you are satisfied with your diagnosis, well and good. If you find that you are wrong, go over the keys again and find wherein you were led astray.

Before you leave the tree take a sample leaf, properly labeled, which you can press between the pages of an old magazine and save for future reference. Do this with other trees which you may find, and when you get home lay them out side by side so that the labels will not show and compare them. A few trials of this kind will serve to form a mental picture of each leaf which you will remember.

A very helpful practice for the beginner is that of making keys based upon various characters. Practice keys of this kind will bring out the differences and likenesses of trees as will no other means, and characters which hitherto have escaped the eye will be brought forward prominently. Nor should the student take his characters from books, but rather should he go to the woods and get his knowledge at first hand.

It is hardly necessary to state that, while the key is a valuable crutch while learning to walk, once the leg is strong enough to bear the weight it should be discarded, lest it become a burden. A key's main function is the guidance of the student through the preliminary steps leading to a more intimate knowledge of the trees. When once he knows a tree, instinctively, because of long acquaintance with it, just as he knows people, then the need for a key will have ceased.

SUMMER KEY TO THE GENERA*

a. Leaves simple. (For aa, see page 26.)
  b. Leaves needle-shaped, awl-shaped, strap-shaped, or scale-like.
    c. Leaves in clusters of 2-many.
      d. Leaves in clusters of 2-5, sheathed, persistent for several years.............................PINUS, p. 37
      dd. Leaves mostly in fascicles of 8-many, on short, lateral branchlets, or scattered singly along leading shoots, deciduous in autumn....................LARIX, p. 49

    cc. Leaves solitary, not clustered.
      d. Leaves opposite.
        e. Twigs flattened; leaves all of one kind, scale-like, decurrent on the stem; fruit a small, pale brown cone...............................THUJA, p. 63
        ee. Twigs essentially terete; leaves of two kinds, either scale-like, or else awl-shaped, often both kinds on the same branch, not decurrent on the stem; fruit berry-like, bluish...............JUNIPERUS, p. 65

      dd. Leaves alternate or spirally-whorled.
        e. Leaves flattened, soft to the touch.
          f. Leaves ½-1¼ inches long, sessile, aromatic; cones 2-4 inches long; bark of trunk with raised blisters containing resin....................ABIES, p. 59
          ff. Leaves seldom over ½ inch long, short-petioled, not aromatic; cones about ¾ inch long; bark of trunk without raised blisters.......TSUGA, p. 61
        ee. Leaves 4-sided, harsh to the touch.....PICEA, p. 51

  bb. Leaves broad and flat.
    c. Leaves alternate or clustered, never opposite nor whorled. (For cc, see page 26.)
      d. Margin of leaves entire or only slightly undulate.

---

*See page 18.

e. Leaves heart-shaped or rounded; fruit a legume......
......................................CERCIS, p. 199
ee. Leaves oval, ovate or obovate; fruit not a legume.
  f. Branches armed with stout, straight spines; fruit large, orange-like..............MACLURA, p. 165
  ff. Branches without spines; fruit small, not orange-like.
    g. Fruit an acorn...............QUERCUS, p. 128
    gg. Fruit a drupe or berry.
      h. Twigs spicy-aromatic when bruised; leaves of many shapes on the same branch.............
      ....SASSAFRAS, p. 171
      hh. Twigs not spicy-aromatic; leaves not of many shapes on the same branch.
        i. Leaves thick, abruptly pointed, very lustrous above, not clustered at the ends of the branches...................NYSSA, p. 241
        ii. Leaves thin, long-pointed, not lustrous above, clustered at the ends of the branches........
        ....CORNUS, p. 235
dd. Margin of leaves serrate, toothed or lobed.
  e. Margin of leaves serrate to toothed. (For ee, see page 25.)
    f. Branches armed with stiff, sharp thorns..........
    ....CRATAEGUS, p. 183
    ff. Branches not armed.
      g. Base of leaves decidedly oblique.
        h. Leaf-blades about as long as they are broad, heart-shaped..................TILIA, p. 233
        hh. Leaf-blades 1½-2 times as long as they are broad, oval to ovate.
          i. Leaves thin, coarsely but singly serrate; fruit a globular drupe, ripe in autumn; pith chambered.....................CELTIS, p. 163
          ii. Leaves thick, coarsely and doubly serrate; fruit a samara, ripe in spring; pith homogeneous.....................ULMUS, p. 155
      gg. Base of leaves essentially symmetrical.
        h. Leaf serrations coarse, 2-5 per inch of margin.
          i. Leaves very glabrous both sides; fruit a prickly bur.

j. Leaves 3-5 inches long, very lustrous beneath; bark close, smooth, steel-gray......
.... FAGUS, p. 125
jj. Leaves 6-8 inches long, not lustrous beneath; bark fissured, brownish...........
.....................CASTANEA, p. 127
ii. Leaves pubescent or white-tomentose, at least beneath; fruit not a prickly bur.
j. Leaves 2-4 inches long, broadly ovate to suborbicular; fruit a very small capsule, falling in spring........POPULUS, p. 76
jj. Leaves 4-7 inches long, oblong-lanceolate to obovate; fruit an acorn, falling in autumn..................QUERCUS, p. 128
hh. Leaf serrations fine, 6-many per inch of margin.
i. Leaf-petioles laterally compressed; leaves tremulous................POPULUS, p. 76
ii. Leaf-petioles terete; leaves not tremulous.
j. Leaf-blades at least 3 times as long as they are broad.
k. Twigs brittle; fruit a very small capsule, falling in spring..........SALIX, p. 67
kk. Twigs tough; fruit a fleshy drupe, falling in late summer or autumn..............
......................PRUNUS, p. 184
jj. Leaf-blades not more than twice as long as they are broad.
k. Leaf-blades about twice as long as they are broad.
l. Margin of leaves singly serrate; fruit fleshy.
m. Lenticels conspicuous; pith whitish or brownish; bark easily peeled off in papery layers; buds ovoid........
...................PRUNUS, p. 184
mm. Lenticels inconspicuous; pith greenish; bark not separable into papery layers; buds narrow-conical........
..........AMELANCHIER, p. 181
ll. Margin of leaves doubly serrate; fruit not fleshy.

— 24 —

m. Trunk fluted; fruit inclosed within a halberd-shaped involucre.........

...............CARPINUS, p. 115

mm. Trunk not fluted; fruit not inclosed within a halberd-shaped involucre.

n. Bark of trunk gray-brown, broken into narrow, flattish pieces loose at the ends, giving a shreddy appearance; fruit in hop-like strobiles............OSTRYA, p. 113

nn. Bark of trunk white, yellow or dark brown, platy or cleaving off in papery layers, not shreddy; fruit not in hop-like strobiles.........

...............BETULA, p. 117

kk. Leaf-blades almost as broad as they are long.

1. Lower side of leaves more or less downy; sap milky; leaves not crowded on short, spur-like branchlets; fruit berry-like, black......MORUS, p. 167

ll. Lower side of leaves glabrous; sap not milky; leaves crowded on short, spur-like branchlets; fruit a large, green pome...........PYRUS, p. 175

ee. Margin of leaves lobed.

f. Fruit an acorn................QUERCUS, p. 128

ff. Fruit not an acorn.

g. Leaves fan-shaped, with many fine veins radiating from the base of the blade.......GINKGO, p. 35

gg. Leaves not fan-shaped, without many fine veins radiating from the base of the blade.

h. Leaf-lobes entire.

i. Leaf-petioles 5-6 inches long; leaves lustrous above; twigs not aromatic when bruised....

.................LIRIODENDRON, p. 169

ii. Leaf-petioles about 1 inch long; leaves dull above; twigs spicy-aromatic when bruised...

.....................SASSAFRAS, p. 171

hh. Leaf-lobes sinuate-toothed to serrate.

d. Trunk and large branches armed with stout spines;
leaflets ¾-1½ inches long.........GLEDITSIA, p. 197
dd. Trunk and large branches unarmed; leaflets 2-2½
inches long...............GYMNOCLADUS, p. 195
bb. Leaves opposite.
c. Leaves pinnately compound; fruit a samara.
d. Leaflets 3-5; samaras paired.............ACER, p. 205
dd. Leaflets 7-11, exceptionally 5; samaras not paired....
...............................FRAXINUS, p. 243
cc. Leaves digitately compound; fruit a prickly bur........
...............................AESCULUS, p. 227

WINTER KEY TO THE GENERA*

a. Leaves persistent and green throughout the winter, needle-
shaped, awl-shaped or scale-like.
b. Leaves in clusters of 2-5, sheathed............PINUS, p. 37
bb. Leaves solitary, not clustered.
c. Leaves opposite.
d. Twigs flattened; leaves all of one kind, scale-like, decurrent on the stem; fruit a small, pale brown cone......
....................................THUJA, p. 63
dd. Twigs essentially terete; leaves of two kinds, either
scale-like, or else awl-shaped, often both kinds on the
same branch, not decurrent on the stem; fruit berry-
like, bluish.....................JUNIPERUS, p. 65
cc. Leaves alternate or spirally-whorled.
d. Leaves flattened, soft to the touch.
e. Leaves ½-1¼ inches long, sessile, aromatic; cones
2-4 inches long; bark of trunk with raised blisters
containing resin.....................ABIES, p. 59
ee. Leaves seldom over ½ inch long, short-petioled, not
aromatic; cones about ¾ inch long; bark of trunk
without raised blisters...............TSUGA, p. 61
dd. Leaves 4-sided, harsh to the touch......PICEA, p. 51

---

*See page 18.

aa. Leaves not persistent and green throughout the winter, but deciduous in early autumn.

b. Twigs, branches or trunk armed with stiff, sharp prickles, spines or thorns.

c. Thorns or spines not exceeding ½ inch in length on the branches.

d. Spines in pairs at each node; buds rusty-hairy, 3-4 superposed; fruit a flat pod........ROBINIA, p. 201

dd. Spines one at each node; buds glabrous, not superposed; fruit orange-like.................MACLURA, p. 165

cc. Thorns or spines much exceeding ½ inch in length on the branches.

d. Thorns on twigs often branched, situated above the nodes; lateral buds superposed, the lower covered by bark; fruit a flat pod.............GLEDITSIA, p. 197

dd. Thorns on twigs unbranched, situated at the nodes; lateral buds not superposed, not covered by bark; fruit a small pome.................CRATAEGUS, p. 183

bb. Twigs, branches or trunk unarmed.

c. Leaf-scars mainly crowded on short, stout, lateral shoots.

d. Bundle-scar 1; fruit a cone, usually present...........
....LARIX, p. 49

dd. Bundle-scars 2; fruit a globose drupe, falling in autumn............................GINKGO, p. 35

cc. Leaf-scars distributed along the lateral branches.

d. Leaf-scars, or some of them, 3 at a node, i.e., whorled..
...............................CATALPA, p. 255

dd. Leaf-scars 1-2 at a node, i.e., not whorled.

e. Leaf-scars 2 at a node, i.e., opposite.

f. Terminal buds ½-1½ inches long, resin-coated; twigs very stout..............AESCULUS, p. 227

ff. Terminal buds rarely exceeding ½ inch in length, not resin-coated; twigs not conspicuously stout.

g. Leaf buds with 1 pair of scales visible.

h. Buds scurfy-pubescent....VIBURNUM, p. 261

hh. Buds glabrous...............CORNUS, p. 235

gg. Leaf buds with 2 or more pairs of scales visible.

h. Bundle-scars usually 3, distinct, separated....
.............................ACER, p. 206

hh. Bundle-scars many, minute, more or less confluent in a U-shaped line.....................
........................FRAXINUS, p. 243
cc. Leaf-scars 1 at a node, i.e., alternate.
  f. Bundle-scars 1-3. (For ff, see page 31.)
    g. Bundle-scar only 1, or appearing as 1.
      h. Twigs bright green, spicy-aromatic; bundle-
         scar appearing as a horizontal line; terminal
         bud present; pith homogeneous...............
         ....SASSAFRAS, p. 171
      hh. Twigs brownish, not spicy-aromatic; bundle-
          scar appearing as a large dot; terminal bud
          absent; pith chambered........CELTIS, p. 163
    gg. Bundle-scars 3 or in 3 compound, but distinct
        groups.
      h. Terminal bud present.
        i. Stipule-scars present.
          j. First (outermost) scale of lateral buds
             directly in front, i.e., exactly above the
             center of the leaf-scar; twigs brittle; pith
             somewhat star-shaped in cross-section....
             ....POPULUS, p. 77
          jj. First (outermost) scale of lateral buds not
              directly in front, i.e., to one side of the
              center of the leaf-scar; twigs not brittle;
              pith circular in cross-section.............
              ....PRUNUS, p. 185
        ii. Stipule-scars absent.
          j. Buds bright to dark red, the terminal ⅛-¼
             inch long.
            k. Branches contorted, bearing many short,
               spur-like branchlets; fruit an apple an
               inch or more in diameter, light green...
               ....PYRUS, p. 175
            kk. Branches not contorted, not bearing
                short, spur-like branchlets; fruit berry-
                like, ½ inch long, blue-black............
                ....NYSSA, p. 241

— 29 —

jj. Buds brownish to gray, the terminal exceeding ¼ inch in length.

  k. Buds narrow-conical, sharp-pointed; leaf-
scars small, narrowly crescent-shaped;
twigs about ¹⁄₁₆ inch thick; pith homogeneous; fruit berry-like, not present ..
..............AMELANCHIER, p. 181

  kk. Buds broadly conical to ovoid, blunt-
pointed; leaf-scars conspicuous, broadly
heart-shaped; twigs about ¼ inch thick;
pith chambered; fruit a nut, often present.................JUGLANS, p. 93

hh. Terminal bud absent (sometimes present on
short shoots of *Betula*).

  i. Stipule-scars present.

    j. Bud-scale only 1 visible; twigs brittle....
.........................SALIX, p. 67

    jj. Bud-scales 2 or more; twigs not brittle.

      k. Bark smooth, close, warty or peeling
into papery layers, but not flaky nor
rough-ridged.

        l. Tip of buds appressed; fruit berry-like
....................CELTIS, p. 163

        ll. Tip of buds not appressed; fruit not
berry-like.

          m. Trunk fluted; catkins not present
in winter; lenticels not elongated
horizontally; low tree or bushy
shrub.........CARPINUS, p. 115

          mm. Trunk not fluted; catkins usually
present in winter; lenticels elongated
horizontally; large trees...........
.................BETULA, p. 117

      kk. Bark flaky or rough-ridged, not warty
nor peeling off in papery layers.

        l. Bundle-scars depressed, conspicuous;
bark thick, more or less deeply furrowed, not shreddy...ULMUS, p. 155

ll. Bundle-scars not depressed, inconspicuous; bark thin, broken into narrow,
flattish strips, loose at the ends, giving
a shreddy appearance...............
...................OSTRYA, p. 113
ii. Stipule-scars absent.
j. Buds silky-pubescent, depressed; twigs
stout, clumsy, blunt, with conspicuous leaf-
scars.........GYMNOCLADUS, p. 195
jj. Buds glabrous, not depressed; twigs slender, with inconspicuous leaf-scars.
k. Buds ⅛ inch long, obtuse, somewhat
flattened and appressed; pith with reddish longitudinal streaks..............
.....................CERCIS, p. 199
kk. Buds ⅛-¼ inch long, acute, not flattened nor appressed; pith without reddish streaks..........PRUNUS, p. 185
ff. Bundle-scars 4-many.
g. Bundle-scars in a single U-shaped line.
h. Terminal bud present; fruit berry-like; a shrub
or small tree.................PYRUS, p. 175
hh. Terminal bud absent; fruit not berry-like;
large trees.
i. Stipule-scars present; twigs slender.
j. Stipule-scars encircling the twig; leaf-scars
nearly surrounding the bud; bark peeling
off in thin plates, exposing the lighter
colored inner bark....PLATANUS, p. 173
jj. Stipule-scars not encircling the twig; leaf-
scars not nearly surrounding the bud; bark
thick, rough-ridged, not exposing the inner
bark....................ULMUS, p. 155
ii. Stipule-scars absent; twigs very stout.
j. Bundle-scars usually not more than 5....
..............GYMNOCLADUS, p. 195
jj. Bundle-scars usually 6-12 ....
...................AILANTHUS, p. 203

gg. Bundle-scars variously grouped or scattered, but not in a single line.
  h. Terminal bud present.
    i. Stipule-scars present.
      j. Stipule-scars encircling the twig; visible bud-scales 2, united.....................
      ...............LIRIODENDRON, p. 169
      jj. Stipule-scars not encircling the twig; visible bud-scales more than 2, not united.
        k. Buds 4 times as long as broad, not clustered at the tips of vigorous shoots; fruit a prickly bur......FAGUS, p. 125
        kk. Buds not 4 times as long as broad, usually clustered at the tips of vigorous shoots; fruit an acorn................
        ....QUERCUS, p. 130
    ii. Stipule-scars absent..........CARYA, p. 99
  hh. Terminal bud absent (occasionally present in *Castanea*).
    i. Bud at end of twig very obliquely unsymmetrical, mucilaginous when chewed..........
    ....TILIA, p. 233
    ii. Bud at end of twig symmetrical, not mucilaginous when chewed.
      j. Bud-scales 2-3 visible; pith star-shaped in cross-section; sap not milky; fruit a prickly bur, present; large tree...............
      ....CASTANEA, p. 127
      jj. Bud-scales 4-8 visible; pith not star-shaped in cross-section; sap milky; fruit berry-like, not present; small tree.............
      ....MORUS, p. 167

MANUAL OF TREES

———

DESCRIPTION OF SPECIES

WITH

SUMMER AND WINTER KEYS
TO THE SPECIES

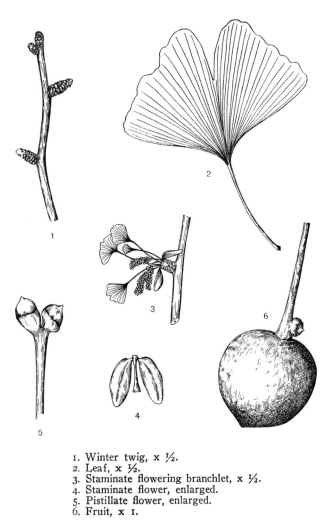

1. Winter twig, x ½.
2. Leaf, x ½.
3. Staminate flowering branchlet, x ½.
4. Staminate flower, enlarged.
5. Pistillate flower, enlarged.
6. Fruit, x 1.

GINKGOACEAE
Ginkgo. Maidenhair Tree
Ginkgo biloba L. [*Salisburia adiantifolia* Smith]

HABIT.—A slender, spire-like tree in youth, with the branches having a tendency to hug the stem; later, the lowermost branches grow out horizontally and the crown becomes more spreading; probably 60-80 feet high, with a trunk diameter of 2-4 feet.

LEAVES.—Clustered at the ends of short, spur-like shoots, or scattered alternately on the long terminal branches; simple; 2-5 inches broad; more or less fan-shaped; usually bilobed and irregularly crenate at the upper extremity; thin and leathery; glabrous, pale yellow-green on both sides; petioles long, slender; turning a clear, golden yellow before falling in autumn.

FLOWERS.—May, with the leaves; dioecious; the staminate in short-stalked, pendulous catkins, 1-1½ inches long, yellow; the pistillate more or less erect on the shoot, long-stalked, consisting of 2 naked ovules, one of which usually aborts.

FRUIT.—Autumn; a more or less globose drupe, orange-yellow to green, about 1 inch in diameter, consisting of an acrid, foul-smelling pulp inclosing a smooth, whitish, somewhat flattened, almond-flavored nut.

WINTER-BUDS.—Terminal bud about ⅛ inch long, conical, smooth, light chestnut-brown; lateral buds divergent, usually only on rapid-growing shoots.

BARK.—Twigs gray-brown and smooth; thick, ash-gray and somewhat roughened on the trunk, becoming more or less fissured in old age.

WOOD.—Light, soft, weak, close-grained, yellow-white to light red-brown, with thin, lighter colored sapwood.

DISTRIBUTION.—Introduced from China; frequently planted in city parks and on spacious lawns.

HABITAT.—Almost any good soil.

NOTES.—The sole surviving genus of an ancient order of plants intermediate between the ferns and conifers. Extensively cultivated in temperate countries. The fruit is esteemed as a delicacy in China and Japan; but it must be said that the flesh is slippery and dangerous when it drops to the sidewalk or pavement, for which reason staminate trees only are to be recommended for street-planting. Slow of growth, but very disease-resistant, and little harmed by city smoke. Easily propagated from seed. Probably hardy throughout the southern half of the Lower Peninsula.

THE PINES—PINUS

The Pines are the largest and most useful group of trees included in the great cone-bearing family, *Pinaceae.* Of the thirty-four species which are found in the United States, only three are native to Michigan. Formerly the northern part of the state was a vast forest of White Pine and of Red or Norway Pine, intermixed with hardwoods. The exploitation of these great timber reserves played a very important rôle in our economic and industrial development. To our sorrow, these forests no longer exist; but in their place are great stretches of sand, desolation, and thickets of inferior broad-leaved trees and the scrubby Jack Pine. Some day all this will be changed, forests will again be established, and a new period of prosperity will ensue.

The Pines, like the other members of this family, produce their seeds in cones. They are peculiar, however, in that their cones require two years for maturing. The flowers also take the form of cones, the pollen-bearing and the ovule-bearing clusters being separated, though both may be found on the same tree. The yellow pollen matures in May or June, when it is scattered in great abundance, to be borne to its destination by the wind. Most of the seed-bearing cones develop on the upper branches, and the nut-like seeds escape from them during the second autumn. The empty cones with opened scales thereafter may cling to the tree for some time or they may fall soon.

The leaves of all the evergreens cling to the branches several years. The leaves of the White Pine, for example, drop when they are two or three years old. The arrangement of the leaves, or needles, in clusters of from two to five, with the base of each cluster encased in a delicate sheath, offers a simple means of distinguishing the species.

Besides the native Pines, a number of introduced species have been planted, either for ornamental, or for forestry purposes. Of these, two European Pines, the Austrian and the Scotch, were among the first to be so used, and large trees of these species are seen frequently.

The Swiss Mountain Pine, *Pinus mugo* Turra, and its var. *mughus* Zenari, known as the Mugho Pine, are usually seen as spreading shrubs with ascending branches and stiff, stubby branchlets, although they sometimes form dwarf trees from 6-15 feet high. They are among the most important low pines for parks and gardens, or as single specimens on lawns, being perfectly hardy and adapted to a variety of soils and exposures. Their native home is the mountains of Switzerland. The leaves are in clusters of two, ¾-2 inches long, stout, bright or dark green. The cones are yellow to brown in color and ¾-2¼ inches long, the cone-scales ending in a sharp point which is surrounded by a blackish ring.

SUMMER AND WINTER KEY TO THE SPECIES OF PINUS

a. Leaves 5 in a cluster; cones 4-10 inches long ....
....*P. strobus,* p. 39
aa. Leaves 2 in a cluster; cones less than 4 inches long.
  b. Leaves 1-3 inches long.
    c. Leaves about 1 inch long, divergent; cones sessile, pointing forward towards the tip of the branch, persistent 10-15 years, opening very unevenly..........*P. banksiana,* p. 41
    cc. Leaves 1½-3 inches long, slightly divergent; cones stout-stalked, pointing away from the tip of the branch, opening evenly in the autumn of the second season and falling as soon as ripe........................*P. sylvestris,* p. 45
  bb. Leaves 3-6 inches long.
    c. Bark of trunk red-brown; cones about 2 inches long, opening in the autumn of the second season and falling the next summer; cone-scales thickened at the apex, but unarmed.............................*P. resinosa,* p. 47
    cc. Bark of trunk gray to nearly black; cones 2-3 inches long, maturing in the autumn of the second season, but not opening until two years after full size is attained and remaining on the tree for several years; cone-scales thickened at the apex and topped with a short spine......
..............................*P. laricio austriaca,* p. 43

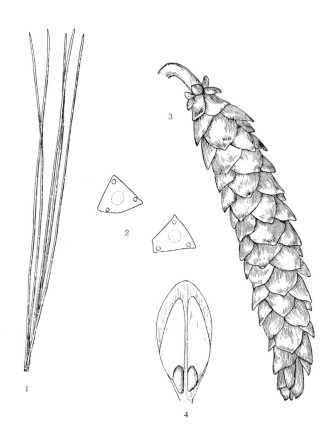

1. Cluster of leaves, **x** 1.
2. Cross-sections of leaves, enlarged.
3. Partly opened cone, **x** ¾.
4. Cone-scale with seeds, **x** 1.

PINACEAE

White Pine
Pinus strobus L.

HABIT.—A large tree 60-80 feet high, with a trunk diameter of 2-4 feet; forming a wide, pyramidal crown. Formerly trees 100-150 feet in height and 5-7 feet in trunk diameter were not exceptional.

LEAVES.—In clusters of five; 3-5 inches long; slender, straight, needle-shaped, 3-sided, mucronate; pale blue-green. Persistent about 2 years.

FLOWERS.—June; monoecious; the staminate in ovoid clusters, ⅓ inch long, composed of many sessile, yellow anthers imbricated upon a central axis; the ovulate in long-stalked, subglobose clusters, ¼ inch long, composed of many pinkish purple scales spirally arranged upon a central axis.

FRUIT.—Autumn of second season, falling during the winter and succeeding spring; pendent, short-stalked, narrow-cylindrical, often curved, greenish cones, 4-10 inches long; scales rather loose, slightly thickened at the apex; seeds red-brown, ¼ inch long, with wings 1 inch long.

WINTER-BUDS.—Oblong-ovoid, sharp-pointed, yellow-brown, ¼-½ inch long.

BARK.—Twigs at first rusty-tomentose, later smooth and light brown, finally thin, smooth, greenish; thick, dark gray on the trunk, shallowly fissured into broad, scaly ridges.

WOOD.—Light, soft, weak, compact, straight-grained, easily worked, light brown, with thin, whitish sapwood. See p. 309.

DISTRIBUTION.—Upper Peninsula and Lower Peninsula north of Allegan, Eaton and St. Clair Counties. Often planted as an ornamental tree farther south.

HABITAT.—Prefers a light, fertile loam; sandy soils of granite origin.

NOTES.—Widely used in reforestation, and very attractive for shade and ornament. Small seedlings are readily transplanted. Adapts itself to a great variety of soil conditions and grows rapidly. The white-pine blister rust, requiring wild or cultivated currants and gooseberries as the alternate host, was introduced into America some years ago and has since become widespread and highly destructive both to old trees and young growth.

1. Cluster of leaves, x 1.
2. Cross-section of leaf, enlarged.
3. Branchlet with unopened cone, x 1.
4. Branchlet with opened cone, x 1.
5. Cone-scale with seeds, x 1.

PINACEAE

Jack Pine. Scrub Pine

Pinus banksiana Lamb. [*Pinus divaricata* (Ait.)
Du Mont de Cours.]

HABIT.—Usually a small tree 20-30 feet high, with a trunk diameter of 8-12 inches; forming a crown varying from open and symmetrical to scrubby, stunted, and variously distorted.

LEAVES.—In clusters of two; about 1 inch long; narrow-linear, with sharp-pointed apex; stout, curved or twisted, divergent from a short sheath; dark gray-green. Persistent 2-3 years.

FLOWERS.—May-June; monoecious; the staminate in cylindrical clusters, ½ inch long, composed of many sessile, yellow anthers imbricated upon a central axis; the ovulate in sub-globose clusters, composed of many carpel-like, purple scales (subtended by small bracts) spirally arranged upon a central axis.

FRUIT.—Autumn of second or third season, but remaining closed for several years and persistent on the tree for 10-15 years; erect, usually incurved, oblong-conical, sessile cones, 1½-2 inches long; scales thickened at the apex; seeds triangular, nearly black, ⅜ inch long, with wings ⅓ inch long.

WINTER-BUDS.—Terminal bud ¼ inch long, ovoid, with rounded apex, pale brown; lateral buds smaller.

BARK.—Twigs yellow-green, becoming purple, finally dark red-brown and rough with the persistent bases of fallen leaves; thin, dark red-brown on the trunk, with shallow, rounded ridges, rough-scaly on the surface.

WOOD.—Light, soft, weak, close-grained, light brown, with thick, whitish sapwood.

DISTRIBUTION.—Common from Clare County northward; occurs sparingly along the lake shore as far south as Grand Haven on the west and Port Austin on the east.

HABITAT.—Sandy, sterile soil.

NOTES.—Cones open unevenly. Slow of growth. Difficult to transplant. A stunted tree, with sprawling habit. The wood is used for fuel, and occasionally for railroad ties and fence posts.

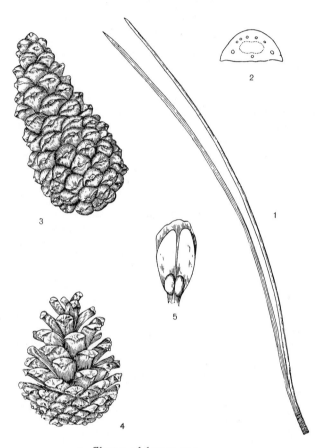

1. Cluster of leaves, x 1.
2. Cross-section of leaf, enlarged.
3. Unopened cone, x 1.
4. Partly opened cone, x ½.
5. Cone-scale with seeds, x 1.

PINACEAE

Austrian Pine. Black Pine

Pinus laricio austriaca Endl. [*Pinus austriaca* Höss.]
[*Pinus nigra austriaca* Asch. & Graebn.]

HABIT.—A large tree 60-80 feet high, with a trunk diameter of 2-4 feet; forming a massive, spreading crown of stiff, strong branches.

LEAVES.—In clusters of two; 3-6 inches long; slender, rigid, sharp-pointed, curved towards the twig; deep green on both faces. Persistent 3-6 years.

FLOWERS.—May-June; monoecious; the staminate in cylindrical, subsessile clusters, about ¾ inch long, composed of many bright yellow anthers imbricated upon a central axis; the ovulate in small, cylindrical, subsessile, bright red, cone-like clusters.

FRUIT.—Autumn of second season, opening two years after full size is attained and remaining on the tree several years; erect, sessile, long-ovoid cones, 2-3 inches long; scales smooth, lustrous, thickened at the apex and topped with a short spine in the center; seeds red-brown, ¼ inch long, with wings ¾ inch long.

WINTER-BUDS.—Oblong-conical, sharp-pointed, red-brown, resinous, about ½ inch long.

BARK.—Twigs brownish to olive-brown and smooth, becoming darker with age; thick, gray to nearly black on old trunks and coarsely and deeply fissured.

WOOD.—Light, strong, very resinous, red-brown, with thick, yellowish to reddish white sapwood.

DISTRIBUTION.—Introduced from Europe; frequently cultivated as an ornamental tree, and to some extent used in forest planting.

HABITAT.—Prefers good soil.

NOTES.—Perfectly hardy. Adapts itself to a variety of soils. Well adapted to screens and windbreaks. Easily transplanted when small. Grows rapidly.

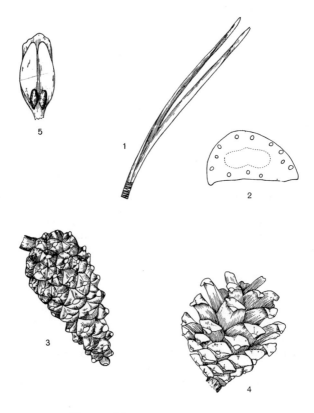

1. Cluster of leaves, x 1.
2. Cross-section of leaf, enlarged.
3. Unopened cone, x 1.
4. Partly opened cone, x 1.
5. Cone-scale with seeds, x 1.

PINACEAE

Scotch Pine. Scotch Fir

Pinus sylvestris L.

HABIT.—A large tree 50-70 feet high, with a trunk diameter of 1-2 feet; the side branches persist, forming a massive, wide-spreading crown.

LEAVES.—In clusters of two; 1½-3 inches long; stiff, more or less twisted, spreading slightly from a short sheath; bluish- or often glaucous-green. Persistent 3-4 years.

FLOWERS.—May-June; monoecious; the staminate in ovoid, short-stalked clusters, about ¼ inch long, composed of many sessile, yellowish anthers imbricated upon a central axis; the ovulate in short-stalked, reddish, cone-like clusters, about ¼ inch long.

FRUIT.—Autumn of second season, falling as soon as ripe; pendent, stout-stalked, ovoid-conical cones, 1½-2½ inches long; scales dull gray-brown, thickened at the apex into 4-sided, recurved points; seeds red-brown, nearly ¼ inch long, with wings about ¾ inch long.

WINTER-BUDS.—Oblong-ovoid, sharp-pointed, red-brown, resinous, about ¼ inch long.

BARK.—Twigs reddish to orange-brown, becoming grayish; thick, dark orange-brown on old trunks and coarsely and deeply fissured.

WOOD.—Light, stiff, straight-grained, strong, hard, resinous, red-brown, with thick, yellow to reddish white sapwood.

DISTRIBUTION.—Introduced from Europe; frequently planted.

HABITAT.—Prefers deep, well-drained, sandy loam.

NOTES.—Grows very rapidly in youth, but later more slowly. Reaches perfection only in cold or elevated regions. Adapts itself to a variety of soils, even dry, sterile sand. A valuable ornamental tree, but inferior to native species for forestry purposes. Useful for screens or shelter belts.

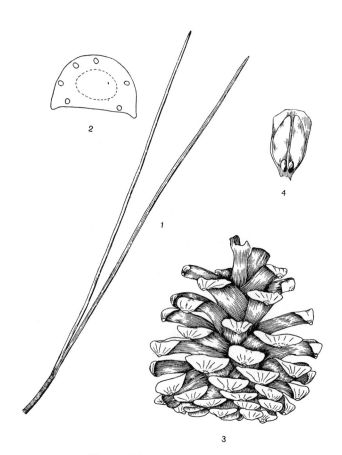

1. Cluster of leaves, x 1.
2. Cross-section of leaf, enlarged.
3. Opened cone, x 1.
4. Cone-scale with seeds, x 1.

PINACEAE
Red Pine. Norway Pine
Pinus resinosa Ait.

HABIT.—A large tree, usually 50-75 feet high, with a trunk diameter of 2-3 feet; stout, horizontal branches form a broad, rounded, rather open crown.

LEAVES.—In clusters of two; 4-6 inches long; slender, straight, needle-shaped, sharp-pointed, flexible, from elongated, persistent sheaths; lustrous dark green. Persistent 4-5 years.

FLOWERS.—April-May; monoecious; the staminate in dense, cylindrical clusters, ½-¾ inch long, composed of many sessile, purple anthers imbricated upon a central axis; the ovulate in subglobose clusters of scarlet scales spirally arranged upon a central axis, borne on stout peduncles covered with pale brown bracts.

FRUIT.—Autumn of second season, falling the next summer; ovoid-conical, nearly sessile cones, about 2 inches long; scales thickened at the apex; seeds oval, compressed, light mottled-brown, with wings ½-¾ inch long.

WINTER-BUDS.—About ¾ inch long, ovoid or conical, acute, red-brown, with rather loose scales.

BARK.—Twigs orange-brown, becoming rough with the persistent bases of leaf-buds; thick and red-brown on the trunk, shallowly fissured into broad, flat ridges.

WOOD.—Light, hard, very close-grained, pale red, with thin, yellow to white sapwood. See p. 309.

DISTRIBUTION.—Very abundant in Clare County and northward; frequent on the east side of the state as far south as Port Huron.

HABITAT.—Sandy plains and dry, gravelly ridges.

NOTES.—Rapid of growth on the better soils. Difficult to transplant. A prolific seeder, and therefore adapted to natural regeneration. The name Red Pine is appropriate both because of the pale red color of the heartwood and the distinctly reddish cast of the bark. This species does not grow in Norway or elsewhere in Europe, and it is said that it received the name from the town of Norway, Maine. The name Norway Pine has so little fitness as applied to this tree, and evidently is so misleading, that its use is to be discouraged. The picturesqueness and individuality of the Red Pine commend it for wider use as an ornamental tree.

Tamarack

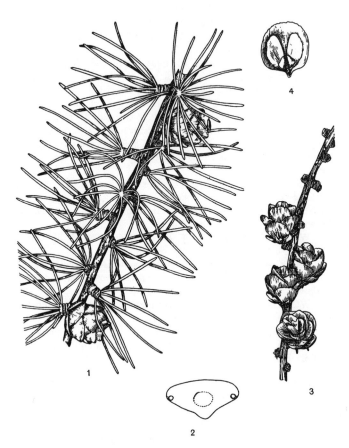

1. Autumn branchlet, with leaves and cónes, x 1.
2. Cross-section of leaf, enlarged.
3. Fruiting branchlet in winter, x 1.
4. Cone-scale with seeds, x 2.

PINACEAE

Tamarack

Larix laricina (DuRoi) Koch [*Larix americana* Michx.]

HABIT.—A tree usually 40-60 feet high, with a trunk diameter of 1-2 feet; forming a broad, open, irregular crown of horizontal branches.

LEAVES.—Scattered singly along the leading shoots or clustered on the short lateral branchlets; linear, with blunt apex; rounded above, keeled beneath; about 1 inch long; bright green; sessile. Deciduous in early autumn.

FLOWERS.—May, with the leaves; monoecious; the staminate in sessile, subglobose, yellow clusters, composed of many short-stalked anthers spirally arranged about a central axis; the ovulate in short-stalked clusters, composed of orbicular, green scales (subtended by red bracts) spirally arranged about a central axis.

FRUIT.—Autumn of first season, but persistent on the tree for a year longer; ovoid, obtuse, light brown, short-stalked cones, ½-¾ inch long; seeds ⅛ inch long, with pale brown wings widest near the middle.

WINTER-BUDS.—Small, globose, lustrous, dark red.

BARK.—Twigs at first grayish, glaucous, later light orange-brown, and finally dark brown; red-brown and scaly on the trunk.

WOOD.—Heavy, hard, very strong, coarse-grained, very durable, light brown, with thin, nearly white sapwood. See p. 311.

DISTRIBUTION.—Common throughout the state.

HABITAT.—Prefers cold, deep swamps, or in the north coming out on the drier uplands.

NOTES.—Becomes a picturesque tree in old age. Should be transplanted while dormant. Grows slowly in swamps, but more rapidly on well-drained soils. It has a very destructive enemy, the larch sawfly, which has recently destroyed a large number of trees in our swamp areas. The European Larch, *Larix decidua* Mill., is being planted extensively in this country, and in most respects it is preferable to our native species. It has stouter, yellower twigs, more abundant and somewhat longer leaves and larger cones than our native Tamarack, is adapted to drier situations and grows very rapidly.

THE SPRUCES—PICEA

The Spruces have tall, gradually-tapering trunks, thickly covered with branches, forming compact, pyramidal or conical crowns. They are confined wholly to the cold and temperate regions of the northern hemisphere, where they often form extensive forests. It is therefore our northern plains and cold swamps which furnish conditions suitable for their best development. The leaves are for the most part four-sided, spirally arranged on the branches and persist for 5-10 years. The seeds are usually light, with rather large wings, by means of which they are blown over great distances by the wind. The wood, formerly looked upon with disfavor, is now an important article of commerce, large quantities being consumed annually for the manufacture of paper pulp.

Eight species of Spruces are found in North America, of which two, the White Spruce and the Black Spruce, are native to Michigan. The White Spruce is an important timber tree, besides being planted for ornamental purposes. The Black Spruce is a smaller tree, is short-lived and is not to be recommended for ornamental planting, since other species far surpass it for this purpose.

Besides the native Spruces, several introduced species are much planted. The Norway Spruce is probably the best known of these, coming to us from Europe, where it is especially abundant in Norway. It has been planted mostly for ornamental purposes and for windbreaks, but in the future it also will be planted freely as a forest tree.

The Colorado Blue Spruce, *Picea pungens* Engelm., a native of the Rocky Mountains, is commonly planted as an ornamental tree on lawns and in parks. It grows in all soils, is quite hardy and is easily raised from seed. It is of very slow growth until about a foot high, then it advances more rapidly, to form a strong, symmetrical, upright tree which keeps its lower branches well to the ground. The Colorado Blue Spruce is striking in its foliage; the branchlets are in horizontal layers and the leaves of each new season are pale blue or silvery, contrasting with the darker blue-green of the older foliage. The narrow-cylindrical cones are about 3 inches long, with thin scales having blunt, ragged tips, and generally they do not remain on the tree after the second winter.

The Engelmann Spruce, *Picea engelmanni* Engelm., also from the Rocky Mountains, somewhat resembles our native White Spruce, but it is more beautiful in color and texture of its foliage, the leaves being a silver-blue. In general habit this tree resembles the Colorado Blue Spruce. It has cones which are about 2 inches long, with the thin, flexible scales toothed on the margin. It is perfectly hardy, but should be planted on northern exposures.

SUMMER AND WINTER KEY TO THE SPECIES OF PICEA

a. Leaves ⅛-⅜ inch long, blunt-pointed; twigs rusty-pubescent..
....*P. mariana,* p. 55

aa. Leaves ¾-1 inch long, sharp-pointed; twigs glabrous.

   b. Cones 1-2 inches long, falling during the autumn or early winter of the first season; cone-scales with nearly entire margin; leaves ill-scented when bruised..*P. canadensis,* p. 53

   bb. Cones 3-6 inches long, falling in the spring or summer of the second season; cone-scales with finely toothed margin; leaves not ill-scented when bruised..........*P. abies,* p. 57

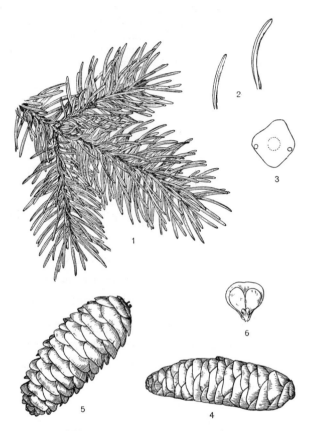

1. Winter branchlet, x 1.
2. Leaves, x 1.
3. Cross-section of leaf, enlarged.
4. Unopened cone, x 1.
5. Partly opened cone, x 1.
6. Cone-scale with seeds, x 1.

PINACEAE

White Spruce

Picea canadensis (Mill.) BSP. [*Picea alba* Link]

HABIT.—A tree 60-70 feet high, with a trunk diameter of 1-2 feet; forming a rather broad, open, pyramidal crown.

LEAVES.—Spirally arranged, but crowded on the upper side of the branches by the twisting of those on the under side; awl-shaped, 4-sided, incurved; dark blue-green; about ¾ inch long; ill-scented when bruised. Persistent for 7-10 years.

FLOWERS.—May and early June; monoecious; the staminate in oblong-cylindrical, long-stalked clusters, ½-¾ inch long, composed of many spirally arranged, red anthers; the ovulate in oblong-cylindrical clusters, composed of broad, reddish scales (subtended by orbicular bracts) spirally arranged upon a central axis.

FRUIT.—Autumn of first season, falling soon after discharging the seeds; pendent, slender, oblong-cylindrical, nearly sessile cones, 1-2 inches long; cone-scales with nearly entire margin; seeds nearly ⅛ inch long, with large wings oblique at the apex.

WINTER-BUDS.—Broadly ovoid, obtuse, light brown, ⅛-¼ inch long.

BARK.—Twigs smooth, gray-green, becoming orange-brown, finally dark gray-brown; thin, light gray-brown on the trunk, separating into thin, plate-like scales.

WOOD.—Light, soft, weak, straight-grained, light yellow, with sapwood of the same color. See p. 311.

DISTRIBUTION.—Common in the northern half of the Lower Peninsula and throughout the Upper Peninsula.

HABITAT.—Low, damp woods; banks of streams; borders of lakes; high rocky or sandy slopes; loves the cold winters.

NOTES.—A vigorous and beautiful tree in regions sufficiently cold. In recent years much growing timber has been destroyed by the attacks of a leaf-eating insect, the spruce budworm.

1. Winter branchlet, x 1.
2. Leaves, x 2.
3. Cross-sections of leaves, enlarged.
4–5. Opened cones, x 1.
6. Cone-scale with seeds, x 1.

PINACEAE

Black Spruce

Picea mariana (Mill.) BSP. [*Picea nigra* Link]

HABIT.—A small tree 20-30 feet high, with a trunk diameter of 6-10 inches; forming a narrow-based, conical, more or less irregular crown of short, slender, horizontal branches; often small and stunted.

LEAVES.—Spirally arranged, spreading in all directions; awl-shaped, 4-sided, blunt at the apex, more or less incurved; stiff; dark blue-green and glaucous; ⅛-⅜ inch long. Persistent for 7-10 years.

FLOWERS.—May and early June; monoecious; the staminate in subglobose clusters, about ½ inch long, composed of many spirally arranged dark red anthers; the ovulate in oblong-cylindrical clusters, composed of broad, purple scales (subtended by rounded, toothed, purple bracts) spirally arranged upon a central axis, about ½ inch long.

FRUIT.—Autumn of first season, but persistent on the branch for many years; pendent, short-stalked, ovoid cones, about 1 inch long; seeds about ⅛ inch long, with pale brown wings ½ inch long.

WINTER-BUDS.—Ovoid, acute, light red-brown, puberulous, ⅛ inch long.

BARK.—Twigs at first green and rusty-pubescent, becoming dull red-brown and rusty-pubescent; thin, gray-brown on the trunk, separating into thin, appressed scales.

WOOD.—Light, soft, weak, pale yellow-white, with thin, pure white sapwood.

DISTRIBUTION.—Occurs sparingly in southern Michigan; more abundant in the northern portions.

HABITAT.—Cold, sphagnous bogs and swamps; shores of lakes.

NOTES.—Short-lived. Undesirable for ornamental planting, as the lower branches die early, making an unattractive evergreen. Often cut for Christmas trees. Growing to its largest size in the far north.

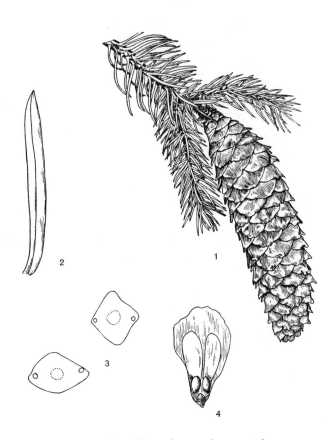

1. Branchlet with partly opened cone, x ½.
2. Leaf, x 3.
3. Cross-sections of leaves, enlarged.
4. Cone-scale with seeds, x 1.

PINACEAE

Norway Spruce

Picea abies (L.) Karst. [*Picea excelsa* Link]

HABIT.—A tree 50-70 feet high, with a trunk diameter of 1-3 feet; forming a dense, conical, spire-topped crown of numerous, drooping branches which persist nearly to the ground.

LEAVES.—Spirally arranged along the twig; crowded; ¾-1 inch long; rigid, curved, acute; lustrous, dark green. Persistent for 5-7 years.

FLOWERS.—May; monoecious; the staminate in ovoid to subglobose, long-stalked, reddish to yellowish clusters, ¾-1 inch long; the ovulate in cylindrical, sessile, erect clusters, 1½-2 inches long.

FRUIT.—Autumn of first season; sessile, cylindrical cones, 3-6 inches long, pendent from the tips of the uppermost branches; cone-scales with finely toothed margin; seeds red-brown, rough, ⅛ inch long, with long wings.

WINTER-BUDS.—Ovoid, acute, red-brown, not resinous, about ⅜ inch long.

BARK.—Twigs red- or orange-brown, smooth or corrugated; becoming thin and gray-brown on old trunks, slightly fissured, scaly.

WOOD.—Light, strong, tough, elastic, soft, fine-grained, white, with thick, indistinguishable sapwood.

DISTRIBUTION.—Introduced from Europe.

HABITAT.—Prefers rather rich, moist soils; does not thrive on very dry, very sterile or extremely rich vegetable soil.

NOTES.—Grows to a height of 120-150 feet in northern Europe and Asia. Perfectly hardy in Michigan, though somewhat susceptible to drought, wind and late frosts. Easily transplanted, grows rapidly, but is short-lived in our country. Desirable for ornamental planting, hedges and windbreaks. There are a number of horticultural varieties.

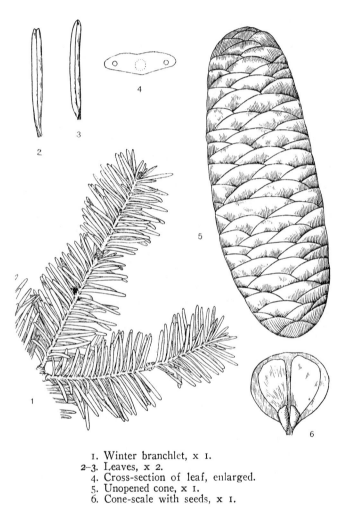

1. Winter branchlet, x 1.
2–3. Leaves, x 2.
4. Cross-section of leaf, enlarged.
5. Unopened cone, x 1.
6. Cone-scale with seeds, x 1.

PINACEAE

Balsam Fir

Abies balsamea (L.) Mill.

HABIT.—A slender tree 40-60 feet high, with a trunk diameter of 12-18 inches; branches in whorls of 4-6, forming a symmetrical, open crown widest at the base and tapering regularly upward.

LEAVES.—Scattered, spirally arranged in rows, on young trees extending from all sides of the branch, on old trees covering the upper side of the branch; narrowly linear, with apex acute or rounded; ½-1¼ inches long; lustrous, dark green above, pale beneath; sessile; aromatic. Persistent for 8-10 years.

FLOWERS.—May; monoecious; the staminate in oblong-cylindrical clusters, ¼ inch long, composed of yellow anthers (subtended by scales) spirally arranged upon a central axis; the ovulate in oblong-cylindrical clusters, 1 inch long, composed of orbicular, purple scales (subtended by yellow-green bracts) spirally arranged upon a central axis.

FRUIT.—Autumn of first season; oblong-cylindrical, erect, puberulous, dark purple cones, 2-4 inches long and 1 inch in diameter; seeds ¼ inch long, shorter than their light brown wings.

WINTER-BUDS.—Globose, orange-green, resinous, ⅛-¼ inch in diameter.

BARK.—Twigs at first grayish and pubescent, becoming gray-brown and smooth; thin and smooth on young trunks, pale gray-brown and marked by swollen resin chambers; red-brown on old trunks and somewhat roughened by small, scaly plates.

WOOD.—Very light, soft, weak, coarse-grained, perishable, pale brown, with thick, lighter colored sapwood. See p. 313.

DISTRIBUTION.—Occasional in the southern half of the Lower Peninsula, frequent in the northern half; abundant in the Upper Peninsula.

HABITAT.—Prefers cool, moist, rich soil; low, swampy ground; well-drained hillsides.

NOTES.—Grows rapidly. Short-lived. Easily transplanted. There is a characteristic fragrance from the bruised leaves and they are much prized for making pillows. An excellent Christmas tree. The Canada balsam of commerce is obtained from this tree.

The White Fir, *Abies concolor* Lindl. & Gord., a native of the Rocky Mountains, is grown extensively for ornamental purposes. It is perfectly hardy, grows in any kind of soil and forms a stately, pyramidal tree, 75-100 or more feet high. It withstands heat and drought well. The leaves are 1½-3 inches long, flat, and vary in color from a pale green or silver to a deep blue. The bark is smooth, gray, on old trees fissured and scaly. The cones are erect, cylindrical, 3-5 inches long, greenish or purple before maturity.

Hemlock

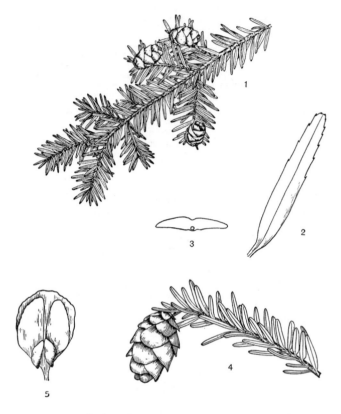

1. Fruiting branch viewed from beneath, x ½.
2. Leaf, x 3.
3. Cross-section of leaf, enlarged.
4. Branchlet with partly opened cone, x 1.
5. Cone-scale with seeds, x 3.

PINACEAE
Hemlock
Tsuga canadensis (L.) Carr.

HABIT.—A large tree 60-80 feet high, with a trunk 2-4 feet in diameter; forming a rather broad, open, somewhat irregular-pyramidal crown of slender, horizontal branches.

LEAVES.—Spirally arranged around the branch, but appearing 2-ranked by the twisting of their petioles; linear, flat, rounded at the apex; about ½ inch long; dark yellow-green and shining above, hoary beneath; short-petioled. Persistent for about 3 years.

FLOWERS.—April-May; monoecious; the staminate in axillary, short-stalked, light yellow, subglobose clusters of stamens, about ⅜ inch long; the ovulate in terminal, oblong-cylindrical, pale green clusters of short, pinkish scales, ⅛ inch long.

FRUIT.—Autumn of first season, gradually losing their seeds during the winter and falling the next spring; oblong-ovoid, acute, short-stalked, red-brown cones, about ¾ inch long; seeds ⅛ inch long, with wings about twice as long.

WINTER-BUDS.—Ovoid, obtuse, red-brown, slightly puberulous, ¹⁄₁₆ inch long.

BARK.—Twigs at first pale brown and pubescent, becoming glabrous, gray-brown; thick, red-brown or gray on the trunk, deeply divided into narrow, rounded, scaly ridges.

WOOD.—Light, soft, weak, brittle, coarse- and crooked-grained, not durable, ill-smelling, light red-brown, with thin, darker colored sapwood. See p. 313.

DISTRIBUTION.—Throughout the state, with the exception of the south-eastern portion; scarce on the east side of the state, more common on the west, becoming very abundant in Emmet County.

HABITAT.—Prefers well-drained uplands and slopes of ravines.

NOTES.—Slow of growth and rather difficult to establish by planting. A favorite hedge plant, and useful for ornamental planting in shady situations.

Closely related to the Hemlock is the giant tree of western America, *Pseudotsuga taxifolia* Britt., commonly called the Douglas Fir, but known also as Douglas Spruce and Red Fir. As in our native Hemlock, the leaves are flat; they are slightly narrowed, but not distinctly stalked, at the base, and obtuse at the apex, dark yellow-green to blue-green, with two white lines on the lower surface, ¾-1¼ inches long. The branches are horizontal, very irregularly whorled, and they turn up gracefully at the ends; forming a handsome, pyramidal crown. The bark is thick, dark red-brown and ridged. The cones are pendulous on long, stout stalks, 2-4½ inches long, with broad, rounded scales and narrow, protecting bracts which are 2-lobed at the apex and have the rigid midrib projecting into a point. The Douglas Fir is perfectly hardy, is easily transplanted, is rapid of growth, and is worthy of more extensive planting.

1. Fruiting branchlet, x 1.
2. Tip of branchlet, enlarged.
3. Cone-scale with seeds, x 3.

PINACEAE

Arborvitae. White Cedar
Thuja occidentalis L.

HABIT.—A tree 30-50 feet high, with a short, often buttressed trunk 1-2 feet in diameter, often divided into 2-3 secondary stems; forming a rather dense, wide-based, pyramidal crown.

LEAVES.—Opposite, 4-ranked, scale-like, appressed; ovate, obtuse or pointed, keeled in the side pairs, flat in the others; ⅛-¼ inch long; yellow-green, often becoming brown in winter; strongly aromatic when crushed. Persistent for 1-2 years.

FLOWERS.—April-May; usually monoecious; the staminate in minute, globose, yellow clusters, composed of 4-6 stamens arranged oppositely on a short axis; the ovulate in small, oblong-cylindrical, reddish clusters, composed of 8-12 scales arranged oppositely on a short axis.

FRUIT.—Early autumn of first season, but persistent on the branch through the winter; erect, short-stalked, oblong-ovoid, pale brown cones, about ½ inch long, composed of 8-12 loose scales; seeds ⅛ inch long, ovoid, acute, winged.

WINTER-BUDS.—Naked, minute.

BARK.—Twigs yellow-green, becoming light red, finally smooth, lustrous, dark orange-brown; thin, light red-brown on the trunk, slightly furrowed or deciduous in ragged strips.

WOOD.—Light, soft, brittle, rather coarse-grained, durable, fragrant, pale yellow-brown, with thin, whitish sapwood. See p. 315.

DISTRIBUTION.—Throughout the Upper Peninsula; Lower Peninsula as far south as Montcalm County.

HABITAT.—Prefers moist soil in low swamps and along river-banks.

NOTES.—Slow of growth. Tolerant of all soils and exposures. Especially useful for hedges or narrow evergreen screens. There are at least fifty or more varieties of Arborvitae in cultivation.

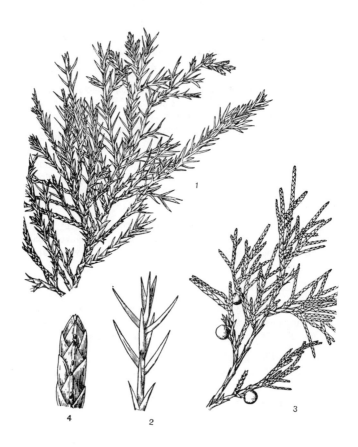

1. Branchlet with awl-shaped leaves, x 1.
2. Tip of branchlet, showing awl-shaped leaves, enlarged.
3. Fruiting branchlet with scale-like leaves, x 1.
4. Tip of branchlet, showing scale-like leaves, enlarged.

PINACEAE

Red Juniper. Red Cedar

Juniperus virginiana L.

HABIT.—A medium-sized tree 30-40 feet high, with a trunk diameter of 1-2 feet; forming an irregular, pyramidal or rounded crown.

LEAVES.—Opposite, of two kinds: (1) sessile, scale-like, closely appressed, overlapping, 4-ranked, ovate, acute, $\frac{1}{16}$ inch long; (2) sessile, awl-shaped, loosely arranged, $\frac{1}{4}$-$\frac{1}{2}$ inch long. Persistent for 5-6 years.

FLOWERS.—April-May; usually dioecious; minute; the staminate in oblong-ovoid clusters, composed of 4-6 shield-like scales, each bearing 4-5 yellow, globose pollen sacs; the ovulate in ovoid clusters, composed of about 3 pairs of fleshy, bluish scales, united at the base and bearing 2 ovules.

FRUIT.—Autumn of first or second season; subglobose, berry-like strobile, about $\frac{1}{4}$ inch in diameter, dark blue and glaucous; flesh sweet and resinous; seeds 2-3.

WINTER-BUDS.—Naked, minute, covered by the leaves.

BARK.—Twigs greenish to red-brown and smooth; thin, light red-brown on the trunk, exfoliating lengthwise into long, narrow, persistent strips, exposing the smooth, brown inner bark.

WOOD.—Light, soft, close-grained, brittle, weak, durable, very fragrant, dull red, with thin, whitish sapwood. See p. 315.

DISTRIBUTION.—Occurs sparingly throughout the state; most abundant in the southern portion.

HABITAT.—Prefers loamy soil on sunny slopes; dry, rocky hills; also borders of lakes and streams and peaty swamps.

NOTES.—Slow of growth. Long-lived. Should be transplanted with ball of earth. Tolerant of varied soils and situations. Extremely hardy and suitable for planting in cold exposures. Many ornamental varieties have been developed, some of which are highly prized for landscape work. See p. 263 for a description of the Chinese Juniper.

THE WILLOWS—SALIX

The genus *Salix* is represented in Michigan by thirty or more distinct species, and there are many more hybrids. The majority of these are shrubs, only a few becoming truly arborescent. Because of the similarity of their botanical characters, the frequency with which they hybridize and the facility with which they respond to their environment, only an expert is competent to identify the species so abundant along our water courses and on the banks of our lakes and swamps. The scope of this work being necessarily limited, it has been deemed best to describe but two of our native Willows and two of our foreign neighbors which are planted frequently.

Willows are introduced commonly as shade trees because they are propagated so easily by cuttings. Care should be taken, however, to select the stamen-bearing trees, both because these are more ornamental when in flower and because they do not produce the cottony fruit which often is disagreeable when Willows are growing near dwellings.

SUMMER KEY TO THE SPECIES OF SALIX*

a. Leaf petioles without glands.

   b. Leaves ¼-¾ inch broad; petioles broad and flat ....
....*S. nigra,* p. 69

   bb. Leaves ¾-1¼ inches broad; petioles slender and terete....
....................................*S. amygdaloides,* p. 71

aa. Leaf-petioles glandular above.

   b. Leaves ¼-½ inch broad, sharp-serrate; tree with weeping
habit................................*S. babylonica,* p. 75

   bb. Leaves ½-1½ inches broad, blunt-serrate; tree with upright
habit....................................*S. fragilis,* p. 73

WINTER KEY TO THE SPECIES OF SALIX

The classification of the Willows is a task for the specialist, even when leaves and both staminate and pistillate flowers are obtainable. It is impracticable for the novice to attempt the determination of species of *Salix* from winter characters alone. Consequently the usual winter key is omitted.

---

*It is not intended that this key shall serve as a means of identification of any species of *Salix* found in Michigan, but it is added simply to give a ready comparison of the four species which are described.

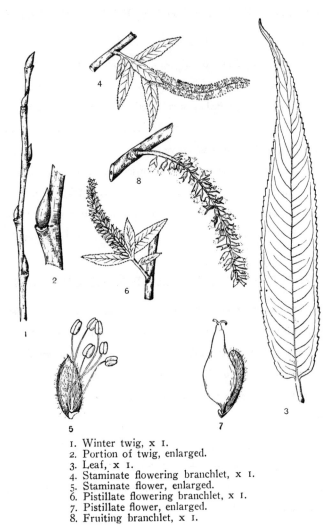

1. Winter twig, x 1.
2. Portion of twig, enlarged.
3. Leaf, x 1.
4. Staminate flowering branchlet, x 1.
5. Staminate flower, enlarged.
6. Pistillate flowering branchlet, x 1.
7. Pistillate flower, enlarged.
8. Fruiting branchlet, x 1.

SALICACEAE

Black Willow

Salix nigra Marsh.

HABIT.—A tree 30-50 feet high, with a short trunk, 1-2 feet in diameter; stout, spreading branches form a broad, rather irregular, open crown. Often a shrub.

LEAVES.—Alternate, simple, 3-6 inches long, ¼-¾ inch broad; lanceolate, very long-pointed, often curved at the tip; finely serrate; thin; bright green and rather lustrous above, paler and often hairy beneath; petioles very short, more or less pubescent.

FLOWERS.—April-May, with the leaves; dioecious; borne in crowded, slender, hairy catkins, 1-3 inches long; calyx 0; corolla 0; scales yellow, villous, with 3-6 stamens; ovary ovoid-conical, short-stalked, with stigmas nearly sessile.

FRUIT.—June; ovoid-conical capsule, ⅛ inch long, containing many minute seeds which are furnished with long, silky, white hairs.

WINTER-BUDS.—Terminal bud absent; lateral buds narrow-conical, acute, lustrous, red-brown, ⅛ inch long.

BARK.—Twigs glabrous or pubescent, bright red-brown, becoming darker with age; thick, dark brown or nearly black on old trunks, deeply divided into broad, flat ridges, often becoming shaggy.

WOOD.—Light, soft, weak, close-grained, light red-brown, with thin, whitish sapwood.

DISTRIBUTION.—Common throughout the state.

HABITAT.—Banks of streams and lake-shores.

NOTES.—Branchlets very brittle at the base, and these, broken off by the wind, are carried down stream, often catching in the muddy banks and there taking root.

Almondleaf Willow

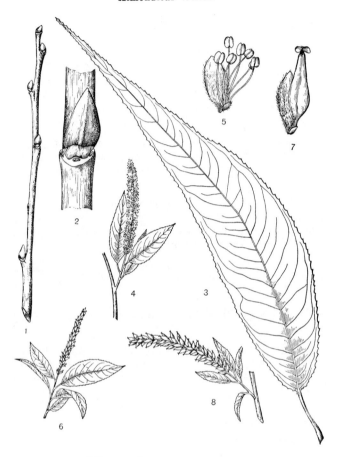

1. Winter twig, x 1.
2. Portion of twig, enlarged.
3. Leaf, x 1.
4. Staminate flowering branchlet, x ½.
5. Staminate flower, enlarged.
6. Pistillate flowering branchlet, x ½.
7. Pistillate flower, enlarged.
8. Fruiting branchlet, x ½.

SALICACEAE

Almondleaf Willow

Salix amygdaloides Anders.

HABIT.—A tree 30-40 feet high, with a straight, columnar trunk, 1-2 feet in diameter; straight, ascending branches form a rather narrow, rounded crown.

LEAVES.—Alternate, simple, 2-6 inches long, ¾-1¼ inches broad; lanceolate to ovate-lanceolate, long-pointed; finely serrate; thin and firm; light green and shining above, pale and glaucous beneath; petioles slender, ½-¾ inch long.

FLOWERS.—April, with the leaves; dioecious; borne in crowded, slender, pubescent catkins, 2-3 inches long; calyx o; corolla o; scales yellow, villous both sides; stamens 5-9; ovary oblong-conical, with stigmas nearly sessile.

FRUIT.—May; 1-celled, globose-conical capsule ¼ inch long, containing many minute seeds which are furnished with long, silky, white hairs.

WINTER-BUDS.—Terminal bud absent; lateral buds broadly ovid, gibbous, lustrous, dark brown, ⅛ inch long.

BARK.—Twigs glabrous, lustrous, dark orange or red-brown, becoming darker orange-brown; thick and brown on old trunks, irregularly fissured into flat, connected ridges.

WOOD.—Light, soft, weak, close-grained, light brown, with thick, whitish sapwood.

DISTRIBUTION.—Common throughout the state.

HABITAT.—Banks of streams.

NOTES.—Hybridizes freely with other willows, making its identification difficult.

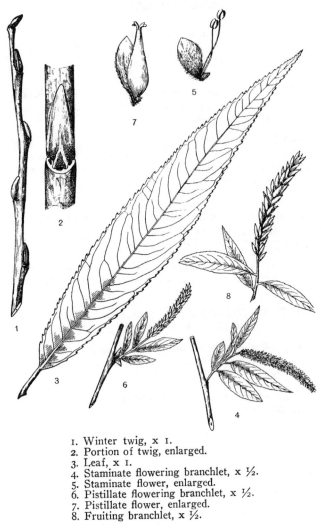

1. Winter twig, x 1.
2. Portion of twig, enlarged.
3. Leaf, x 1.
4. Staminate flowering branchlet, x ½.
5. Staminate flower, enlarged.
6. Pistillate flowering branchlet, x ½.
7. Pistillate flower, enlarged.
8. Fruiting branchlet, x ½.

SALICACEAE

Crack Willow. Brittle Willow
Salix fragilis L.

HABIT.—A tree 50-60 feet high, with a short, stout trunk, 3-4 feet in diameter; stout, spreading branches form a broad, open crown.

LEAVES.—Alternate, simple, 3-6 inches long, ½-1½ inches broad; lanceolate, long-pointed; finely glandular-serrate; thin and firm; lustrous, dark green above, paler beneath, glabrous both sides; petioles short, stout, with 2 glands at the junction of blade and petiole.

FLOWERS.—April-May, with the leaves; dioecious; borne in slender, pubescent catkins, 1-3 inches long; calyx o; corolla o; scales blunt, somewhat pubescent; stamens usually 2; ovary abortive, with stigmas nearly sessile. Staminate trees rare.

FRUIT.—May-June; 1-celled, long-conical, short-stalked capsule, about ¼ inch long, containing many minute seeds which are furnished with long, silky, white hairs.

WINTER-BUDS.—Terminal bud absent; lateral buds long-conical, pointed, glabrous, bright red-brown, about ¼ inch long.

BARK.—Twigs pubescent, yellow-green, often reddish, becoming glabrous, lustrous, brown; thick, gray on the trunk, smooth on young trees, very rough and irregularly scaly-ridged on old trees.

WOOD.—Light, soft, tough, close-grained, red-brown, with thick, whitish sapwood.

DISTRIBUTION.—Introduced from Europe and Asia, where it is a valuable timber tree, and naturalized in America.

HABITAT.—Prefers rich, damp soil.

NOTES.—Hardy throughout the state. Easily grown from cuttings. Of very rapid growth. The shoots are used in the manufacture of baskets and furniture. The twigs are very brittle at the base and are easily broken by the wind, hence the name Brittle Willow.

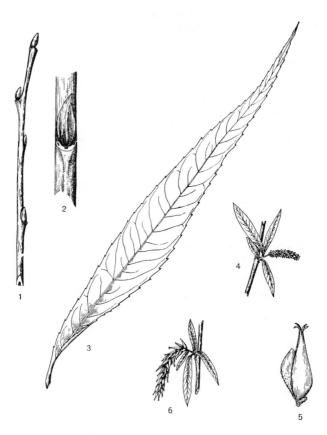

1. Winter twig, x 1.
2. Portion of twig, enlarged.
3. Leaf, x 1.
4. Pistillate flowering branchlet, x ½.
5. Pistillate flower, enlarged.
6. Fruiting branchlet, x ½.

SALICACEAE

Weeping Willow. Napoleon's Willow

Salix babylonica L.

HABIT.—A tree 40-50 feet high, with a short, stout trunk, 3-4 feet in diameter; the long, slender branchlets, often many feet in length, droop in graceful festoons, giving to the tree a weeping habit.

LEAVES.—Alternate, simple, 3-7 inches long, ¼-½ inch broad; linear to linear-lanceolate, long-pointed; finely sharp-serrate; thin and firm; glabrous, dark green above, paler beneath; petioles ½ inch or less in length, glandular above, often hairy.

FLOWERS.—April-May, with the leaves; dioecious; borne in slender, nearly glabrous catkins, 1-2 inches long; calyx o; corolla o; scales ovate-lanceolate, slightly hairy; ovary ovoid-conical, very short-stalked, with stigmas longer than the style. Staminate trees apparently do not occur in the United States.

FRUIT.—May-June; 1-celled, narrow-ovoid, sessile capsule, about ³⁄₁₆ inch long, containing many minute seeds which are furnished with long, silky, white hairs.

WINTER-BUDS.—Terminal bud absent; lateral buds narrow-conical, sharp-pointed, somewhat flattened, brownish, ⅛-¼ inch long.

BARK.—Twigs glabrous, olive-green; thick and gray on old trunks, rather smooth, or irregularly fissured into shallow, firm ridges.

WOOD.—Light, soft, weak, close-grained, light brown, with thick, whitish sapwood.

DISTRIBUTION.—Introduced from Asia and Europe; widely cultivated in America, and in many places established through natural cuttings.

HABITAT.—A moisture-loving tree thriving along streams and about lakes and ponds.

NOTES.—Much planted for ornament and shade in cemeteries and parks, in moist places, especially about ponds and lakes and along streams. Easily propagated from cuttings. Rapid of growth in rich, damp soil. Sometimes winter-killed because the wood is not ripened. A number of horticultural varieties are recognized.

THE POPLARS—POPULUS

The genus *Populus* belongs to the Willow family, and the Poplars resemble the Willows, especially in flower and fruit characters. The pendulous, worm-like catkins of flowers are borne upon different trees, and, opening before the leaves have appeared, are conspicuous objects in early spring. As in the Willows, the seeds are very light, and they are produced in great abundance. They are furnished with a dense covering of long, white hairs or "cotton," which aids in their dispersal. Escaping early in the season, they float in the wind, becoming objectionable when the trees are growing in the vicinity of dwellings. On this account the trees are called Cottonwoods in the West.

The Poplars are distributed widely, extending from the Arctic Circle to Mexico and from the Atlantic to the Pacific. Eleven species occur within the boundaries of the United States, of which five are native to Michigan. Two introduced species are quite commonly cultivated, the Lombardy Poplar and the White or Silver-leaf Poplar, both of which are described and illustrated.

SUMMER KEY TO THE SPECIES OF POPULUS

a. Leaf-petioles essentially terete.
  b. Petioles and lower sides of leaves pubescent; leaves heart-shaped....................................*P. candicans,* p. 87
  bb. Petioles and lower sides of leaves glabrous; leaves ovate-lanceolate...............................*P. balsamifera,* p. 85
aa. Leaf-petioles strongly flattened.
  b. Petioles and lower sides of leaves tomentose; twigs pubescent.......................................*P. alba,* p. 79
  bb. Petioles and lower sides of leaves glabrous; twigs glabrous.
    c. Leaves distinctly deltoid in shape.
      d. Leaves broader than they are long, abruptly acuminate at the apex; marginal teeth not conspicuously incurved; branches erect and more or less appressed to the main stem, forming a narrow, spire-like crown.
      ....*P. nigra italica,* p. 91

dd. Leaves longer than they are broad, more or less taper-pointed at the apex; marginal teeth rather conspicuously incurved; branches spreading, forming a broad crown.............................*P. deltoides,* p. 89
cc. Leaves ovate to nearly orbicular in shape.
    d. Margin of leaves coarsely sinuate-toothed; leaves 3-5 inches long.....................*P. grandidentata,* p. 83
    dd. Margin of leaves finely serrate; leaves less than 3 inches long.......................*P. tremuloides,* p. 81

WINTER KEY TO THE SPECIES OF POPULUS

a. Branches erect, more or less appressed to the main stem, forming a narrow, spire-like crown......*P. nigra italica,* p. 91
aa. Branches spreading, forming a broad crown.
  b. Terminal buds ⅛-¼ inch long, not resinous.
    c. Buds and twigs more or less conspicuously white-downy; twigs green.............................*P. alba,* p. 79
    cc. Buds and twigs not conspicuously white-downy; twigs usually red-brown.
      d. Terminal buds about ⅛ inch long, puberulous, dusty-looking; lateral buds widely divergent; twigs rather coarse.........................*P. grandidentata,* p. 83
      dd. Terminal buds about ¼ inch long, glabrous, lustrous; lateral buds more or less appressed; twigs rather slender.........................*P. tremuloides,* p. 81
  bb. Terminal buds ½-1 inch long, sticky-resinous.
    c. Terminal buds about ½ inch long; buds not fragrant; twigs usually yellow, more or less strongly angled......
      ....*P. deltoides,* p. 89
    cc. Terminal buds nearly 1 inch long; buds fragrant; twigs usually red-brown and seldom strongly angled.........
      ....*P. balsamifera,** p. 85
                               P. candicans,* p. 87

---

*It is difficult to distinguish between these species in the absence of summer characters. If leaves can be found on or beneath a tree which is sufficiently segregated from similar trees as to avoid any chance for error, the summer key may be used.

1. Winter twig, x 1.
2. Portion of twig, enlarged.
3. Leaf, x 2.
4. Staminate flowering branchlet, x ½.
5. Staminate flower, enlarged.
6. Pistillate flowering branchlet, x ½.
7. Pistillate flower, enlarged.
8. Fruiting catkin, x ½.

SALICACEAE
White Poplar. Silver-leaf Poplar
Populus alba L.

HABIT.—A large tree 60-80 feet high, with a trunk diameter of 2-4 feet, forming a large, spreading, rounded or irregular crown of large, crooked branches and sparse, stout branchlets.

LEAVES.—Alternate, simple, 2-4 inches long and almost as broad; broadly ovate to suborbicular; irregularly sinuate-toothed; glabrous, dark green above, white-tomentose to glabrous beneath; petioles long, slender, flattened, tomentose.

FLOWERS.—April-May, before the leaves; dioecious; the staminate catkins thick, cylindrical, 2-4 inches long; the pistillate catkins slender, 1-2 inches long; calyx o; corolla o; stamens 6-16, with purple anthers; stigmas 2, branched, yellow.

FRUIT.—May-June; ovoid, 2-valved capsules, ⅛-¼ inch long, borne in drooping catkins, 2-4 inches long; seeds light brown, surrounded by long, white hairs.

WINTER-BUDS.—Ovoid, pointed, not viscid, downy, about ¼ inch long.

BARK.—Twigs greenish, covered with a white down, becoming greenish gray and marked with darker blotches; dark gray and fissured at the base of old trunks.

WOOD.—Light, soft, weak, difficult to split, reddish yellow, with thick, whitish sapwood.

DISTRIBUTION.—Introduced from Europe and Asia; commonly planted for shade and ornament.

HABITAT.—Prefers rich, moist soil, but will thrive in poorer, drier situations.

NOTES.—Perfectly hardy. Grows rapidly in good soils. The deep roots produce numerous suckers for a considerable distance from the tree. Undesirable for planting in dirty, smoky situations. The type form of *Populus alba* is less frequently planted than are two of its varieties, both of which have 3-5-lobed leaves, which are white velvety-tomentose beneath, and cottony twigs. *Populus alba*, v. *nivea* Wesm. has a spreading habit, like the type, while *Populus alba*, v. *pyramidalis* Bunge, known as Bolle's Poplar, has a narrow, spire-like crown of erect branches, thus resembling the Lombardy Poplar in general habit, and the leaves are more deeply lobed than are those of v. *nivea*. Bolle's Poplar is attractive for bold effects, but is sometimes attacked by borers.

Aspen

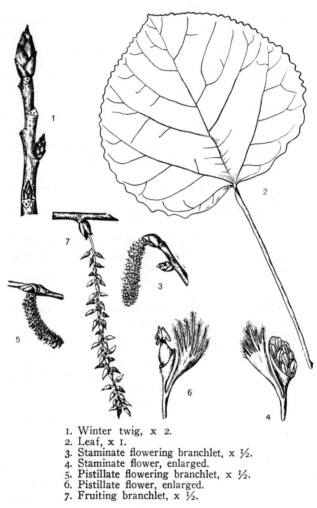

1. Winter twig, x 2.
2. Leaf, x 1.
3. Staminate flowering branchlet, x ½.
4. Staminate flower, enlarged.
5. Pistillate flowering branchlet, x ½.
6. Pistillate flower, enlarged.
7. Fruiting branchlet, x ½.

SALICACEAE

Aspen

Populus tremuloides Michx.

HABIT.—A small, slender tree generally 35-45 feet high, with a trunk diameter of 8-15 inches; forming a loose, rounded crown of slender branches.

LEAVES.—Alternate, simple, 1½-2½ inches long and broad; broadly ovate to suborbicular; finely serrate; thin and firm; lustrous, dark green above, dull and pale beneath; petioles slender, laterally compressed. Tremulous with the slightest breeze.

FLOWERS.—March-April, before the leaves; dioecious; the staminate catkins 1½-3 inches long; the pistillate at first about the same length, gradually elongating; calyx 0; corolla 0; stamens 6-12; stigmas 2, 2-lobed, red.

FRUIT.—May-June; 2-valved, oblong-cylindrical, short-pedicelled capsules, ¼ inch long; seeds light brown, white-hairy.

WINTER-BUDS.—Terminal bud about ¼ inch long, narrow-conical, acute, red-brown, lustrous; lateral buds often appressed.

BARK.—Twigs very lustrous, red-brown, becoming grayish and roughened by the elevated leaf-scars; thin, yellowish or greenish and smooth on the trunk, often roughened with darker, horizontal bands or wart-like excrescences, becoming thick, fissured and almost black at the base of old trunks.

WOOD.—Light, soft, weak, close-grained, not durable, light brown, with thin, whitish sapwood. See p. 317.

DISTRIBUTION.—Common throughout the state, but most abundant in the Upper Peninsula.

HABITAT.—Prefers moist, sandy soil and gravelly hillsides.

NOTES.—One of the first trees to cover cut- and burned-over lands. Grows rapidly. Usually short-lived. Propagated from seed or cuttings. Largely used with Spruce and Hemlock for pulpwood.

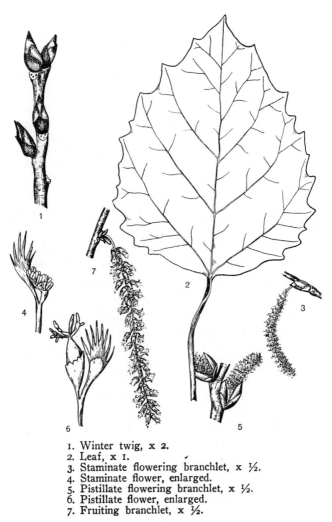

1. Winter twig, x 2.
2. Leaf, x 1.
3. Staminate flowering branchlet, x ½.
4. Staminate flower, enlarged.
5. Pistillate flowering branchlet, x ½.
6. Pistillate flower, enlarged.
7. Fruiting branchlet, x ½.

SALICACEAE

Largetooth Aspen
Populus grandidentata Michx.

HABIT.—A medium-sized tree 30-50 feet high, with a slender trunk 12-20 inches in diameter; forming a loose, ovoid or rounded crown of slender, spreading branches and coarse spray.

LEAVES.—Alternate, simple, 3-5 inches long, two-thirds as broad; orbicular-ovate; coarsely and irregularly sinuate-toothed; thin and firm; densely white-tomentose beneath when young, becoming with age dark green above, paler beneath, glabrous both sides; petioles long, slender, laterally compressed.

FLOWERS.—March-April, before the leaves; dioecious; the staminate in short-stalked catkins, 1-3 inches long; the pistillate in loose-flowered, long-stalked catkins, at first about the same length, but gradually elongating; calyx 0; corolla 0; stamens 6-12, with red anthers; stigmas 2, 2-lobed, red.

FRUIT.—May; 2-valved, conical, acute, hairy capsules, ⅛ inch long, borne in drooping catkins, 4-6 inches long; seeds minute, dark brown, hairy.

WINTER-BUDS.—Terminal bud ⅛ inch long, ovoid to conical, acute, light chestnut, puberulous, dusty-looking.

BARK.—Twigs greenish gray and at first hoary-tomentose, becoming lustrous, orange or red-brown and finally greenish gray; thick, dark red-brown or blackish at the base of old trunks, irregularly fissured, with broad, flat ridges.

WOOD.—Light, soft, weak, close-grained, light brown, with thin, whitish sapwood.

DISTRIBUTION.—A common tree in the northern portions of the Lower Peninsula, but rare in the Upper Peninsula.

HABITAT.—Prefers rich, moist, sandy soil; borders of swamps; river-banks; hillsides.

NOTES.—Grows rapidly in many soils. Easily transplanted. Short-lived. Useful for temporary effect. Propagated from seed or cuttings.

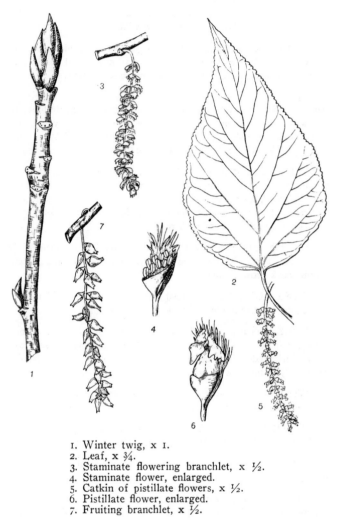

1. Winter twig, x 1.
2. Leaf, x ¾.
3. Staminate flowering branchlet, x ½.
4. Staminate flower, enlarged.
5. Catkin of pistillate flowers, x ½.
6. Pistillate flower, enlarged.
7. Fruiting branchlet, x ½.

SALICACEAE

Balm of Gilead. Balsam

Populus balsamifera L.

HABIT.—A tree 60-75 feet high, with a trunk diameter of 1-3 feet; forming a rather narrow, open, pyramidal crown of few, slender, horizontal branches.

LEAVES.—Alternate, simple, 3-6 inches long, about one-half as broad; ovate to ovate-lanceolate; finely crenate-serrate; thin and firm; lustrous, dark green above, paler beneath; petioles 1¼ inches long, slender, terete, smooth.

FLOWERS.—April-May, before the leaves; dioecious; the staminate in long-stalked catkins, 3-4 inches long; the pistillate in loose-flowered, long-stalked catkins, 4-5 inches long; calyx o; corolla o; stamens 20-30, with bright red anthers; ovary short-stalked; stigmas 2, wavy-margined.

FRUIT.—May-June; 2-valved, ovoid, short-pedicelled capsules, ¼ inch long, borne in drooping catkins, 4-6 inches long; seeds light brown, hairy.

WINTER-BUDS.—Terminal bud about 1 inch long, ovoid, long-pointed, brownish, resin-coated, sticky, fragrant.

BARK.—Twigs red-brown, becoming dark orange, finally green-gray; thick, grayish on old trunks and shallowly fissured into broad, rounded ridges, often roughened by dark excrescences.

WOOD.—Light, soft, weak, close-grained, light red-brown, with thick, nearly white sapwood.

DISTRIBUTION.—Occurs throughout the entire state, but is more abundant and of greater size in the northern portions.

HABITAT.—Prefers river bottom-lands and borders of swamps.

NOTES.—Rapid of growth. Spreads from the roots. Most useful for shelter-belts. Easily transplanted. Propagated from cuttings. It is subject to great variation in the form of the leaves. Some are almost triangular with a deeply heart-shape base, while others are very slender with a wedge-shape base.

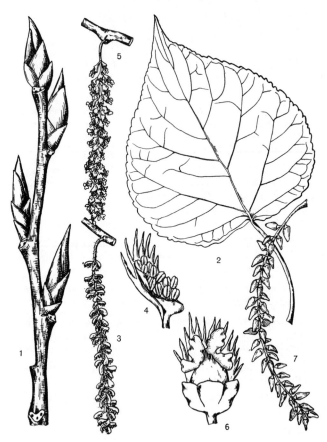

1. Winter twig, x 1.
2. Leaf, x ½.
3. Staminate flowering branchlet, x ½.
4. Staminate flower, enlarged.
5. Pistillate flowering branchlet, x ½.
6. Pistillate flower, enlarged.
7. Fruiting catkin, x ½.

SALICACEAE

Hairy Balm of Gilead. Balsam

Populus candicans Ait. [*Populus balsamifera candicans*
(Ait.) Gray]

HABIT.—A tree 50-70 feet high, with a trunk diameter of
1-3 feet; more spreading branches than in *P. balsamifera,* forming
a broader and more open crown.

LEAVES.—Resemble those of *P. balsamifera,* but more
broadly heart-shaped and more coarsely serrate; more or less
pubescent when young; petioles pubescent.

FLOWERS.—Similar to those of *P. balsamifera.*

FRUIT.—Similar to that of *P. balsamifera.*

WINTER-BUDS.—Terminal bud about 1 inch long, ovoid,
long-pointed, dark red-brown, resinous throughout, viscid, very
aromatic.

BARK.—Twigs reddish or olive-green, with occasional longitudinal gray lines, covered with a fragrant, gummy secretion,
becoming gray-green; dark gray, rough, irregularly striate and
firm on old trunks.

WOOD.—Resembles that of *P. balsamifera,* but is somewhat
heavier.

DISTRIBUTION.—Indigenous to the northern portions of
the state, but often cultivated and occasionally escaping in the
southern portion.

HABITAT.—In a great variety of soils and situations.

NOTES.—Grows rapidly in all soils and situations. Spreads
rapidly by suckers from the roots. Propagated from cuttings.
Short-lived and becomes unsightly with age; hence not to be
recommended for shade or ornament.

Cottonwood

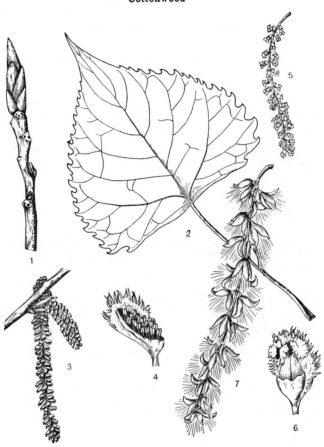

1. Winter twig, x 1.
2. Leaf, x ½.
3. Staminate flowering branchlet, x ½.
4. Staminate flower, enlarged.
5. Pistillate catkin, x ½.
6. Pistillate flower, enlarged.
7. Fruiting catkin, x ½.

SALICACEAE

Cottonwood

Populus deltoides Marsh. [*Populus monilifera* Ait.]

HABIT.—A stately tree attaining a height of 60-80 feet and a trunk diameter of 3-5 feet; forming a spreading, open, symmetrical crown of massive, horizontal branches and stout, more or less angled branchlets.

LEAVES.—Alternate, simple, 3-6 inches long, nearly as broad; broadly deltoid-ovate; coarsely crenate-serrate above the entire base; thick and firm; lustrous, dark green above, paler beneath; petioles 2-3 inches long, slender, compressed laterally.

FLOWERS.—April-May, before the leaves; dioecious; the staminate in short-stalked, densely-flowered catkins, 3-4 inches long; the pistillate in short-stalked, few-flowered catkins, elongating to 6-8 inches; calyx 0; corolla 0; stamens very numerous, with red anthers; stigmas 3-4, spreading.

FRUIT.—May; 2-4-valved, short-stalked capsules, borne in drooping catkins 8-10 inches long; seeds light brown, densely cottony.

WINTER-BUDS.—Terminal bud ½-¾ inch long, conical, acute, very resinous, shining, brownish.

BARK.—Twigs and young stems smooth, yellow-green; old trunks ashy gray, deeply divided into straight furrows with broad, rounded ridges.

WOOD.—Light, soft, weak, close-grained, dark brown, with thick, whitish sapwood; warps badly and is difficult to season.

DISTRIBUTION.—Entire Michigan; rare in the northern portions.

HABITAT.—Prefers rich, moist soil; river-banks; river-bottoms; lake-shores; grows well in drier situations.

NOTES.—Rapid of growth, consequently an excellent tree for immediate effect. Propagated from cuttings.

A tree, long known as Carolina Poplar, has been planted extensively in cities because it grows very rapidly and is not injured by smoke and drought. The identity of this tree is a matter of some doubt. Some consider it to be a staminate form of the Cottonwood, while others believe it to be a cross between *Populus nigra* and *Populus balsamifera,* in which case the scientific names, *Populus canadensis* Moench. or *Populus eugenei* Hort. ex Dode, are applied. Where other trees can be substituted with success, the planting of Carolina Poplar should be discouraged, for it is short-lived, it sheds many branches during the autumn rains, and the larger roots, which spread out near the surface, are known to heave up the sidewalks and pavement, while the finer rootlets penetrate and clog drain-pipes and sewers.

—89—

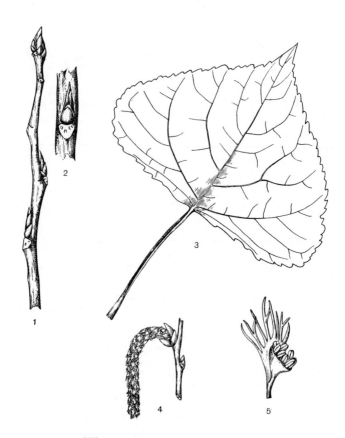

1. Winter twig, x 1.
2. Portion of twig, enlarged.
3. Leaf, x ¾.
4. Staminate flowering branchlet, x ½.
5. Staminate flower, enlarged.

SALICACEAE

Lombardy Poplar

Populus nigra italica DuRoi [*Populus fastigiata* Desf.]
[*Populus dilatata* Ait.]

HABIT.—A tree 75-100 feet high, with a short, ridged and buttressed trunk 4-6 feet in diameter and a narrow, spire-like crown of erect branches.

LEAVES.—Alternate, simple, 2-4 inches long, and usually somewhat broader than long; broad-deltoid, abruptly acuminate at the apex; finely but bluntly crenate-serrate; thick and firm; dark green and shining above, lighter and more or less lustrous beneath; petioles slender, laterally compressed, 1-2 inches long.

FLOWERS.—April-May, before the leaves; dioecious; the staminate in sessile, dark red, cylindrical catkins, about 3 inches long; the pistillate not present in the United States; calyx o; corolla o; stamens about 8, with white filaments and purple anthers.

FRUIT.—Not formed in the United States in the absence of pistillate flowers.

WINTER-BUDS.—Terminal bud conical, slightly angled, taper-pointed, glutinous, about ⅜ inch long; lateral buds smaller, appressed.

BARK.—Twigs glabrous, shining yellow, becoming gray; thick and gray-brown on old trunks, deeply and irregularly furrowed.

WOOD.—Light, soft, easily worked, not liable to splinter, weak, not durable, light red-brown, with thick, nearly white sapwood.

DISTRIBUTION.—Introduced from Europe; thought to be a native of Afghanistan, and cultivated in western Asia in early times; said to have been the first ornamental tree to be introduced into the United States, and a familiar sight in practically every part of the country.

HABITAT.—Grows in a variety of soils and exposures.

NOTES.—Very rapid of growth, but short-lived. Valuable for landscape effects. Its limbs die early, and these remain, causing the tree to become unsightly in a very few years. Spreads by means of suckers from the roots and by fallen branches.

THE WALNUTS—JUGLANS

Every school boy in southern Michigan has some acquaintance with the Walnuts, at least with the more common Black Walnut. The Walnuts have pinnately compound leaves, which are arranged alternately on the branches. The staminate flowers appear in May and hang in graceful, slender catkins 3-5 inches long. These are generally found on the growth of the preceding season, while the pistillate flowers are borne on the growth of the new season. The fruit matures at the end of the first year, and consists of a sculptured nut inclosed in a fleshy husk which does not split open into regular segments. The meat of the nut is 2-4-lobed, large and oily. The nuts are scattered mainly by squirrels, which bury them for food, and by streams of water which carry them along their courses. The pith of the twigs is a never-failing means of identification, being chambered, i.e., it consists of thin plates separated by air cavities. That of the Black Walnut is cream colored, while the Butternut has a chocolate-brown pith.

About ten species of Walnuts are known, four of which occur in the United States, and two are native to Michigan. In addition to the native species, an introduction from Europe, known as the Persian or English Walnut, *Juglans regia* L., is widely planted in the United States as an ornamental tree and very occasionally may be found in the southernmost part of the state, where it is subject to winter-injury, especially in youth. The English Walnut has pinnately-compound leaves, consisting of 7-9 glabrous and almost entire leaflets, 2-5 inches long. The twigs and buds are glabrous also, and there is no downy pad above the leaf-scar. The pith is coarsely chambered, light brown. The bark is gray and smooth for a long time. The thin-shelled nuts are familiar in our markets, and the wood is used extensively in the manufacture of furniture, under the name Circassian Walnut.

SUMMER KEY TO THE SPECIES OF JUGLANS

a. Leaflets 11-17, the terminal usually present; pith of twigs chocolate-brown; bark of trunk rather ·smooth, or fissured, with broad, flat, whitish ridges; fruit elongated, sticky-downy....................................*J. cinerea*, p. 95

aa. Leaflets 13-23, the terminal often lacking; pith of twigs cream colored; bark of trunk rough, brownish or blackish; deeply furrowed by broad, rounded ridges; fruit globose, not sticky-downy.......................................*J. nigra,* p. 97

WINTER KEY TO THE SPECIES OF JUGLANS

a. Pith chocolate-brown; leaf-scar with downy pad above; fruit elongated, sticky-downy, terminal bud ½-¾ inch long; bark rather smooth, or fissured, with broad, flat, whitish ridges....
....*J. cinerea,* p. 95

aa. Pith cream colored; leaf-scar without downy pad above; fruit globose, not sticky-downy; terminal bud ⅓ inch long; bark rough, brownish or blackish, deeply furrowed by broad, rounded ridges..............................*J. nigra,* p. 97

Butternut

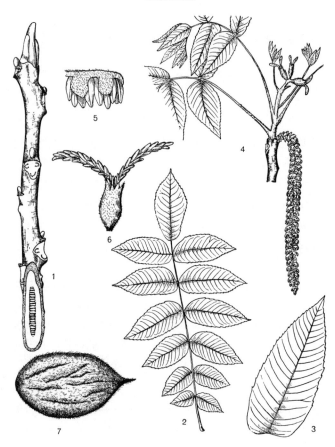

1. Winter twig, x 1.
2. Leaf, x ⅙.
3. Leaflet, x ½.
4. Flowering branchlet, x ½.
5. Staminate flower, enlarged.
6. Pistillate flower, enlarged.
7. Fruit, x ½.

JUGLANDACEAE

Butternut

Juglans cinerea L.

HABIT.—A medium-sized tree 30-50 feet high, with a short trunk 2-3 feet in diameter; forming a wide-spreading crown of large, horizontal branches and stout, stiff branchlets.

LEAVES.—Alternate, pinnately compound, 15-30 inches long. Leaflets 11-17, 2-4 inches long and one-half as broad; sessile, except the terminal; oblong-lanceolate; finely serrate; thin; yellow-green and rugose above, pale and soft-pubescent beneath. Petioles stout, hairy.

FOWERS.—May, with the leaves; monoecious; the staminate in cylindrical, greenish, drooping catkins, 3-5 inches long; calyx 6-lobed, borne on a hairy bract; corolla o; stamens 8-12, with brown anthers; the pistillate solitary, or several on a common peduncle, about ⅓ inch long, their bracts and bractlets sticky-hairy; calyx 4-lobed, hairy; corolla o; styles 2; stigmas 2, fringed, spreading, bright red.

FRUIT.—October; about 2½ inches long, cylindrical, pointed, greenish, sticky-downy, solitary, or borne in drooping clusters of 3-5; nuts with rough shells, inclosing a sweet, but oily kernel; edible.

WINTER-BUDS.—Terminal bud ½-¾ inch long, oblong-conical, obliquely blunt, somewhat flattened, brownish, pubescent.

BARK.—Twigs orange-brown or bright green, rusty-pubescent, becoming smooth and light gray; gray and smoothish on young trunks, becoming brown on old trunks, narrow-ridged, with wide furrows.

WOOD.—Light, soft, weak, coarse-grained, light brown, with thin, lighter colored sapwood.

DISTRIBUTION.—Of common occurrence in the southern half of the Lower Peninsula.

HABITAT.—Prefers low, rich woods; river-banks; low hill-sides.

NOTES.—Leaves appear late and fall early. Pith chambered, chocolate-brown. Large trees usually scraggy and unsound. Not easily transplanted.

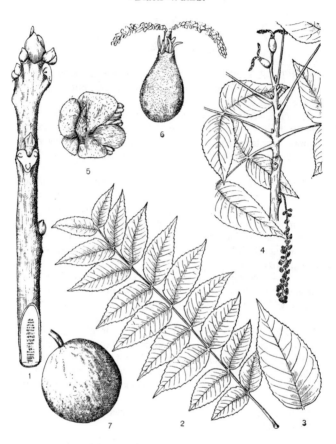

1. Winter twig, x 1.
2. Leaf, x ⅙.
3. Leaflet, x ½.
4. Flowering branchlet, x ½.
5. Staminate flower, back view, enlarged.
6. Pistillate flower, enlarged.
7. Fruit, x ½.

JUGLANDACEAE

Black Walnut
Juglans nigra L.

HABIT.—A large tree 60-80 feet high, with a massive trunk 2-4 feet in diameter; forming an open, capacious crown of heavy branches and coarse branchlets.

LEAVES.—Alternate, pinnately compound, 1-2 feet long. Leaflets 13-23, the terminal often lacking, 2-4 inches long and one-half as broad; sessile; ovate-lanceolate, taper-pointed; sharp-serrate; thin; yellow-green and glabrous above, lighter and soft-pubescent beneath. Petioles stout, pubescent. Foliage aromatic when bruised.

FLOWERS.—May, with the leaves; monoecious; the staminate in cylindrical, greenish, drooping catkins, 3-5 inches long; calyx 6-lobed, borne on a hairy bract; corolla o; stamens numerous, with purple anthers; the pistillate solitary, or several on a common peduncle, about ¼ inch long, their bracts and bractlets hairy; calyx 4-lobed, pubescent; corolla o; styles and stigmas 2.

FRUIT.—October; globose, 1½-2 inches in diameter, smooth, not viscid; solitary, or borne in clusters of 2-3; nuts with irregularly furrowed shell, inclosing a sweet, edible kernel. .

WINTER-BUDS.—Terminal bud ⅓ inch long, ovoid, obliquely blunt, slightly flattened, silky-tomentose.

BARK.—Twigs brownish and hairy, becoming darker and smooth; thick, brownish or blackish on the trunk and deeply furrowed by broad, rounded ridges.

WOOD.—Heavy, hard, strong, close-grained, very durable in contact with the soil, rich dark brown, with thin, lighter colored sapwood. See p. 319.

DISTRIBUTION.—Lower Peninsula as far north as Bay City, but more abundant in the southern portion of its range.

HABITAT.—Prefers rich bottom-lands and fertile hillsides.

NOTES.—Leaves appear late and fall early. Fruit very aromatic. Pith chambered, cream colored. The juices from the husk stain the hands brown. Not easily transplanted. Often infested with caterpillars. One of the most valuable timber trees of eastern United States, rapidly becoming scarce. The planting of nuts wherever they will grow is to be encouraged. Of decided ornamental value.

THE HICKORIES—CARYA

The Hickories belong to the same family as the Walnuts. Previous to the appearance of the Ice Age, forests of Hickory existed in Europe and Greenland. Today Europe has no native Hickories, and they are found nowhere in the world except in North America; and of the dozen species known, eleven occur within the boundaries of the United States. Six of these are native to Michigan.

The Hickories are among our most important timber trees. This is not for the reason that they produce large quantities of wood, but because they yield an exceptional quality of wood. It is used in the manufacture of wagons, automobile wheels, axe handles, agricultural implements, and in places where strength and elasticity are required it is almost unrivaled. The Hickories are stately trees, with deep root systems, and they are characterized by having bark which is extremely hard and compact. The leaves are compound, but composed of fewer leaflets than the Walnuts, and they are of a firm, somewhat leathery texture. The flowers, arranged in catkins of the two kinds, appear in late spring after the unfolding of the leaves.

The fruit matures in the autumn of the first season, and consists of a nut inclosed in a husk which is 4-valved. A hard frost brings them down in profusion. In most of the species the husk splits open when dry at least to the middle, but in some it separates very little. The nuts are sought out by the squirrels, and some of them find their way into our markets. Nut-gathering long has been a favorite pastime with the younger generation, and country boys are quick to distinguish between the edible kinds and the Pignut and Bitternut variety.

SUMMER KEY TO THE SPECIES OF CARYA

a. Bark of trunk essentially smooth, not deeply furrowed nor shaggy; husk of fruit less than ⅛ inch thick.
  b. Leaflets usually 5-7, glabrous beneath; buds dome-shaped, greenish; kernel of nut sweet.
    c. Twigs long-hairy; fruit less than 1 inch long............
.................................*C. microcarpa*, p. 107

cc. Twigs glabrous or nearly so; fruit 1½-2 inches long....
....*C. glabra,* p. 109
bb. Leaflets usually 7-11, more or less downy beneath; buds
elongated, bright yellow; kernel of nut bitter............
...................................*C. cordiformis,* p. 111
aa. Bark of trunk deeply furrowed or shaggy; husk of fruit more
than ⅛ inch thick.
b. Twigs more or less pubescent; leaflets 5-7, more or less
pubescent beneath.
c. Twigs brownish; buds densely hairy; fruit 1½-2 inches
long.....................................*C. alba,* p. 105
cc. Twigs orange; buds merely puberulous; fruit 1¾-2½
inches long; (leaflets usually 7).......*C. laciniosa,* p. 103
bb. Twigs tending to be glabrous; leaflets usually 5, glabrous
beneath.................................*C. ovata,* p. 101

WINTER KEY TO THE SPECIES OF CARYA

a. Bark of trunk essentially smooth, not deeply furrowed nor
shaggy; husk of fruit less than ⅛ inch thick.
b. Terminal bud narrow, long-pointed, flattish, bright yellow;
kernel of nut bitter.................*C. cordiformis,* p. 111
bb. Terminal bud broad, dome-shaped, not bright yellow; kernel
of nut sweet.
c. Buds greenish; twigs glabrous; fruit 1½-2 inches long....
....*C. glabra,* p. 109
cc. Buds red-brown; twigs long-hairy; fruit less than 1 inch
long.............................*C. microcarpa,* p. 107
aa. Bark of trunk deeply furrowed or shaggy; husk of fruit
more than ⅛ inch thick.
b. Twigs more or less pubescent; buds more or less pubescent.
c. Buds ½-¾ inch long, densely hairy; outer bud-scales
deciduous in autumn; twigs brownish; fruit 1½-2 inches
long.....................................*C. alba,* p. 105
cc. Buds about 1 inch long, merely puberulous; outer bud-
scales persistent until spring; twigs orange colored; fruit
1¾-2½ inches long...................*C. laciniosa.* p. 103
bb. Twigs tending to be glabrous; buds glabrous or nearly so..
....*C. ovata,* p. 101

1. Winter twig, x 1.
2. Portion of twig, enlarged.
3. Leaf, x ⅓.
4. Flowering branchlet, x ½.
5. Staminate flower, enlarged.
6. Pistillate flower, enlarged.
7. Fruit, x ½.

JUGLANDACEAE

Shagbark Hickory. Shellbark Hickory

Carya ovata (Mill.) K. Koch [*Hicoria ovata* (Mill.) Britt.]
[*Carya alba* Nutt.]

HABIT.—A tree 60-80 feet high, with a slender, columnar trunk 1-2 feet in diameter; forming a narrow, somewhat open crown of stout, slightly spreading limbs and stout branchlets.

LEAVES.—Alternate, compound, 8-14 inches long. Leaflets usually 5, the upper 5-7 inches long and 2-3 inches broad; sessile, except the terminal; obovate to oblong-lanceolate; finely serrate; thick and firm; glabrous, dark green above, paler beneath and glabrous or puberulous. Petioles stout, glabrous or hairy. Foliage fragrant when crushed.

FLOWERS.—May and early June, after the leaves; monoecious; the staminate hairy, greenish, in pendulous, ternate catkins, 4-5 inches long, on a common peduncle about 1 inch long; scales 3-parted, bristle-tipped; stamens 4, with bearded, yellow anthers; the pistillate in 2-5-flowered spikes, $\frac{1}{3}$ inch long, brown-tomentose; calyx 4-lobed, hairy; corolla 0; stigmas 2, large, fringed.

FRUIT.—October; globular, 1-2 inches long, with thick husk separating completely; nut usually 4-ridged, with thick shell and large, sweet, edible kernel.

WINTER-BUDS.—Terminal bud $\frac{1}{2}$-$\frac{3}{4}$ inch long, broadly ovoid, obtuse, dark brown, pale-tomentose or nearly glabrous.

BARK.—Twigs brownish, more or less downy, becoming smooth and grayish; thick and grayish on old trunks, separating into thick strips 1-3 feet long, free at one or both ends, giving a characteristic shaggy appearance.

WOOD.—Heavy, very hard and strong, tough, close-grained, elastic, light brown, with thin, whitish sapwood. See p. 319.

DISTRIBUTION.—Common in the Lower Peninsula as far north as Roscommon County.

HABITAT.—Prefers light, well-drained, loamy soil; low hillsides; river-banks.

NOTES.—Hardy throughout its range. Moderately rapid in growth. Difficult to transplant on account of the long tap root. Produces the common hickory nut of commerce.

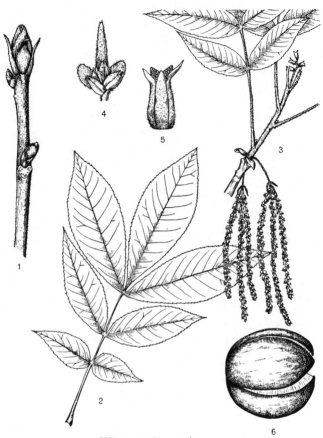

1. Winter twig, x ½.
2. Leaf, x ¼.
3. Flowering branchlet, x ½.
4. Staminate flower, enlarged.
5. Pistillate flower, enlarged.
6. Fruit, x ½.

JUGLANDACEAE

Shellbark Hickory. King Nut

Carya laciniosa (Michx. f.) Loud. [*Hicoria laciniosa* (Michx. f.) Sarg.] [*Carya sulcata* Nutt.]

HABIT.—A tree 60-80 feet high, with a tall, slender trunk 2-3 feet in diameter; forming a narrow, oblong-cylindrical crown of small, spreading branches.

LEAVES.—Alternate, compound, 1-2 feet long. Leaflets usually 7, the upper 5-9 inches long, 3-5 inches broad, larger than the lowest pair; sessile or short-stalked; oblong-lanceolate to obovate, taper-pointed; finely serrate; thick and firm; lustrous, dark green above, paler and soft-pubescent beneath. Petioles stout, glabrous or pubescent, often persistent on the branches during the winter. Foliage fragrant when crushed.

FLOWERS.—May and early June, after the leaves; monoecious; the staminate in pendulous, ternate catkins, 5-8 inches long, slender, yellow-green, on common peduncles 1 inch long; scales 3-lobed, tomentose; stamens 4, with yellow, hairy anthers; the pistillate in crowded, 2-5-flowered spikes, tomentose; calyx 3-toothed, hairy; corolla o; stigmas 2, light green.

FRUIT.—October; oblong to subglobose, 1¾-2½ inches long, with very thick, woody husk, splitting to the base; nut 4-6-ridged, with thick, hard shell and large, sweet kernel.

WINTER-BUDS.—Terminal bud about 1 inch long, ovoid, obtuse, dark brown, puberulous.

BARK.—Twigs orange and more or less pubescent, becoming darker in the first winter, and finally grayish; on the trunk 1-2 inches thick, light gray, separating into broad, thick plates 3-4 feet long, persistent on the trunk for many years.

WOOD.—Heavy, very hard, strong, tough, close-grained, very elastic, dark brown, with thin, whitish sapwood.

DISTRIBUTION.—Occurs in the southern portion of the Lower Peninsula, but is rather a rare tree.

HABITAT.—Prefers deep, rich bottom-lands.

NOTES.—Rapid in growth. May be distinguished from other Hickories by the orange colored branchlets.

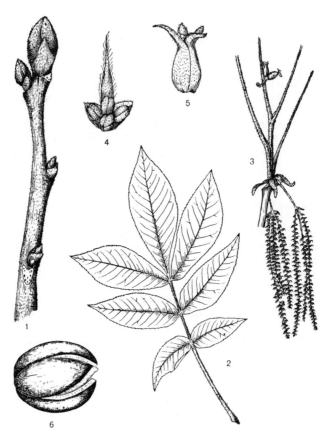

1. Winter twig, x 1.
2. Leaf, x ⅓.
3. Flowering branchlet, x ½.
4. Staminate flower, enlarged.
5. Pistillate flower, enlarged.
6. Fruit, x ½.

JUGLANDACEAE

Mocker Nut Hickory

Carya alba (L.) K. Koch [*Hicoria alba* (L.) Britt.]
[*Carya tomentosa* Nutt.]

HABIT.—A tree 50-70 feet high, with a trunk diameter of 1-2½ feet; forming a wide crown of strong, upright branches and stout branchlets.

LEAVES.—Alternate, compound, 8-12 inches long. Leaflets usually 5-7, sometimes 9, the upper 5-8 inches long, 3-4 inches broad; sessile, except the terminal; oblong- to obovate-lanceolate; minutely or sometimes coarsely serrate; thick and firm; lustrous, dark yellow-green above, paler and more or less pubescent beneath. Petioles pubescent. Foliage fragrant when crushed.

FLOWERS.—May and early June, after the leaves; monoecious; the staminate in pendulous, ternate catkins, 4-5 inches long, slender, green, hairy; scales 3-lobed, hairy; stamens 4-5, with red anthers; the pistillate in crowded, 2-5-flowered, tomentose spikes; calyx toothed, hairy; corolla o; stigmas 2, hairy.

FRUIT.—October; globose to globose-oblong, 1½-2 inches long, with thick husk splitting nearly to the base; nut 4-ridged, red-brown, with very thick, hard shell and small, sweet kernel.

WINTER-BUDS.—Terminal bud ½-¾ inch long, broadly ovoid, red-brown, pilose; outermost scales fall in early autumn.

BARK.—Twigs at first brown-tomentose, becoming smooth and grayish; on the trunk thick, hard, grayish, slightly ridged by shallow, irregular fissures, becoming rugged on very old trunks.

WOOD.—Very heavy, hard, strong, tough, close-grained, elastic, dark brown, with thick, whitish sapwood.

DISTRIBUTION.—Southern Peninsula as far north as Grand Rapids and Flint. Infrequent.

HABITAT.—Prefers rich, well-drained soil, but grows well in various situations, if they are not too wet.

NOTES.—Hardy throughout its range. Difficult to transplant on account of the long tap root.

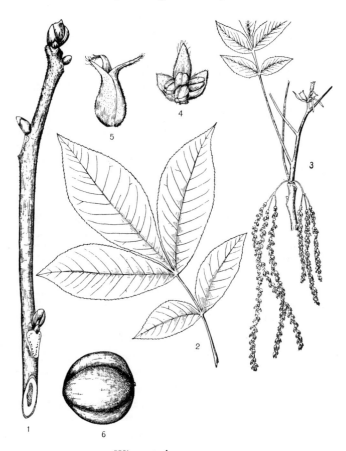

1. Winter twig, x 1.
2. Leaf, x ⅓.
3. Flowering branchlet, x ½.
4. Staminate flower, enlarged.
5. Pistillate flower, enlarged.
6. Fruit, x 1.

JUGLANDACEAE

Small Pignut Hickory

Carya microcarpa Nutt. [*Hicoria odorata* (Marsh.) Sarg.]
[*Hicoria microcarpa* (Nutt.) Britt.] [*Hicoria glabra*, v. *odorata* Sarg.]

HABIT.—A tree usually 50-70 feet high, with a trunk diameter of 1-3 feet; forming an oblong-cylindrical or sometimes rounded crown of slender, spreading branches.

LEAVES.—Alternate, compound, 8-12 inches long. Leaflets usually 5-7, the upper 3-6 inches long, 2-2½ inches broad; sessile, except the terminal; oblong to ovate-lanceolate, long-pointed; sharply serrate; thick and firm; glabrous, dark yellow-green above, lighter beneath. Petioles long, glabrous. Foliage fragrant when crushed.

FLOWERS.—May and June, after the leaves; monoecious; the staminate in pendulous, ternate catkins, 3-7 inches long, slender, greenish, glabrous; stamens 4, with orange anthers; the pistillate in 2-5-flowered spikes, ¼ inch long; calyx 4-toothed, hairy; corolla o; stigmas 2, yellow.

FRUIT.—September; subglobose or globose-oblong, less than 1 inch long, with thin husk splitting tardily nearly to the base; nut obscurely 4-ridged, with thin shell and small, sweet kernel.

WINTER-BUDS.—¼-½ inch long, dome-shaped, red-brown, smooth.

BARK.—Twigs greenish, long-hairy, becoming reddish and finally gray; thick, hard and grayish on the trunk, divided by shallow fissures into narrow plates, and more or less shaggy.

WOOD.—Heavy, hard, strong, tough, close-grained, elastic, dark brown, with thick, whitish sapwood.

DISTRIBUTION.—Confined to the most southern portions of the Lower Peninsula.

HABITAT.—Prefers well-drained slopes and hillsides.

NOTES.—Resembles *Carya glabra,* but the nut is much smaller.

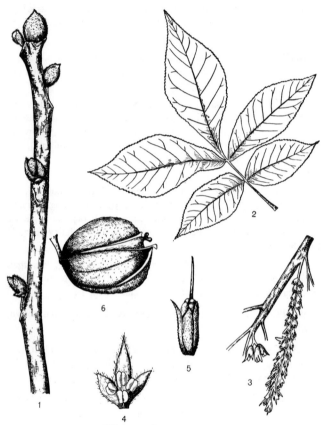

1. Winter twig, x 1.
2. Leaf, x ¼.
3. Flowering branchlet, x 1.
4. Staminate flower, enlarged.
5. Pistillate flower, enlarged.
6. Fruit, x ⅔.

JUGLANDACEAE

Pignut Hickory

Carya glabra (Mill.) Spach. [*Hicoria glabra* (Mill.) Britt.]
[*Carya porcina* Nutt.]

HABIT.—A tree usually 50-65 feet high, with a trunk diameter of 1-3 feet; forming a low, rather narrow, open crown of slender, often contorted branches.

LEAVES.—Alternate, compound, 8-12 inches long. Leaflets usually 5-7, the upper 3-6 inches long, 2-2½ inches broad; subsessile, except the terminal; oblong to obovate-lanceolate, taper-pointed; sharply serrate; thick and firm; glabrous, dark yellow-green above, paler beneath. Petioles long, slender, glabrous or pubescent. Foliage fragrant when crushed.

FLOWERS.—May-June, after the leaves; monoecious; the staminate in pendulous, ternate catkins, 3-7 inches long, slender, yellow-green, tomentose; scales 3-lobed, nearly glabrous; stamens 4, with orange anthers; the pistillate in crowded, 2-5-flowered spikes, ¼ inch long; calyx 4-toothed, hairy; corolla o; stigmas 2, yellow.

FRUIT.—October; variable in size and shape, 1½-2 inches long, with thin husk splitting half-way and sometimes nearly to the base; nut obscurely 4-ridged, with thin or thick, hard shell and small, sweet or slightly bitter kernel which is hard to remove.

WINTER-BUDS.—Terminal bud ¼-½ inch long, dome-shaped, greenish or grayish, smooth or finely downy.

BARK.—Twigs greenish, nearly glabrous, becoming reddish, and finally grayish; thick, hard and grayish on the trunk, with a firm, close surface divided by small fissures and sometimes broken into plates.

WOOD.—Heavy, hard, very strong, tough, close-grained, elastic, dark brown, with thick, whitish sapwood.

DISTRIBUTION.—Occurs only in the extreme southern portion of the Lower Peninsula. Common within its range.

HABITAT.—Prefers deep, rich loam, but grows in any well-drained soil; dry ridges and hillsides.

NOTES.—Hardy and desirable for ornamental purposes. Difficult to transplant on account of the long tap root. Produces a valuable grade of timber.

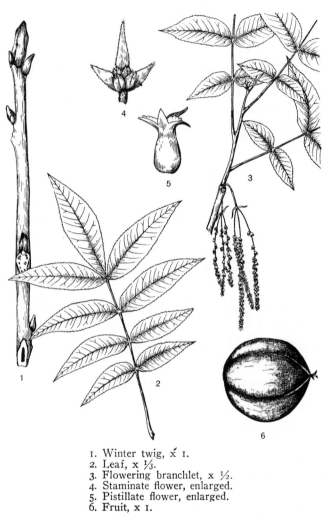

1. Winter twig, x 1.
2. Leaf, x ⅓.
3. Flowering branchlet, x ½.
4. Staminate flower, enlarged.
5. Pistillate flower, enlarged.
6. Fruit, x 1.

JUGLANDACEAE

Bitternut Hickory

Carya cordiformis (Wang.) K. Koch [*Hicoria minima* (Marsh.) Britt.] [*Carya amara* Nutt.]

HABIT.—A tall, slender tree 50-75 feet high, with a trunk diameter of 1-2½ feet; forming a broad crown of slender, stiff, upright branches, widest near the top.

LEAVES.—Alternate, compound, 6-10 inches long. Leaflets 5-11, the upper 4-6 inches long and one-fourth as broad; sessile, except the terminal; lanceolate to oblong-lanceolate, long-pointed; coarsely serrate; thin and firm; glabrous, bright green above, paler and more or less downy beneath. Petioles slender, hairy. Foliage fragrant when crushed.

FLOWERS.—May or early June, after the leaves; monoecious; the staminate slightly pubescent, in pendulous, ternate catkins, 3-4 inches long, on a common peduncle about 1 inch long; scales 3-lobed, hairy; stamens 4, with bearded, yellow anthers; the pistillate in 2-5-flowered spikes, ½ inch long, scurfy-tomentose; calyx 4-lobed, pubescent; corolla 0; stigmas 2, greenish.

FRUIT.—October; obovoid to globular, about 1 inch long, coated with yellow, scurfy pubescence, with very thin husk splitting half-way to the base, the sutures winged at the top; nut quite smooth, with thin shell and small, bitter kernel.

WINTER-BUDS.—Terminal bud about ¾ inch long, long-pointed, flattish, granular-yellow; lateral buds more or less 4-angled.

BARK.—Twigs greenish and more or less downy, becoming brownish, and finally grayish; gray, close, smooth on the trunk, often reticulately ridged, but rarely broken into plates.

WOOD.—Heavy, very hard, strong, tough, close-grained, dark brown, with thick, lighter colored sapwood.

DISTRIBUTION.—Of common occurrence in the southern half of the Lower Peninsula.

HABITAT.—Prefers a rich, loamy or gravelly soil; low, wet woods; along the borders of streams; but also found on high, dry uplands.

NOTES.—Grows most rapidly of all the Hickories, but is apt to show dead branches. Should be propagated from the seed, as it is not easily transplanted on account of the long tap root.

1. Winter twig, x 1.
2. Portion of twig, enlarged.
3. Leaf, x ½.
4. Flowering branchlet, x ½.
5. Staminate flower, enlarged.
6. Pistillate flower, enlarged.
7. Fruit, x ½.

BETULACEAE

Hornbeam. Ironwood

Ostrya virginiana (Mill.) K. Koch

HABIT.—A small tree usually 20-30 feet high, with a trunk diameter of 8-12 inches; forming a broad, rounded crown of many long, slender branches and a slender, stiff spray.

LEAVES.—Alternate, simple, 3-5 inches long, about one-half as broad; oblong-ovate; sharply doubly serrate; thin and very tough; dull, dark green above, paler and more or less pubescent beneath; petioles short, slender, pubescent.

FLOWERS.—April-May, with the leaves; monoecious; the staminate in drooping, cylindrical catkins from wood of the previous season, usually in threes; stamens 3-14, crowded on a hairy torus; the pistillate in erect, lax catkins on the season's shoots, usually in pairs, each flower inclosed in a hairy, sac-like involucre.

FRUIT.—September; strobiles, resembling clusters of hops, 1-2½ inches long, borne on slender, hairy stems; nuts small and flat, inclosed by sac-like involucres.

WINTER-BUDS.—Terminal bud absent; lateral buds ⅛-¼ inch long, ovoid, acute, red-brown.

BARK.—Twigs at first light brown, becoming lustrous, red-brown, and finally dull dark brown; thin, gray-brown on the trunk, broken into narrow, flattish pieces loose at the ends, giving a shreddy appearance.

WOOD.—Heavy, very strong and hard, tough, close-grained, durable, light red-brown, with thick, whitish sapwood.

DISTRIBUTION.—Common throughout the entire state.

HABITAT.—Prefers dry, gravelly slopes and ridges.

NOTES.—Often grows in the shade of other trees. Not easily transplanted. Rather slow of growth. Too small for street use. Well adapted to planting on lawns or in parks. The wood is used for levers, tool-handles, mallets, fence posts and fuel.

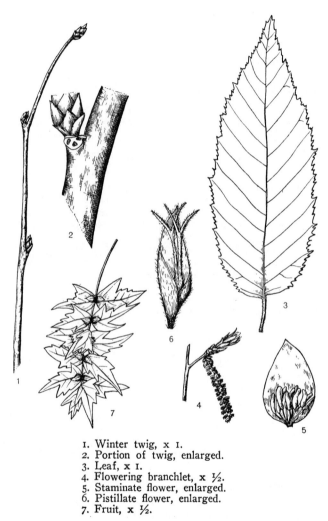

1. Winter twig, x 1.
2. Portion of twig, enlarged.
3. Leaf, x 1.
4. Flowering branchlet, **x** ½.
5. Staminate flower, enlarged.
6. Pistillate flower, enlarged.
7. Fruit, **x** ½.

BETULACEAE

Blue Beech. Water Beech

Carpinus caroliniana Walt.

HABIT.—Usually a low, bushy tree or large shrub 10-30 feet high, with a trunk diameter of 6-12 inches; trunk short, usually fluted; slender zigzag branches and a fine spray form a close, flat-topped crown.

LEAVES.—Alternate, simple, 2-4 inches long and one-half as broad; ovate to oval, long-pointed; sharply doubly serrate; thin and firm; dull green above, lighter beneath, turning scarlet and orange in autumn; petioles short, slender, hairy.

FLOWERS.—April-May, with the leaves; monoecious; apetalous; the staminate catkins 1-1½ inches long, their scales greenish, boat-shaped, each bearing 3-20 stamens; the pistillate catkins ½-¾ inch long, their scales hairy, greenish, each bearing 2 pistils with long, scarlet styles.

FRUIT.—Ripens in midsummer, but often remains on the tree long after the leaves have fallen; in loose, terminal strobiles; involucre halberd-shaped, inclosing a small, ovoid, brownish nut.

WINTER-BUDS.—Terminal bud absent; lateral buds ⅛ inch long, narrow-ovoid, acute, puberulous, brownish.

BARK.—Twigs pale green, hairy, becoming lustrous, dark red the first winter; thin, smooth and close on the trunk and large limbs, dark bluish gray, often mottled with lighter or darker patches.

WOOD.—Heavy, hard, tough, very strong, close-grained, light brown, with thick, whitish sapwood.

DISTRIBUTION.—Common throughout the state.

HABITAT.—Prefers a deep, rich, moist soil along the borders of streams and swamps. Often found in drier situations in the shade of other trees.

NOTES.—Propagated from seed. Not easily transplanted. Slow of growth. Seldom found in masses. Attractive as an ornamental tree in moist situations.

THE BIRCHES—BETULA

The Birches are distributed widely over the Old and the New Worlds, being most abundant in the higher latitudes. Ten species of tree size occur in North America, three of which are native to Michigan. They are all graceful trees with slender, flexuous branches and delicate foliage. The bark is characterized by horizontally-elongated lenticels, and in some of the species it peels off in thin, papery layers. The Indian stripped off the bark of the Paper Birch to use in the construction of his canoe and to inclose his wigwam. It furnished cups, pails, pots, pans and many other useful articles for the early settler. The wood, being dense and hard, has a high fuel value, and it is used also for interior finish, furniture, wood-pulp and numerous small articles.

The leaves of the Birches are doubly serrate on the margin and arranged alternately on the branches. Often they appear in pairs on the short, spur-like branchlets of the older growth. The flowers appear in the spring, before or with the developing leaves. They are unisexual, borne in separate clusters, but both kinds are found on the same tree. The staminate catkins are produced early in the preceding season, standing straight on the twigs during the winter, but becoming long and pendulous when they open the following spring. The pistillate flowers appear below the staminate, from buds of the season, in small, slender catkins. The fruit is a cone-like structure, called a strobile, which consists of a central axis to which numerous scales, bearing the small, winged nuts, are attached. The nuts are light and are easily scattered by the wind.

The European White Birch, *Betula pendula* Roth (*Betula alba* L.), of which the native Paper Birch is considered to be a variety, was formerly much planted for shade and ornament in this country. It is a small to medium-sized tree of graceful habit, which may grow to a height of 30-40 feet. The branches ascend, but the very slender branchlets are more or less drooping, forming a rather open, ovoid crown. The young twigs are reddish and glandular-dotted, while the bark of the trunk is silvery white, peeling off in papery layers, finally becoming furrowed and almost black near the ground. The leaves are 1½-3 inches long, acuminate at the apex, doubly serrate to somewhat lobed, and have long, slender petioles. The strobili are cylindrical, about an inch long, and the nuts are provided with rather wide wings. Unfortunately, the European White Birch is short-lived. Perhaps this is due to the fact that the root system is weak and shallow. Many formerly fine specimens on lawns and in parks have been removed in the past few years. The tree is also subject to the attacks of borers. The variety, *dalecarlica* (L.f.) Schneider, better known as the Cut-leaf Weeping Birch, is more frequently planted, and there are a number of other varieties, differing in form of leaf or habit, known to the trade.

SUMMER KEY TO THE SPECIES OF BETULA

a. Bark of trunk white, separating freely into thin, papery layers; twigs without wintergreen taste; leaves usually solitary, not aromatic.........................*B. alba papyrifera,* p. 123
aa. Bark of trunk not white, usually dark colored, not separating freely into papery layers; twigs with more or less wintergreen taste; leaves solitary or in pairs, aromatic.
  b. Bark dirty yellow, breaking into strips more or less curled at the edges; leaves solitary or in pairs, slightly aromatic; twigs with slight wintergreen taste .... *B. lutea,* p. 121
  bb. Bark dark red-brown, cleaving off in thick, irregular plates (resembles bark of Black Cherry); leaves in pairs, strongly aromatic; twigs with strong wintergreen taste............
    .... *B. lenta,* p. 119

WINTER KEY TO THE SPECIES OF BETULA

a. Bark of trunk white, separating freely into thin, papery layers; twigs without wintergreen taste .... *B. alba papyrifera,* p. 123
aa. Bark of trunk not white, usually dark colored, not separating into papery layers; twigs with more or less wintergreen taste.
  b. Bark dirty yellow, breaking into strips more or less curled at the edges; twigs with slight wintergreen taste ....
    .... *B. lutea,* p. 121
  bb. Bark dark red-brown, cleaving off in thick, irregular plates (resembles bark of Black Cherry); twigs with strong wintergreen taste .... *B. lenta,* p. 119

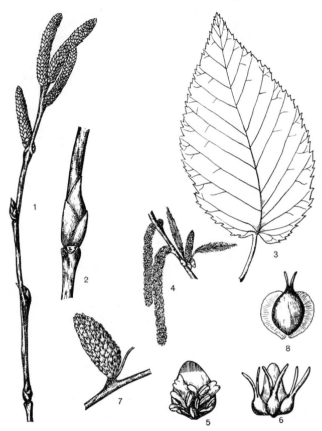

1. Winter twig, x 1.
2. Portion of twig, enlarged.
3. Leaf, x ½.
4. Flowering branchlet, x ½.
5. Staminate flower, enlarged.
6. Bract with pistillate flowers, enlarged.
7. Fruiting branchlet, x ½.
8. Fruit, enlarged.

BETULACEAE

Sweet Birch. Black Birch. Cherry Birch
Betula lenta L.*

HABIT.—A medium-sized tree 50-75 feet high, with a trunk diameter of 1-3 feet; slender, wide-spreading, pendulous branches, forming a narrow, rounded, open crown.

LEAVES.—Alternate in pairs, simple, 3-4 inches long and one-half as broad; outline variable, ovate to oblong-ovate; sharply doubly serrate, with slender, incurved teeth; dull, dark green above, light yellow-green beneath; petioles short, stout, hairy, deeply grooved above; aromatic.

FLOWERS.—April-May, before the leaves; monoecious; the staminate catkins 3-4 inches long, slender, pendent, yellowish; the pistillate catkins ½-¾ inch long, erect or suberect, greenish.

FRUIT.—Ripens in autumn; sessile, glabrous, erect strobiles, 1-1½ inches long; scales glabrous; nuts slightly broader than their wings.

WINTER-BUDS.—Terminal bud absent; lateral buds about ¼ inch long, conical, sharp-pointed, red-brown, divergent.

BARK.—Twigs light green, becoming lustrous, red-brown in their first winter; very dark on old trunks, cleaving off in thick, irregular plates. Resembles bark of Black Cherry. Inner bark aromatic, spicy.

WOOD.—Heavy, very hard and strong, close-grained, dark red-brown, with thin, lighter colored sapwood.

DISTRIBUTION.—Scattered throughout the state; rare in the south, more abundant and of larger size in the north.

HABITAT.—Grows in any situation, but prefers moist, rocky slopes and rich uplands.

NOTES.—Hardy throughout its range. Easily transplanted. Of slow growth. An oil sold as a substitute for wintergreen is distilled from the wood, and birch beer can be made by fermenting the sap.

*A discussion has arisen as to whether *Betula lenta* actually exists in the state, some botanists preferring the name *Betula alleghanensis* Britt. for the tree we have so long called Black Birch. Pending further investigation the authors have thought best to retain the old name.

Reference.—Britton: North American Trees, pp. 257-8.

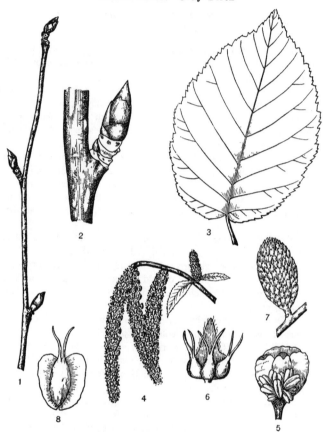

1. Winter twig, x 1.
2. Portion of twig, enlarged.
3. Leaf, x ½.
4. Flowering branchlet, x ½.
5. Staminate flower, enlarged.
6. Bract with pistillate flowers, enlarged.
7. Fruiting branchlet, x ½.
8. Fruit, x 10.

BETULACEAE

Yellow Birch. Gray Birch

Betula lutea Michx. f.

HABIT.—A tree 60-80 feet high and 2-4 feet in trunk diameter; numerous slender, pendulous branches form a broad, open, rounded crown.

LEAVES.—Alternate, solitary or in pairs, simple, 3-5 inches long and one-half as broad; ovate to oblong-ovate; sharply doubly serrate; dull dark green above, yellow-green beneath; petioles short, slender, grooved, hairy; slightly aromatic.

FLOWERS.—April, before the leaves; monoecious; the staminate catkins 3-4 inches long, slender, pendent, purplish yellow; the pistillate catkins sessile or nearly so, erect, almost 1 inch long, greenish.

FRUIT.—Ripens in autumn; sessile or short-stalked, erect, glabrous strobiles about 1 inch long; scales downy on the back and edges; nut about as broad as the wing.

WINTER-BUDS.—Terminal bud absent; lateral buds about ¼ inch long, conical, acute, chestnut-brown, more or less appressed; bud-scales more or less pubescent.

BARK.—Twigs, branches and young stems smooth, very lustrous, silvery gray or light orange; becoming silvery yellow-gray as the trunk expands and breaking into strips more or less curled at the edges; old trunks becoming gray or blackish, dull, deeply and irregularly fissured into large, thin plates; somewhat aromatic, slightly bitter.

WOOD.—Heavy, very strong and hard, close-grained, light brown tinged with red, with thin, whitish sapwood. See p. 321.

DISTRIBUTION.—Throughout the state, but more abundant and of larger size northward.

HABITAT.—Prefers rich, moist uplands, but grows in wet or dry situations.

NOTES.—One of the largest deciduous-leaved trees of Michigan. Easily transplanted, but not desirable as a street tree.

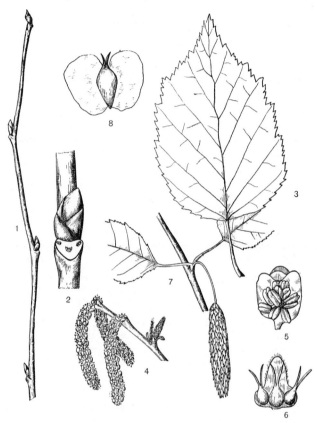

1. Winter twig, x 1.
2. Portion of twig, enlarged.
3. Leaf, x 1.
4. Flowering branchlet x ½.
5. Staminate flower, enlarged.
6. Bract with pistillate flowers, enlarged.
7. Fruiting branchlet, x ½.
8. Fruit, x 5.

BETULACEAE

Paper Birch. Canoe Birch. White Birch
Betula alba papyrifera (Marsh.) Spach. [*Betula papyrifera* Marsh.

HABIT.—A tree 50-75 feet high, with a trunk diameter of 1-2 feet, forming in youth a compact, pyramidal crown of many slender branches, becoming in old age a long, branchless trunk with a broad, open crown, composed of a few large limbs ascending at an acute angle, with almost horizontal branches and a slender, flexible spray.

LEAVES.—Alternate, simple, 2-3 inches long, 1½-2 inches broad; ovate; coarsely, more or less doubly serrate; thick and firm; glabrous, dark green above, lighter beneath and covered with minute black glands; petioles stout, yellow, glandular, glabrous or pubescent.

FLOWERS.—April-May, before or with the leaves; monoecious; the staminate catkins clustered or in pairs, 3-4 inches long, slender, pendent, brownish; the pistillate catkins about 1½ inches long, slender, erect or spreading, greenish; styles bright red.

FRUIT.—Ripens in autumn; long-stalked, cylindrical, glabrous, drooping strobiles, about 1½ inches long; scales hairy on the margin; nut narrower than its wing.

WINTER-BUDS.—Terminal bud absent; lateral buds ¼ inch long, narrow-ovoid, acute, flattish, slightly resinous, usually divergent.

BARK.—Twigs dull red, becoming lustrous, orange-brown; bark of trunk and large limbs cream-white and lustrous on the outer surface, bright orange on the inner, separating freely into thin, papery layers; becoming furrowed and almost black near the ground.

WOOD.—Light, hard, strong, tough, very close-grained, light brown tinged with red, with thick, whitish sapwood.

DISTRIBUTION.—Lansing and northward. Common in central Michigan as a small tree. Of larger size in the Upper Peninsula.

HABITAT.—Prefers rich, moist hillsides; borders of streams, lakes and swamps; but is also found in drier situations.

NOTES.—Rapid of growth in youth. The bark is used by the Indians and woodsmen for canoes, wigwams, baskets, torches, etc. Suitable for ornamental planting, replacing the once popular European White Birch (see p. 116).

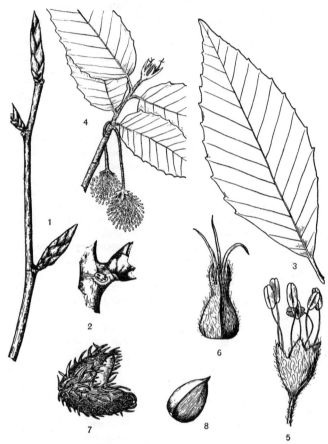

1. Winter twig, x 1.
2. Portion of twig, enlarged.
3. Leaf, x 1.
4. Flowering branchlet, x ¾.
5. Staminate flower, enlarged.
6. Pistillate flower, enlarged.
7. Bur, opened, x 1.
8. Nut, x 1.

FAGACEAE
Beech. White Beech

Fagus grandifolia Ehrh. [*Fagus atropunicea* (Marsh.) Sudw.]
[*Fagus ferruginea* Ait.] [*Fagus americana* Sweet]

HABIT.—A beautiful tree, rising commonly to a height of 50-75 feet, with a trunk diameter of 2-4 feet; in the forest tall and slender, with short branches forming a narrow crown; in the open with a short, thick trunk and numerous slender, spreading branches, forming a broad, compact, rounded crown.

LEAVES.—Alternate, simple, 3-5 inches long, one-half as broad; oblong-ovate, acuminate; coarsely serrate, a vein terminating in each tooth; thin; dull green above, light yellow-green and very lustrous beneath; petioles short, hairy.

FLOWERS.—April-May, with the leaves; monoecious; the staminate in globose heads, 1 inch in diameter, on long, slender, hairy peduncles, yellow-green; calyx campanulate, 4-7-lobed, hairy; corolla o; stamens 8-10; the pistillate on short, hairy peduncles in 2-flowered clusters surrounded by numerous awl-shaped, hairy bracts; calyx urn-shaped, 4-5-lobed; corolla o; ovary 3-celled; styles 3.

FRUIT.—Ripens in autumn; a prickly bur borne on stout, hairy peduncles, persistent on the branch after the nuts have fallen; nuts usually 3, ¾ inch long, sharply tetrahedral, brownish; sweet and edible.

WINTER-BUDS.—Nearly 1 inch long, very slender, cylindrical, gradually taper-pointed, brownish, puberulous.

BARK.—Twigs lustrous, olive-green, finally changing through brown to ashy gray; close, smooth, steel-gray on the trunk, often mottled by darker blotches and bands.

WOOD.—Hard, tough, strong, close-grained, not durable, difficult to season, light or dark red, with thin, whitish sapwood. See p. 321.

DISTRIBUTION.—Common in the Lower Peninsula, especially in the northern portions; locally common in the eastern half of the Upper Peninsula.

HABITAT.—Prefers deep, rich, well-drained loam, but is found and does well on a great variety of soils.

NOTES.—Hardy throughout its range. Desirable for landscape planting because of its clean trunk and limbs, deep shade and freedom from insect pests. Often suckers from the roots.

The European Beech, *Fagus sylvatica* L., is frequently planted for ornament. It can be distinguished from our native Beech by its darker brown bark, by the often villous twigs and puberulent buds and by the leaves, which are shorter, rather blunt and minutely toothed. Among the most useful of the numerous forms are v. *purpurea* Ait. (v. *atropurpurea* Ait.) (v. *atropunicea* West.), the well-known Purple or Copper Beech; v. *heterophylla* Loud. (v. *laciniata* Vignet), the Cut-leaved Beech, with very deeply cut leaves; and v. *pendula* Lodd., the Weeping Beech.

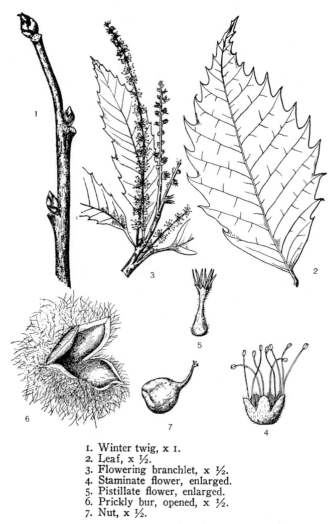

1. Winter twig, x 1.
2. Leaf, x ½.
3. Flowering branchlet, x ½.
4. Staminate flower, enlarged.
5. Pistillate flower, enlarged.
6. Prickly bur, opened, x ½.
7. Nut, x ½.

FAGACEAE

Chestnut

Castanea dentata (Marsh.) Borkh. [*Castanea vesca,* v. *americana* Michx.] [*Castanea sativa,* v. *americana* Sarg.]

HABIT.—A tree 60-80 feet high, forming a short, straight trunk 2-4 feet in diameter, divided not far above the ground into several stout, horizontal limbs and forming a broad, open, rounded crown.

LEAVES.—Alternate, simple, 6-8 inches long, 2-3 inches broad; oblong-lanceolate, long-pointed at the apex; coarsely serrate with stout, incurved, glandular teeth; thin; dull yellow-green above, lighter beneath, glabrous; petioles short, stout, puberulous.

FLOWERS.—June-July, after the leaves; monoecious; the staminate catkins 6-8 inches long, slender, puberulous, bearing 3-7-flowered cymes of yellow-green flowers; calyx 6-cleft, pubescent; stamens 10-20; the androgynous catkins 2½-5 inches long, puberulous, bearing 2-3 prickly involucres of pistillate flowers near their base; calyx campanulate, 6-lobed; styles 6.

FRUIT.—Ripens in autumn; globose, prickly burs about 2 inches in diameter, containing 1-3 nuts; nuts compressed, brownish, coated with whitish down at the apex; sweet and edible.

WINTER-BUDS.—Terminal bud absent; lateral buds ¼ inch long, ovoid, acute, brownish.

BARK.—Twigs lustrous, yellow-green, becoming olive-green and finally dark brown; old trunks gray-brown, with shallow fissures and broad, flat ridges.

WOOD.—Light, soft, coarse-grained, weak, easily split, very durable in contact with the soil, red-brown, with very thin, lighter colored sapwood. See p. 327.

DISTRIBUTION.—South-eastern Michigan, as far north as St. Clair County. Abundant in eastern Monroe County and Wayne County.

HABITAT.—Pastures; hillsides; glacial drift; well-drained, gravelly or rocky soil.

NOTES.—Rapid of growth and long-lived. Difficult to transplant. The Chestnut-bark disease, commonly known as the Chestnut Blight, has made severe inroads on this tree throughout the eastern United States. No means of checking this fatal disease has yet been discovered, and the species is threatened with extinction.

THE OAKS—QUERCUS

The Oaks are remarkable for their massive trunks, their thick, rugged bark and large, strong roots. They are distinguished from all other trees by their cupped fruit, but many who have seen these fruits have not noticed the small, scaly masses of flowers which produce them. The flowers, of two kinds, appear on different parts of the same tree, and often on the same branch. The staminate flowers are small, arranged in long, slender catkins, from buds on the twigs of the preceding season. The pistillate flowers are small and inconspicuous, appearing singly or in groups in the axils of the leaves on the growth of the new season.

The Oaks of our state may be divided into two groups. The White Oaks have leaves with rounded lobes, their acorns mature in the autumn of the first season and their kernels are usually sweet. The Red Oaks have leaves with bristle-pointed lobes, their acorns mature in the autumn of the second season and their kernels are usually bitter.

The Oak genus is a large one, comprising nearly three hundred trees and shrubs widely spread throughout the northern hemisphere. Of the fifty or more species found in North America, eleven are native to Michigan. The Oaks are so numerous and so variable that it is extremely difficult to tell them apart. A number of natural hybrids have been described, and undoubtedly many more exist.

SUMMER KEY TO THE SPECIES OF QUERCUS

a. Leaves deeply cut or lobed.
   b. Leaf-lobes acute, bristle-tipped; fruit maturing in the second season.
      c. Lower surface of leaves more or less pubescent.
         d. Leaf-lobes usually 7; buds hoary-tomentose; bark of trunk deeply furrowed and scaly; inner bark yellow; cup-scales of acorn hoary-pubescent; nut ovoid; large tree, common in Michigan .... *Q. velutina,* p. 149
         dd. Leaf-lobes usually 3 (at apex of the leaf only); buds rusty-hairy; bark of trunk divided into nearly square

plates; inner bark not yellow; cup-scales of acorn rusty-tomentose; nut subglobose; shrubby tree, rare in Michigan .... *Q. marilandica*, p. 151

cc. Lower surface of leaves glabrous or nearly so.

    d. Cup of acorn top-shaped or cup-shaped, inclosing one-third to one-half of the nut.

        e. Kernel of nut yellow; buds glabrous, lustrous, slightly angular; inner bark of trunk yellow; trunk provided with pins or stubs of dead branches near the ground. .... *Q. ellipsoidalis*, p. 147

        ee. Kernel of nut whitish; buds pubescent above the middle, not angular; inner bark of trunk red; trunk not provided with pins nor stubs of branches near the ground .... *Q. coccinea*, p. 145

    dd. Cup of acorn saucer-shaped, inclosing only the base of the nut.

        e. Upper surface of leaves usually lustrous, especially on the lower branches; lowermost branches of trees growing in the open drooping nearly to the ground; nut about ½ inch long .... *Q. palustris*, p. 143

        ee. Upper surface of leaves usually dull; lowermost branches of trees growing in the open not drooping; nut about 1 inch long .... *Q. rubra*, p. 141

bb. Leaf-lobes rounded, not bristle-tipped; fruit maturing in the first season.

    c. Leaves cut nearly to the midrib by a pair of deep sinuses near the middle of the leaf; branches corky-ridged; nut ½-1½ inches long, deeply seated in a large, conspicuously fringed cup .... *Q. macrocarpa*, p. 135

    cc. Leaves not cut by a pair of deep sinuses; branches not corky-ridged; nut about ¾ inch long, about one-fourth covered by a thin, tomentose, warty cup ... *Q. alba*, p. 133

aa. Leaves neither deeply cut nor lobed.

    b. Margin of leaves entire to sinuate-crenate, but not toothed; acorns on stalks ½-4 inches long.

        c. Margin of leaves entire, or only slightly undulate; acorns on peduncles ½ inch long, the nut about ½ inch long; bark on branches not breaking into large, papery scales .. .. *Q. imbricaria*, p. 153

cc. Margin of leaves sinuate-crenate, rarely lobed; acorns on
peduncles 1-4 inches long, the nut about 1 inch long; bark
on branches breaking into large, papery scales which curl
back .... Q. *bicolor*, p. 137
bb. Margin of leaves coarsely toothed; acorns sessile or on
stalks less than ½ inch long .... Q. *muhlenbergii*, p. 139

WINTER KEY TO THE SPECIES OF QUERCUS

a. Terminal buds usually about ⅛ inch long.
  b. Twigs thick-tomentose; entire bud pale-pubescent; branches
corky-ridged; cup of acorn conspicuously fringed at the
rim ....[1]* Q. *macrocarpa*, p. 135
  bb. Twigs glabrous; buds glabrous, or only slightly or partially
pubescent; branches without corky ridges; cup of acorn not
conspicuously fringed at the rim.
    c. Bark on branches breaking into large, papery scales which
curl back; buds pilose above the middle; acorns on pubescent peduncles 1-4 inches long ...... [1] Q. *bicolor*, p. 137
    cc. Bark on branches not breaking into large, papery scales;
buds glabrous; acorns sessile or very short-stalked.
      d. Bark of trunk ash-gray or nearly white, flaky; acorns
maturing in autumn of first season; kernel of nut sweet.
        e. Buds conical, acute; bud-scales scarious on the mar-
gins; nut white-downy at the apex..................
........................[1] Q. *muhlenbergii*, p. 139
        ee. Buds broadly ovoid, obtuse; bud-scales not scarious
on the margins; nut not white-downy at the apex....
................................[1] Q. *alba*, p. 133
      dd. Bark of trunk light to dark brown, smoothish or only
slightly fissured; acorns maturing in autumn of second
season; kernel of nut bitter.

*[1] means that the acorns mature in the autumn of the first
season, hence mature acorns will not be found on the tree, but
on the ground beneath the tree.

[2] means that the acorns mature in the autumn of the second
season, hence immature acorns will be found on the last season's
twigs, and mature acorns on the ground beneath the tree.

e. Lateral buds widely divergent; bud-scales scarious on the margins; lowermost branches of trees growing in the open not drooping nearly to the ground ....
........................[2] *Q. imbricaria,* p. 153
ee. Lateral buds more or less appressed; bud-scales not scarious on the margins; lowermost branches of trees growing in the open drooping nearly to the ground ...
.........................[2] *Q. palustris,* p. 143
aa. Terminal buds usually about ¼ inch long (slightly smaller in *Q. ellipsoidalis*).
  b. Buds conspicuously hairy or tomentose.
    c. Buds rusty-hairy, acute at the apex; cup-scales of acorn rusty-tomentose; inner bark of trunk not yellow; shrubby tree, rare in Michigan .... [2] *Q. marilandica,* p. 151
    cc. Buds hoary-tomentose, obtuse at the apex; cup-scales of acorn hoary-pubescent; inner bark of trunk yellow; large tree, common in Michigan .... [2] *Q. velutina,* p. 149
  bb. Buds glabrous, or pubescent only above the middle.
    c. Buds strictly glabrous throughout, lustrous; inner bark of trunk yellow or whitish.
      d. Buds obtuse at the apex; trunk provided with pins or stubs of dead branches near the ground; inner bark of trunk yellow; nut ½-¾ inch long, inclosed for one-third to one-half of its length in a top-shaped cup; kernel of nut yellow .... [2] *Q. ellipsoidalis,* p. 147
      dd. Buds acute at the apex; trunk not provided with pins nor stubs of branches near the ground; inner bark of trunk whitish; nut about 1 inch long, inclosed only at the base by a shallow, saucer-shaped cup; kernel of nut white .... [2] *Q. rubra,* p. 141
    cc. Buds pale-pubescent above the middle, but usually glabrous below, not lustrous; inner bark of trunk red.......
.................................[2] *Q. coccinea,* p. 145

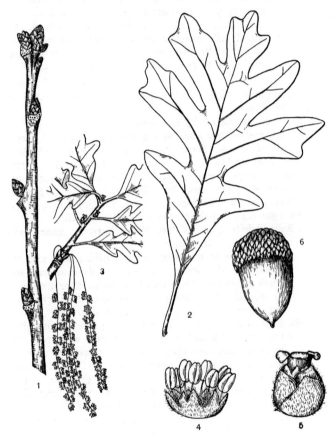

1. Winter twig, x 2.
2. Leaf, x ½.
3. Flowering branchlet, x ½.
4. Staminate flower, enlarged.
5. Pistillate flower, enlarged.
6. Fruit, x 1.

FAGACEAE
White Oak
Quercus alba L.

HABIT.—A large tree 60-80 feet high, with a trunk diameter of 2-4 feet; forming a short, thick trunk with stout, horizontal, far-reaching limbs, more or less gnarled and twisted in old age, and a broad, open crown.

LEAVES.—Alternate, simple, 5-9 inches long, about one-half as broad; obovate to oblong; 5-9-lobed, some with broad lobes and shallow sinuses, others with narrow lobes and deep, narrow sinuses, the lobes usually entire; thin and firm; glabrous, bright green above, pale, or glaucous beneath; often persistent on the tree through the winter.

FLOWERS.—May, with the leaves; monoecious; the staminate in hairy catkins, 2-3 inches long; the pistillate sessile or short-peduncled, reddish, tomentose; calyx campanulate, 6-8-lobed, yellow, hairy; corolla 0; stamens 6-8, with yellow anthers; stigmas red.

FRUIT.—Autumn of first season; sessile or short-stalked acorns; cup with small, brown-tomentose scales, inclosing one-fourth of the nut; nut oblong-ovoid, rounded at the apex, about ¾ inch long, light brown; kernel sweet and edible.

WINTER-BUDS.—Terminal bud ⅛ inch long, broadly ovoid, obtuse; scales glabrous, dark red-brown.

BARK.—Twigs at first bright green, tomentose, later reddish, and finally ashy gray; thick, light gray or whitish on old trunks, shallowly fissured into broad, flat ridges.

WOOD.—Very heavy, strong, hard, tough, close-grained, durable, light brown, with thin, light brown sapwood. See p. 323.

DISTRIBUTION.—Rare in the Upper Peninsula, common in the Lower Peninsula, especially in the lower half.

HABITAT.—Grows well in all but very wet soils, in all open exposures.

NOTES.—Slow and even of growth. Difficult to transplant. The English Oak, *Quercus robur* L. (*Quercus pedunculata* Ehrh.), is sometimes planted. It is a large, spreading tree with dark gray or brownish bark, irregularly fissured into flat ridges without scales. The leaves resemble those of *Quercus alba*, but they are sessile or nearly so, 2½-5 inches long, and at the base they are furnished with ear-shaped appendages. They are dark green above, pale blue-green beneath and glabrous. The acorns are borne on slender peduncles which are 1-3 inches long; the cup-shaped cup, with closely appressed scales, incloses about one-third of the nut, which is about 1 inch long. The twigs are reddish, and the winter-buds are glabrous or nearly so, somewhat angular, with lateral buds diverging. Many varieties of this Oak are known to the trade.

— 133 —

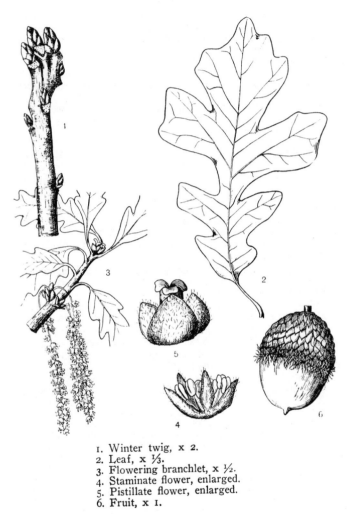

1. Winter twig, x 2.
2. Leaf, x ⅓.
3. Flowering branchlet, x ½.
4. Staminate flower, enlarged.
5. Pistillate flower, enlarged.
6. Fruit, x 1.

FAGACEAE

Bur Oak

Quercus macrocarpa Michx.

HABIT.—A large tree 60-80 feet high, with a trunk 2-4 feet in diameter; great, spreading branches form a broad, rugged crown.

LEAVES.—Alternate, simple, 6-10 inches long and one-half as broad; obovate to oblong, wedge-shaped at the base; crenately lobed, usually cut nearly to the midrib by two opposite sinuses near the middle; thick and firm; dark green and shining above, pale-pubescent beneath; petioles short, stout.

FLOWERS.—May, with the leaves; monoecious; the staminate in slender, hairy catkins, 4-6 inches long; the pistillate sessile or short-stalked, reddish, tomentose; calyx 4-6-lobed, yellow-green, downy; corolla 0; stamens 4-6, with yellow anthers; stigmas bright red.

FRUIT.—Autumn of first season; sessile or short-stalked acorns; very variable in size and shape; cup typically deep, cup-shaped, tomentose, fringed at the rim, inclosing one-third or all of the nut; nut broad-ovoid, ½-1½ inches long, brownish, pubescent; kernel white, sweet and edible.

WINTER-BUDS.—Terminal bud ⅛ inch long, broadly ovoid or conical, red-brown, pale-pubescent.

BARK.—Twigs yellow-brown, thick-tomentose, becoming ash-gray or brownish; branches with corky ridges; thick and gray-brown on the trunk, deeply furrowed.

WOOD.—Heavy, hard, strong, tough, close-grained, very durable, brownish, with thin, pale sapwood.

DISTRIBUTION.—Common throughout both peninsulas.

HABITAT.—Prefers rich, moist soil; bottom-lands; but is tolerant of many soils.

NOTES.—Rather slow of growth. Difficult to transplant. It is occasionally planted as an ornamental tree, but on account of its large size it is suitable only for parks and large estates. Known also as the Mossy-cup or Over-cup Oak.

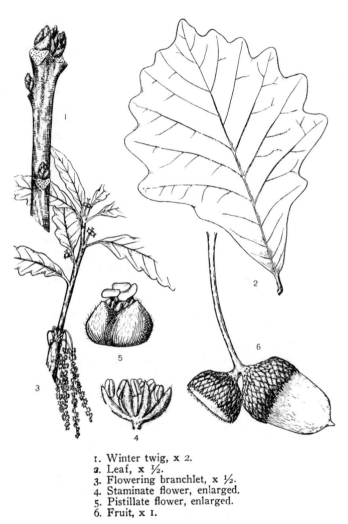

1. Winter twig, x 2.
2. Leaf, x ½.
3. Flowering branchlet, x ½.
4. Staminate flower, enlarged.
5. Pistillate flower, enlarged.
6. Fruit, x 1.

FAGACEAE

Swamp White Oak. Swamp Oak

Quercus bicolor Willd. [*Quercus platanoides* (Lam.) Sudw.]

HABIT.—A large tree 50-70 feet high, with a trunk diameter of 2-3 feet; forming a rather open, rugged crown of tortuous, pendulous branches and short, stiff, bushy spray.

LEAVES.—Alternate, simple, 5-7 inches long, 3-5 inches broad; obovate to oblong-obovate; coarsely sinuate-crenate or shallow-lobed; thick and firm; dark green and shining above, whitish and more or less tomentose beneath; petioles stout, about ½ inch long.

FLOWERS.—May, with the leaves; monoecious; the staminate in hairy catkins, 3-4 inches long; the pistillate tomentose, on long, tomentose peduncles, in few-flowered spikes; calyx deeply 5-9-lobed, yellow-green, hairy; corolla o; stamens 5-8, with yellow anthers; stigmas bright red.

FRUIT.—Autumn of first season; acorns on pubescent peduncles 1-4 inches long, usually in pairs; cup cup-shaped, with scales somewhat loose (rim often fringed), inclosing one-third of the nut; nut ovoid, light brown, pubescent at the apex, about 1 inch long; kernel white, sweet, edible.

WINTER-BUDS.—Terminal bud ⅛ inch long, broadly ovoid to globose, obtuse, light brown, pilose above the middle.

BARK.—Twigs at first lustrous, green, becoming red-brown, finally dark brown and separating into large, papery scales which curl back; thick, gray-brown on the trunk, deeply fissured into broad, flat, scaly ridges.

WOOD.—Heavy, hard, strong, tough, coarse-grained, light brown, with thin, indistinguishable sapwood.

DISTRIBUTION.—Southern half of Lower Peninsula.

HABITAT.—Prefers moist, rich soil bordering swamps and along streams.

NOTES.—Fairly rapid of growth and reasonably easy to transplant. The lateral branches have a tendency to persist, which results in knotty lumber.

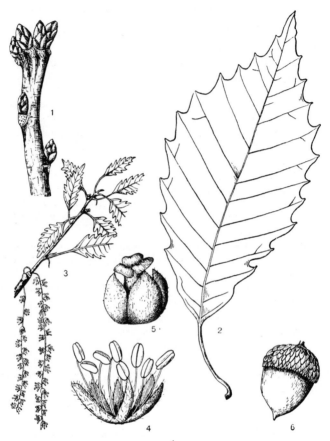

1. Winter twig, x 2.
2. Leaf, x ½.
3. Flowering branchlet, x ½.
4. Staminate flower, enlarged.
5. Pistillate flower, enlarged.
6. Fruit, x 1.

FAGACEAE

Chinquapin Oak. Chestnut Oak. Yellow Oak

Quercus muhlenbergii Engelm. [*Quercus acuminata* (Michx.)
Houba]

HABIT.—A medium-sized tree 40-50 feet high, with a trunk diameter of 1-3 feet; erect, somewhat short branches form a narrow, rounded crown.

LEAVES.—Alternate, simple, 4-7 inches long, 1-4 inches broad; oblong-lanceolate to obovate; coarsely and somewhat sharp-toothed; thick and firm; lustrous, yellow-green above, pale-pubescent beneath; petioles slender, about 1 inch long.

FLOWERS.—May, with the leaves; monoecious; the staminate in hairy catkins, 3-4 inches long; the pistillate sessile or in short spikes, hoary-tomentose; calyx campanulate, 5-8-lobed, yellow, hairy; corolla 0; stamens 5-8, with yellow anthers; stigmas red.

FRUIT.—Autumn of first season; sessile or short-stalked acorns; cup with small scales, hoary-tomentose, inclosing one-half of the nut; nut ovoid, about ¾ inch long, light brown, pubescent at the apex; kernel sweet, sometimes edible.

WINTER-BUDS.—Terminal bud ⅛ inch long, conical, acute; scales chestnut-brown, scarious on the margin.

BARK.—Twigs greenish at first, becoming gray-brown, finally gray or brown; thin, silvery gray or ash colored, shallowly fissured and flaky on the trunk.

WOOD.—Heavy, very hard, strong, close-grained, durable, dark brown, with thin, pale brown sapwood.

DISTRIBUTION.—Confined to the southern half of the Lower Peninsula.

HABITAT.—Prefers a limestone soil; dry hillsides; rich bottom-lands; rocky river-banks.

NOTES.—Grows uniformly until maturity. Leaves resemble those of the Chestnut. A form which differs from the type in having broader, obovate leaves broadest above the middle and a flaky bark has been described and named *Quercus alexanderi* Britton.

A tree with somewhat similar characteristics, also known as the Chestnut Oak, *Quercus prinus* L., is common to the south and east of our range. It differs from the native Chinquapin Oak in that the teeth of the leaves are rounded, the nut of the acorn is lustrous at maturity, the twigs are stout, orange-brown, and the bark of the trunk is dark red-brown to nearly black and characteristically deeply fissured into broad, rounded, continuous, vertical ridges. This species deserves to be planted more extensively.

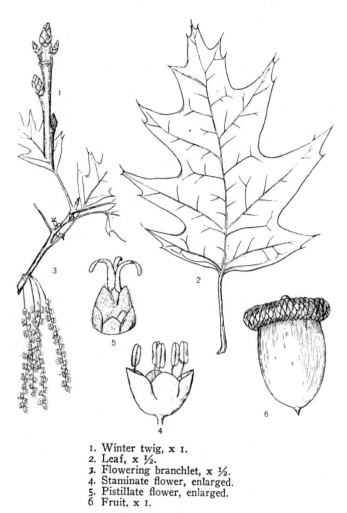

1. Winter twig, x 1.
2. Leaf, x ½.
3. Flowering branchlet, x ½.
4. Staminate flower, enlarged.
5. Pistillate flower, enlarged.
6 Fruit, x 1.

FAGACEAE
Red Oak
Quercus rubra L.

HABIT.—A large tree 70-80 feet high, with a trunk diameter of 2-4 feet; forming a broad, rounded crown of a few large, wide-spreading branches and slender branchlets.

LEAVES.—Alternate, simple, 5-9 inches long, 4-6 inches broad; oval to obovate; 5-11-lobed with coarse-toothed, bristle-tipped lobes tapering from broad bases and wide, oblique, rounded sinuses; thin and firm; dull dark green above, paler beneath; petioles stout, 1-2 inches long.

FLOWERS.—May, when the leaves are half-grown; monoecious; the staminate in hairy catkins, 4-5 inches long; the pistillate on short, glabrous peduncles; calyx 4-5-lobed, greenish; corolla 0; stamens 4-5, with yellow anthers; stigmas long, spreading, bright green.

FRUIT.—Autumn of second season; sessile or short-stalked acorns; cup shallow, saucer-shaped, inclosing only the base of the nut; scales closely appressed, more or less glossy, puberulous, bright red-brown; nut oblong-ovoid with a broad base, about 1 inch long, red-brown; kernel white, very bitter.

WINTER-BUDS.—Terminal bud ¼ inch long, ovoid, acute, light brown, smooth.

BARK.—Twigs lustrous, green, becoming reddish, finally dark brown; young trunks smooth, gray-brown; old trunks darker, shallowly fissured into thin, firm, broad ridges; inner bark light red, not bitter.

WOOD.—Heavy, hard, strong, coarse-grained, pale red-brown, with thin, lighter colored sapwood. See p. 323.

DISTRIBUTION.—Southern portion of Lower Peninsula as far north as Roscommon County, and sparingly in the more northern parts of the state.

HABITAT.—Prefers rich, moist loam; glacial drift; streambanks. Grows well in all well-drained soils.

NOTES.—Grows rapidly. A good tree for street, lawn or woodland planting. Comparatively free from insects and disease. Along our northern border passing into the Gray Oak, *Quercus rubra*, v. *ambigua* (Michx.f.) Fernald, differing in the cup of the acorn, which tends to be deeper and somewhat turbinate, and the nut, which is smaller.

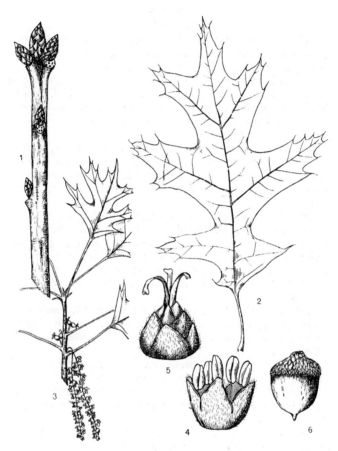

1. Winter twig, x 3.
2. Leaf, x ½.
3. Flowering branchlet, x ½.
4. Staminate flower, enlarged.
5. Pistillate flower, enlarged.
6. Fruit, x 1.

FAGACEAE

Pin Oak

Quercus palustris Muench.

HABIT.—A medium-sized tree 40-50 feet high, with a trunk diameter of 1-2 feet; forming an oblong-cylindrical or pyramidal crown of many upright, spreading branches, the lowermost drooping nearly to the ground.

LEAVES.—Alternate, simple, 4-6 inches long, 2-4 inches broad; obovate to ovate; 5-7-lobed by deep, wide, rounded sinuses, the lobes few-toothed, bristle-tipped; thin and firm; very lustrous, dark green above, paler beneath and glabrous, or often with tufts of pale hairs in the axils of the veins; petioles slender.

FLOWERS.—May, with the leaves; monoecious; the staminate in hairy catkins, 2-4 inches long; the pistillate tomentose, borne on short, tomentose peduncles; calyx 4-5-lobed, hairy; corolla o; stamens 4-5, with yellow anthers; stigmas recurved, bright red.

FRUIT.—Autumn of second season; sessile or short-stalked acorns; cup saucer-shaped with scales closely appressed, dark red-brown, inclosing only the base of the nut; nut nearly hemispherical, about ½ inch in diameter, light brown; kernel bitter.

WINTER-BUDS.—Terminal bud ⅛ inch long, ovoid or conical, acute, light brown, smooth.

BARK.—Twigs dark red and tomentose at first, becoming lustrous, green, finally gray-brown; thick, gray-brown and smoothish on the trunk.

WOOD.—Heavy, hard, strong, coarse-grained, light brown, with thin, darker colored sapwood.

DISTRIBUTION.—Confined to the most southern portions of the Lower Peninsula.

HABITAT.—Prefers moist, rich soil; river-bottoms; borders of swamps.

NOTES.—Grows rapidly and uniformly. Easily transplanted. The tiny branchlets at a distance give the impression of the tree being full of pins. An attractive tree, which should be planted more generally on street and lawn.

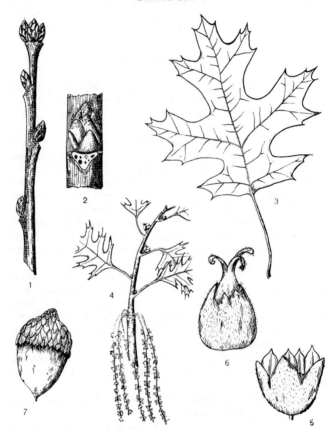

1. Winter twig, **x** 1.
2. Portion of twig, enlarged.
3. Leaf, **x** ½.
4. Flowering branchlet, **x** ½.
5. Staminate flower, enlarged.
6. Pistillate flower, enlarged.
7. Fruit, **x** 1.

FAGACEAE

Scarlet Oak

Quercus coccinea Muench.

HABIT.—A tree 50-70 feet high and 1-2 feet in trunk diameter; long, slender branches form a rather open, rounded crown.

LEAVES.—Alternate, simple, 3-6 inches long and nearly as broad; broadly obovate to oval; 5-9-lobed by deep, wide, rounded sinuses which extend over half-way to the midrib, the lobes toothed and bristle-tipped; thin and firm; shining, bright green above, paler beneath, both sides glabrous; turning brilliant scarlet in autumn; petioles slender, 1-2 inches long.

FLOWERS.—May, with the leaves; monoecious; the staminate in glabrous catkins, 3-4 inches long; the pistillate on pubescent peduncles ½ inch long, bright red, pubescent; calyx 4-5-lobed, reddish, pubescent; corolla o; stamens usually 4, with yellow anthers; stigmas long, spreading, bright red.

FRUIT.—Autumn of second season; sessile or short-stalked acorns; cup top-shaped to cup-shaped, with closely imbricated, slightly puberulous, red-brown scales, inclosing about one-half of the nut; nut usually short-ovoid, ½-¾ inch long, light red-brown; kernel whitish, bitter.

WINTER-BUDS.—Terminal bud about ¼ inch long, broadly ovoid, acute, dark red-brown, pale-pubescent above the middle.

BARK.—Twigs at first scurfy-pubescent, later lustrous, green, finally smooth, light brown; thick, dark gray or brown on old trunks, shallowly fissured, scaly; inner bark red, not bitter.

WOOD.—Heavy, hard, strong, coarse-grained, light red-brown, with thick, darker brown sapwood.

DISTRIBUTION.—Lower Peninsula, southern half.

HABITAT.—Prefers a light, dry, sandy soil.

NOTES.—Rapid of growth. Desirable for ornamental planting. Long-lived, free from serious pests, and should be more commonly planted. The brilliant scarlet coloration of the leaves in autumn makes it one of the most attractive Oaks.

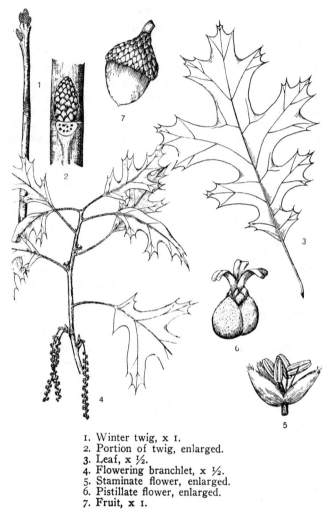

1. Winter twig, x 1.
2. Portion of twig, enlarged.
3. Leaf, x ½.
4. Flowering branchlet, x ½.
5. Staminate flower, enlarged.
6. Pistillate flower, enlarged.
7. Fruit, x 1.

FAGACEAE

Hill's Oak. Northern Pin Oak. Black Oak
Quercus ellipsoidalis E. J. Hill

HABIT.—A tree 50-60 feet high, with a short trunk 2-3 feet in diameter; forming a rather narrow, oblong-cylindrical crown of upright and horizontal branches. Many small, drooping branches are sent out near the ground, which eventually die; and it is to the stubs or pins which persist about the trunk that the appellation Pin Oak is due.

LEAVES.—Alternate, simple, 3-7 inches long and about as broad; oval to nearly orbicular; narrowly 5-7-lobed by deep, wide, rounded sinuses, the lobes few-toothed, bristle-tipped; thin and firm; lustrous, bright green above, paler beneath, both sides glabrous except for the tufts of hairs in the axils of the veins beneath; petioles slender, glabrous.

FLOWERS.—May, with the leaves; monoecious; the staminate in puberulous catkins, 2-3 inches long; the pistillate red, tomentose, borne on stout, tomentose, 1-3-flowered peduncles; calyx 2-5-lobed or -parted, glabrous except at the apex, which is fringed with long, twisted hairs; corolla o; stamens 2-5, with short filaments; stigmas 3, recurved, dark red.

FRUIT.—Autumn of second season; short-stalked or nearly sessile acorns; cup top-shaped, with scales thin, puberulous, inclosing one-third to one-half of the nut; nut ellipsoid, ½-¾ inch long, light brown, puberulous; kernel yellow, bitter.

WINTER-BUDS.—Terminal bud ⅛-¼ inch long, ovoid, rather obtuse, slightly angular, lustrous, red-brown.

BARK.—Twigs bright red-brown, covered with matted, pale hairs, becoming glabrous, dark gray or brown; thin, dull gray to dark brown, rather smooth or closely ribbed on the trunk; inner bark yellow.

WOOD.—Heavy, hard, strong, coarse-grained, red-brown, with thin, paler sapwood.

DISTRIBUTION.—South-western part of the Lower Peninsula, but limits not definitely known.

HABITAT.—Well-drained uplands, especially on clays; occasionally on the borders of ponds and in low woods.

NOTES.—A new and comparatively little known species. It closely resembles *Quercus palustris,* for which it has been mistaken.

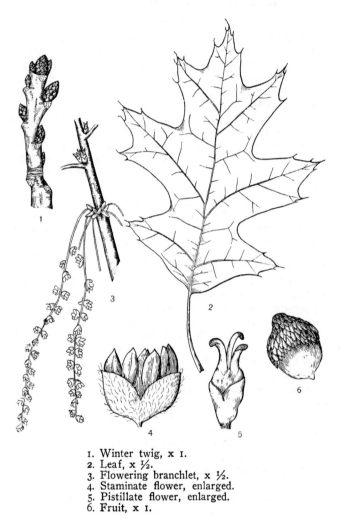

1. Winter twig, x 1.
2. Leaf, x ½.
3. Flowering branchlet, x ½.
4. Staminate flower, enlarged.
5. Pistillate flower, enlarged.
6. Fruit, x 1.

FAGACEAE

Yellow Oak. Black Oak

Quercus velutina Lam.

HABIT.—A large-sized tree 60-75 feet high and 1-3 feet in trunk diameter; slender branches and stout branchlets form a wide-spreading, rounded crown.

LEAVES.—Alternate, simple, 5-10 inches long, 3-8 inches broad; ovate to oblong; usually 7-lobed, some with shallow sinuses and broad, rounded, mucronate lobes, others with wide, rounded sinuses extending half-way to the midrib or farther and narrow-oblong or triangular, bristle-tipped lobes, the lobes more or less coarse-toothed, each tooth bristle-tipped; thick and leathery; dark green and shining above, pale and more or less pubescent beneath; petioles stout, yellow, 3-6 inches long.

FLOWERS.—May, when the leaves are half grown; monoecious; the staminate in pubescent catkins, 4-6 inches long; the pistillate reddish, on short, tomentose peduncles; calyx acutely 3-4-lobed, reddish, hairy; corolla o; stamens usually 4-5, with acute, yellow anthers; stigmas 3, divergent, red.

FRUIT.—Autumn of second season; sessile or short-stalked acorns; cup cup-shaped or turbinate, inclosing about one-half of the nut; scales thin, light brown, hoary; nut ovoid, ½-¾ inch long, red-brown, often pubescent; kernel yellow, bitter.

WINTER-BUDS.—Terminal bud ¼ inch long, ovoid to conical, obtuse, strongly angled, hoary-tomentose.

BARK.—Twigs at first scurfy-pubescent, later glabrous, red-brown, finally mottled gray; thick and nearly black on old trunks, deeply furrowed and scaly; inner bark thick, yellow, very bitter.

WOOD.—Heavy, hard, strong, coarse-grained, bright red-brown, with thin, paler sapwood.

DISTRIBUTION.—Southern half of the Lower Peninsula.

HABITAT.—Prefers glacial drift; dry or gravelly uplands; poor soils.

NOTES.—Rapid of growth. Undesirable for street use. Not attractive as an ornamental tree. Of little importance as a timber species. The wood is used largely for fuel. The inner bark yields a yellow dye.

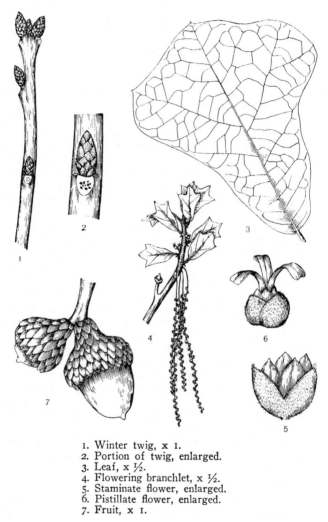

1. Winter twig, **x** 1.
2. Portion of twig, enlarged.
3. Leaf, x ½.
4. Flowering branchlet, x ½.
5. Staminate flower, enlarged.
6. Pistillate flower, enlarged.
7. Fruit, x 1.

FAGACEAE

Black Jack

Quercus marilandica Muench.

HABIT.—A small, shrubby tree 20-30 feet high, with a trunk diameter of 6-14 inches; spreading, often contorted branches form a rounded or obovoid crown.

LEAVES.—Alternate, simple, 5-7 inches long and broad; broad-obovate; more or less 3-lobed at the apex, the lobes entire or toothed, bristle-tipped, very variable in size and shape; thick and leathery; very lustrous and dark green above, yellowish and scurfy-pubescent beneath; petioles short, stout.

FLOWERS.—May, with the leaves; monoecious; the staminate in slender, hoary catkins, 2-4 inches long; the pistillate rusty-tomentose, on short, rusty-tomentose peduncles; calyx 4-5-lobed, thin, scarious, tinged with red, pale-pubescent; corolla o; stamens 4, with apiculate, red anthers; stigmas recurved, dark red.

FRUIT.—Autumn of second season; short-stalked acorns; cup turbinate, with large, red-brown, rusty-tomentose scales, inclosing about one-half of the nut; nut subglobose, about ¾ inch long, yellow-brown, puberulous; kernel yellowish.

WINTER-BUDS.—Terminal bud ¼ inch long, ovoid, acute, prominently angled; scales light red-brown, rusty-hairy.

BARK.—Twigs at first light red and scurfy, later glabrous, red-brown, and finally brown or ashy gray; thick and almost black on the trunk, divided into nearly square plates.

WOOD.—Heavy, hard, strong, dark brown, with thick, lighter colored sapwood.

DISTRIBUTION.—Southern Michigan (Ann Arbor and Lansing).

HABITAT.—Dry, sandy or clay barrens.

NOTES.—Rare in Michigan. Of no commercial importance, but attractive ornamentally.

Shingle Oak

1. Winter twig, **x 2**.
2. Portion of twig, enlarged.
3. Leaf, **x ½**.
4. Flowering branchlet, **x ½**.
5. Staminate flower, enlarged.
6. Pistillate flower, enlarged.
7. Fruit, **x 1**.

THE ELMS—ULMUS

The Elms are among the noblest of our trees, and perhaps no others are better known or more esteemed by American people. Not only are they valuable for their wood, which is heavy, hard and exceedingly tough, but they are attractive ornamentally. The Elms are among the first trees to herald the coming of spring. The tiny, greenish flowers have no petals, but by their great abundance they clothe the tree with delicate green before the leaves appear. The flowers are soon followed by the equally profuse, winged fruits, which mature early and germinate the same season. The leaves of most of the Elms have a peculiar oblique base, full and rounded on one side, more or less wedge-shaped on the other.

Some fifteen species of Elms are known, of which number six species are native to the United States, and three occur in Michigan. A number of introduced species have been planted for shade and ornament, some of which, known to be hardy in our latitude, are briefly indicated below.

The English Elm, *Ulmus campestris* L. (*Ulmus procera* Salisb.), is a large tree with somewhat continuous trunk, but forming a spreading crown. The bark of the trunk is gray, deeply fissured into rectangular flakes. The twigs are a dark red-brown, nearly glabrous or somewhat downy, while the winter-buds are dark smoky brown or almost black, glabrous or with a few scattered hairs. The leaves are 2-3 inches long, scabrous above and soft-pubescent beneath, of a darker green than those of the American Elm. They remain green long after those of the American Elm have dropped to the ground, in which sole respect the English Elm is superior to the American tree.

The Scotch or Wych Elm, *Ulmus glabra* Huds. (*Ulmus montana* With.), is a medium-sized tree whose bark remains smooth for many years. Both the twigs and the black-red winter-buds are pubescent, and the leaves are very short-petioled, 3-6 inches long, very unequal at the base, rough-scabrous above and pubescent beneath. It is more frequently planted in one of its forms, known as the Camperdown or Weeping Elm, v. *camperdownii* Rehd., with pendulous branches and branchlets, forming a small tree 12-15 feet high with a rounded crown. It is usually produced by reverse-grafting on an unright stock, which leads to a peculiar umbrella-like development.

The Siberian, Chinese or Dwarf Elm, *Ulmus pumila* L., is a small, rapidly-growing tree of dense habit with the main branches ascending, attaining a maximum height of 30-45 feet. The bark on the trunk is dark gray or brown, shallowly fissured, and the inner bark is mucilaginous. The winter-twigs are slender, gray-brown, glabrous or somewhat pubescent, and the buds are small, narrow- or broad-ovoid, somewhat pubescent. The flowers appear in March or early in April, before the leaves, and are purplish. The winged fruits are hardly more than ½ inch long, deeply notched at the apex, and are glabrous. Exceptionally handsome in foliage, the leaves are 1½-3½ inches long and about one-half as broad, acute or acuminate at the apex, almost symmetrical at the base, doubly or nearly simply serrate, dark green above and glabrous or nearly so on both sides. It is an excellent tree for a hot, dry climate and soil, and makes a fine screen.

SUMMER KEY TO THE SPECIES OF ULMUS

a. Leaves essentially smooth on both sides; branches often with corky, wing-like ridges; lowermost branches usually short and strongly drooping; main trunk usually continuous into the crown without dividing, giving to the tree a narrow-oblong outline .... *U. racemosa,* p. 161

aa. Leaves usually rough on one or on both sides; branches without corky ridges; lowermost branches not short, not strongly drooping; main trunk usually dividing into several large limbs, giving to the tree a more or less vase-shaped outline.

  b. Leaves usually rough above, but smooth beneath, with petioles glabrous; bark of trunk gray, deeply fissured into broad, scaly ridges; inner bark not mucilaginous................
.... *U. americana,* p. 159

  bb. Leaves usually rough both sides, with petioles hairy; bark of trunk dark red-brown, shallowly fissured into large, loose plates; inner bark mucilaginous .... *U. fulva,* p. 157

WINTER KEY TO THE SPECIES OF ULMUS

a. Buds conspicuously rusty-tomentose; twigs more or less pubescent; inner bark very mucilaginous when chewed.........
.... *U. fulva,* p. 157

aa. Buds not conspicuously rusty-tomentose; twigs glabrous; inner bark not mucilaginous.

  b. Bundle-scars usually 3; buds ⅛ inch long, glabrous; twigs without corky ridges; outline of tree vase-shaped..........
.... *U. americana,* p. 159

  bb. Bundle-scars usually 4-6 in a curved line; buds ¼ inch long, somewhat pilose; twigs often with corky ridges; outline of tree narrow-oblong .... *U. racemosa,* p. 161

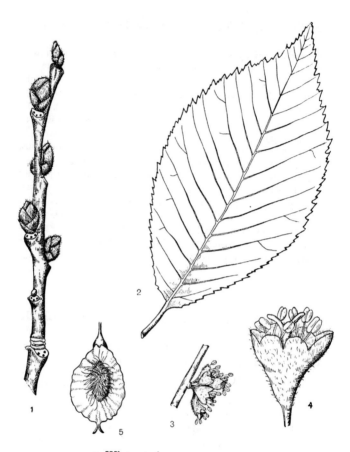

1. Winter twig, x 2.
2. Leaf, x 1.
3. Flowering branchlet, x 1.
4. Perfect flower, enlarged.
5. Fruit, x 1.

URTICACEAE

Slippery Elm. Red Elm

Ulmus fulva Michx. [*Ulmus pubescens* Walt.]

HABIT.—A medium-sized tree 40-60 feet high, with a short trunk 1-2 feet in diameter; spreading branches form a broad, open, flat-topped crown.

LEAVES.—Alternate, simple, 4-7 inches long, about one-half as broad; ovate-oblong; coarsely doubly serrate; thick and firm; dark green and rough above. paler and somewhat rough beneath; petioles short, stout, hairy.

FLOWERS.—March-April, before the leaves; mostly perfect; borne on short pedicels in crowded fascicles; calyx campanulate, 5-9-lobed, green, hairy; corolla o; stamens 5-9, with dark red anthers; stigmas 2, reddish purple.

FRUIT.—May; semi-orbicular, 1-seeded samaras, short-stalked in dense clusters; seed cavity brown-tomentose; wings smooth, nearly ¾ inch long, entire or nearly so at the apex.

WINTER-BUDS.—Terminal bud absent; lateral buds ovoid, obtuse, dark brown, rusty-tomentose, ¼ inch long.

BARK.—Twigs at first bright green and pubescent, becoming light to dark brown or grayish; thick on old trunks, dark red-brown, shallowly fissured into large, loose plates; inner bark mucilaginous.

WOOD.—Heavy, hard, strong, very close-grained, durable, easy to split while green, dark red-brown, with thin, lighter colored sapwood.

DISTRIBUTION.—Of frequent occurrence throughout the state.

HABITAT.—Prefers stream-banks and bottom-lands; rich, moist hillsides; rocky ridges and slopes.

NOTES.—Grows more rapidly than *Ulmus americana* and often mistaken for it. It may always be distinguished from it by the slippery inner-bark, which is valued medicinally, by the leaves which are rough above and by the smooth-margined fruit.

1. Winter twig, x 2.
2. Leaf, x ½.
3. Flowering branchlet, x ½.
4. Flower, enlarged.
5. Fruit, x 2.

URTICACEAE

White Elm. American Elm. Water Elm

Ulmus americana L.

HABIT.—A tree 75-100 feet high, with a trunk diameter of 2-6 feet; commonly dividing 20-30 feet above the ground into a few large branches which rise upward and outward to form a vase-shaped outline.

LEAVES.—Alternate, simple, 4-6 inches long, one-half as broad; obovate-oblong to oval; coarsely doubly serrate; thick and firm; dark green and rough above, pale and pubescent or glabrous beneath; petioles short and stout.

FLOWERS.—March-April, before the leaves; mostly perfect; small, brown to red; borne on slender pedicels in loose fascicles; calyx campanulate, 5-9-lobed; corolla o; stamens 4-9, with bright red anthers; ovary 2-celled; styles 2, green.

FRUIT.—May; ovate, 1-seeded samaras, smooth both sides, hairy on the margin, ½ inch long, deeply notched at the apex, long-stemmed, in crowded clusters.

WINTER-BUDS.—Terminal bud absent; lateral buds ovoid, acute, flattened, glabrous, brown, ⅛ inch long.

BARK.—Twigs at first light green and downy, becoming glabrous, red-brown, finally ash-gray; on old trunks thick, ash-gray, deeply fissured into broad, scaly ridges.

WOOD.—Heavy, hard, strong, tough, difficult to split, coarse-grained, light brown, with thick, lighter colored sapwood. See p. 325.

DISTRIBUTION.—Common throughout the state.

HABITAT.—Prefers deep, rich, moist loam; bottom-lands; stream-banks.

NOTES.—Grows rapidly. Long-lived. The roots run along near the surface of the ground for a great distance. An ideal street tree, and the most commonly planted ornamental, valued for its shade and graceful habit. Unfortunately it is subject to serious injury by many insects, which can be contolled only by costly spraying, and many fine old specimens are being removed on account of insect depredations.

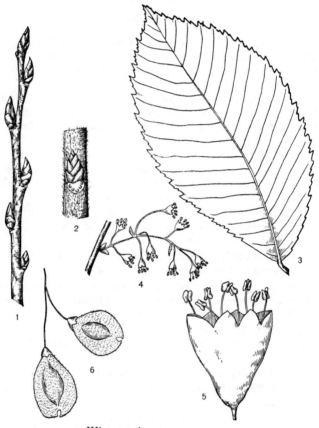

1. Winter twig, x 1.
2. Portion of twig, enlarged.
3. Leaf, x 1.
4. Flowering branchlet, x 1.
5. Flower, enlarged.
6. Fruit, x 1.

URTICACEAE

Cork Elm. Rock Elm

Ulmus racemosa Thomas [*Ulmus Thomasi* Sarg.]

HABIT.—A large tree usually reaching a height of 60-80 feet and a trunk diameter of 2-3 feet; strongly drooping lateral and lower branches form a narrow, oblong-cylindrical crown.

LEAVES.—Alternate, simple, 3-6 inches long, one-half as broad; obovate to oblong-oval, more or less dished; coarsely doubly serrate; thick and firm; lustrous, dark green above, pale-pubescent beneath; petioles pubescent, ¼ inch long.

FLOWERS.—April-May, before the leaves; mostly perfect; greenish; borne on slender, drooping pedicels in loose racemes; calyx campanulate, 7-8-lobed; corolla o; stamens 7-8, with purple anthers; ovary hairy, 2-styled.

FRUIT.—May; ovate, 1-seeded samaras, pubescent all over, ½ inch long, the wings shallowly notched at the apex.

WINTER-BUDS.—Terminal bud absent; lateral buds ovoid, acute, brown, pilose, ¼ inch long.

BARK.—Twigs at first light brown and pubescent, becoming lustrous, red-brown, finally gray-brown, with corky, wing-like ridges; thick and grayish on the trunk, with wide fissures separating broad, flat, scaly ridges.

WOOD.—Heavy, very strong and tough, close-grained, light red-brown, with thick, lighter colored sapwood.

DISTRIBUTION.—Frequent in the southern third of the Lower Peninsula.

HABITAT.—Dry, gravelly uplands; rocky ridges and slopes; heavy clay soils; river-banks.

NOTES.—A good street tree, but less graceful in habit than *Ulmus americana*. Of fairly rapid growth. Tends to produce suckers from the roots, which are often troublesome on the lawn. The wood is considered to be superior to that of the other native Elms. Should be planted more extensively.

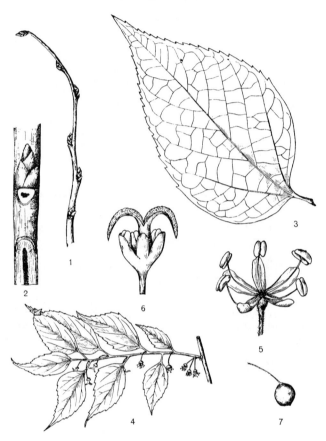

1. Winter twig, x 1.
2. Portion of twig, enlarged.
3. Leaf, x ¾.
4. Flowering branchlet, x ½.
5. Staminate flower, enlarged.
6. Pistillate flower, enlarged.
7. Fruit, x 1.

URTICACEAE
Hackberry. Nettle-tree
Celtis occidentalis L.

HABIT.—A medium-sized tree 40-60 feet high, with a short, straight trunk 1-2 feet in diameter which branches 8-10 feet from the ground into a few large limbs and many slender, horizontal, zigzag branches, forming a broad, rounded crown.

LEAVES.—Alternate, simple, 2-4 inches long and one-half as broad; ovate to ovate-lanceolate, oblique at the base, usually long-pointed; coarsely serrate above the entire base; thin; glabrous, light green above, paler beneath, turning light yellow late in autumn; petioles short, slender, hairy.

FLOWERS.—May, with or soon after the leaves; polygamo-monoecious; greenish; inconspicuous; on slender pedicels; the staminate in clusters at the base of the shoot, the pistillate usually solitary in the axils of the upper leaves; calyx greenish, deeply 5-lobed; corolla o; stamens 5; ovary 1-celled.

FRUIT.—September-October, remaining on the tree through the winter; slender-stalked, fleshy, globular drupes, ¼ inch long, dark purple; edible.

WINTER-BUDS.—Terminal bud absent; lateral buds light brown, ¼ inch long, ovoid, acute, flattened, the tip appressed.

BARK.—Twigs greenish, puberulous, becoming lustrous, red-brown in their first winter; on old trunks thick, light brown or silvery gray, broken into deep, short ridges or warty excrescences.

WOOD.—Heavy, rather soft, coarse-grained, weak, light yellow, with thick, whitish sapwood.

DISTRIBUTION.—Common throughout the Lower Peninsula.

HABITAT.—Prefers rich, moist, well-drained soil, but will grow on gravelly or rocky hillsides. Common along river-banks.

NOTES.—Hardy throughout its range. Grows slowly and irregularly in youth. Easily transplanted. Desirable as a street tree, and appears well in ornamental grounds. Very tolerant of shade. Produces good shade, is vigorous and long-lived, and is free from very serious diseases. Pith small, white, closely chambered.

The variety, *crassifolia* (Lam.) Gray, is of more vigorous growth and becomes a larger tree. It may be distinguished from the species by its pubescent branchlets and by its thicker, darker green leaves, which are scabrous above and pubescent on the veins beneath.

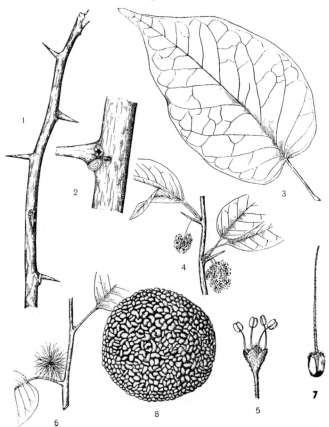

1. Winter twig, x 1.
2. Portion of twig, enlarged.
3. Leaf, x ½.
4. Staminate flowering branchlet, x ½.
5. Staminate flower, enlarged.
6. Pistillate flowering branchlet, x ½.
7. Pistillate flower, enlarged.
8. Fruit, x ¼.

URTICACEAE

Osage Orange

Maclura pomifera (Raf.) Schneider [*Toxylon pomiferum* Raf.]
[*Maclura aurantiaca* Nutt.]

HABIT.—A tree 20-30 feet high, with a short trunk 1-2 feet in diameter; divides into a few large limbs with curving branches, forming a symmetrical, rounded crown.

LEAVES.—Alternate, simple, 3-5 inches long, 2-3 inches broad; ovate to oblong-lanceolate; entire; thick and firm; dark green and shining above, paler beneath; petioles slender, pubescent, 1½-2 inches long.

FLOWERS.—May-June, after the leaves; dioecious; the staminate slender-pedicelled, borne in dense racemes at the end of long, slender, drooping peduncles; the pistillate in dense, globose heads at the end of short, stout peduncles; calyx 4-lobed, hairy; corolla o; stamens 4; style covered with white, stigmatic hairs.

FRUIT.—Autumn; pale green, orange-like, 4-5 inches in diameter, composed of numerous small drupes crowded and grown together.

WINTER-BUDS.—Terminal bud absent; lateral buds depressed-globular, partly hidden in the bark, pale brown.

BARK.—Twigs at first bright green, pubescent, becoming orange-brown and armed with stout, straight, axillary spines; dark orange-brown on the trunk and deeply furrowed.

WOOD.—Heavy, very hard and strong, flexible, ·coarse-grained, very durable, bright orange, with thin, lemon colored sapwood.

NOTES.—A native of the South, but hardy throughout Michigan. A desirable ornamental tree. Extensively planted for hedges. Free from insect and fungous enemies. Difficult to eradicate when once established. A yellow dye is extracted from the bark of the roots.

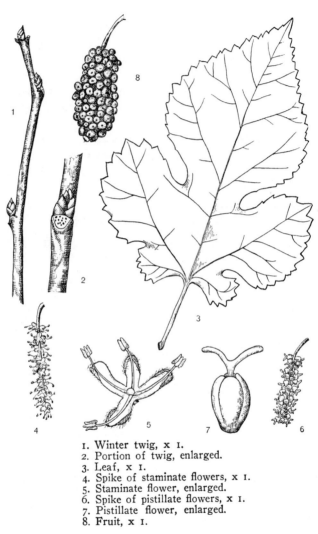

1. Winter twig, x 1.
2. Portion of twig, enlarged.
3. Leaf, x 1.
4. Spike of staminate flowers, x 1.
5. Staminate flower, enlarged.
6. Spike of pistillate flowers, x 1.
7. Pistillate flower, enlarged.
8. Fruit, x 1.

URTICACEAE

Red Mulberry

Morus rubra L.

HABIT.—A small tree 20-40 feet high, with a short trunk 10-15 inches in diameter; forming a dense, round-topped crown of stout, spreading branches and more or less zigzag, slender branchlets.

LEAVES.—Alternate, simple, 3-5 inches long, nearly as broad; outline variable, ovate to semiorbicular, often 3-5-lobed; coarsely serrate; thin; dark blue-green and smooth or rough above, pale and more or less downy beneath; petioles 1-2 inches long, smooth, exuding a milky juice when cut.

FLOWERS.—May or early June, with the leaves; monoecious or dioecious; the staminate in dense spikes, 1-2 inches long, on short, hairy peduncles; the pistillate in dense spikes, about 1 inch long, on short, hairy peduncles; calyx 4-lobed, hairy; corolla 0; stamens 4, with green anthers; stigmas 2, spreading.

FRUIT.—July; 1 inch long; consisting of drupes about $\frac{1}{32}$ inch long, each inclosed in a thickened, fleshy calyx; berry-like; bright red at first, finally blackish; sweet, juicy, edible.

WINTER-BUDS.—Terminal bud absent; lateral buds ovoid, abruptly pointed, $\frac{1}{4}$ inch long, lustrous, light brown, somewhat divergent.

BARK.—Twigs greenish and more or less downy, becoming smooth and brownish; trunk dark brown tinged with red and more or less furrowed.

WOOD.—Light, soft, weak, rather tough, coarse-grained, very durable, pale orange, with thick, lighter colored sapwood.

DISTRIBUTION.—Southern portion of the Lower Peninsula, as far north as the Muskegon River.

HABITAT.—Prefers rich soil in river-bottoms.

NOTES.—Easily transplanted. Grows rapidly in good, moist soil.

The White Mulberry, *Morus alba* L., is a Chinese tree which is used extensively for screening and for underplanting in woodlands. It is a small tree of rapid growth which may be distinguished from the Red Mulberry in summer by its leaves, which are smooth and glossy above and nearly glabrous beneath, and by the white or pinkish white fruit. In winter it may be distinguished by the somewhat shorter lateral buds, which are about $\frac{1}{8}$ inch long and appressed, and by the pale yellow-brown bark.

The Russian Mulberry, *Morus alba*, v. *tatarica* Loud., is a smaller, bushy tree which has great hardiness to withstand cold, drought and neglect. It is useful for low windbreaks and sheared hedges. The leaves are 1½-3 inches long, commonly much lobed, and the fruit is very small, dark red.

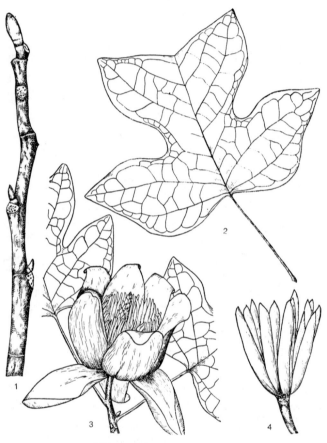

1. Winter twig, x 1.
2. Leaf, x ½.
3. Flowering branchlet, x ½.
4. Fruit (opened and partly disseminated), x ½.

MAGNOLIACEAE

Tulip Poplar. Tulip-tree. White-wood

Liriodendron tulipifera L.

HABIT.—A large tree 50-80 feet high, with a columnar trunk 2-5 feet in diameter; forming a rather open, conical crown of slender branches.

LEAVES.—Alternate, simple, 5-6 inches long and broad; 4-lobed; the lobes entire; lustrous, dark green above, pale or glaucous beneath, turning clear yellow in autumn; petioles slender, angled, 5-6 inches long.

FLOWERS.—May-June, after the leaves; perfect; terminal; solitary on stout peduncles; tulip-shaped, greenish yellow, 2 inches or more across; sepals 3, greenish, early deciduous; petals 6, in 2 rows, greenish yellow with an orange spot at the base, early deciduous; stamens numerous, somewhat shorter than the petals; pistils numerous, clinging together about a central axis; ovary 1-celled.

FRUIT.—September-October; a narrow, light brown cone 2½-3 inches long, composed of numerous carpels; carpels long, flat, with a 1-2-seeded nutlet at the base, separating from the slender spindle at maturity.

WINTER-BUDS.—Terminal bud ½-1 inch long, obtuse, flattish, dark red, covered with a glaucous bloom.

BARK.—Twigs smooth, lustrous, reddish, becoming brownish, and at length gray; ashy gray, thin and scaly on young trunks, becoming thick, brownish and deeply furrowed with age.

WOOD.—Light, soft, brittle, weak, easily worked, light yellow or brown, with thin, cream-white sapwood. See p. 325.

DISTRIBUTION.—Lower Peninsula south of the Grand River. Formerly common, but becoming rare.

HABITAT.—Prefers deep, rich, rather moist soil, but adapts itself readily to any good, light soil.

NOTES.—Difficult to transplant, but rapid of growth when once established. Not disfigured by insect and fungus enemies. Desirable for shade on the lawn and, where there is good soil and plenty of space, makes a good street tree.

The Magnolias, which belong to the same family as the Tulip Tree, are extensively planted in their variety and hybrid forms for their large, showy, and mostly fragrant flowers, which appear in early spring, and their large, tropical-like leaves. In our latitude they need some protection against the rigors of winter. The hardiest Magnolia is the Cucumber Tree, *Magnolia acuminata* L., a native of Ohio and adjacent regions to the south and east. Its leaves are 4-10 inches long, about one-half as broad, acute at the apex, mostly rounded at the base, and entire. The fruit is a red, cone-like mass of fleshy carpels, 2-2½ inches long. The winter-buds are densely covered with pale, silky hairs, and are nearly surrounded by the leaf-scars.

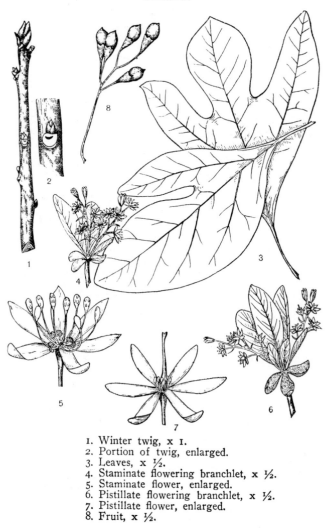

1. Winter twig, **x** 1.
2. Portion of twig, enlarged.
3. Leaves, **x** ½.
4. Staminate flowering branchlet, **x** ½.
5. Staminate flower, enlarged.
6. Pistillate flowering branchlet, **x** ½.
7. Pistillate flower, enlarged.
8. Fruit, **x** ½.

LAURACEAE

Sassafras

Sassafras variifolium (Salisb.) Ktze. [*Sassafras sassafras* (L.) Karst.] [*Sassafras officinale* Nees & Eberm.]

HABIT.—Usually a large shrub, but often a small tree 20-40 feet high, with a trunk diameter of 10-20 inches; stout, often contorted branches and a bushy spray form a flat, rather open crown.

LEAVES.—Alternate, simple, 3-6 inches long, 2-4 inches broad; oval to oblong or obovate; entire or 1-3-lobed with deep, broad sinuses and finger-like lobes; thin; dull dark green above, paler beneath; petioles slender, about 1 inch long.

FLOWERS.—May, with the leaves; dioecious; greenish yellow; on slender pedicels, in loose, drooping, few-flowered racemes, 2 inches long; calyx deeply 6-lobed, yellow-green; corolla o; stamens of staminate flower 9, in 3 rows, of pistillate flower 6, in 1 row; ovary 1-celled.

FRUIT.—September-October; an oblong-globose, lustrous, dark blue berry, ⅜ inch long, surrounded at the base by the scarlet calyx, borne on a club-shaped, bright red pedicel.

WINTER-BUDS.—Terminal bud ⅓ inch long, ovoid, acute, greenish, soft-pubescent, flower-bearing; lateral buds much smaller, sterile or leaf-bearing. Aromatic.

BARK.—Twigs glabrous, lustrous, yellow-green, spicy-aromatic, becoming red-brown and shallowly fissured when 2-3 years old; thick, dark red-brown and deeply and irregularly fissured into firm, flat ridges on old trunks.

WOOD.—Soft, weak, brittle, coarse-grained, very durable in the soil, aromatic, dull orange-brown, with thin, light yellow sapwood.

DISTRIBUTION.—Southern portion of Lower Peninsula as far north as Grayling.

HABITAT.—Prefers well-drained, stony or sandy soil; woods; abandoned fields; peaty swamps.

NOTES.—Rapid of growth. Suckers freely. Difficult to transplant. Propagated easily from seed. Oil of sassafras is distilled from the roots and bark.

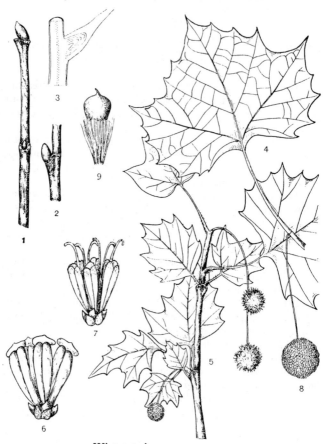

1. Winter twig, x 1.
2. Portion of twig, side view, x 1.
3. Vertical section of twig, summer
   bud and leaf petiole, enlarged.
4. Leaf, x ⅜.
5. Flowering branchlet, x ½.
6. Staminate flower, enlarged.
7. Pistillate flower, enlarged.
8. Fruit, x ⅜.
9. Achene, enlarged.

PLATANACEAE

Sycamore. Button-wood. Buttonball-tree

Platanus occidentalis L.

HABIT.—A large tree 70-100 feet high, with a trunk diameter of 3-8 feet; commonly dividing near the ground into several large secondary trunks, forming a broad, open, irregular crown of massive, spreading branches.

LEAVES.—Alternate, simple, 5-10 inches long and broad; broadly ovate; more or less 3-5-lobed by broad, shallow sinuses, the lobes sinuate-toothed; thin and firm; bright green above, paler beneath, glabrous both sides; petioles stout, puberulous, 1-2 inches long.

FLOWERS.—May, with the leaves; monoecious; borne in dense heads; the staminate dark red, on short, axillary peduncles; the pistillate greenish, on long, slender, terminal peduncles; sepals 3-6, minute; petals 3-6, minute; stamens 3-6; styles long, red.

FRUIT.—October, persistent on the limbs throughout the winter; brown heads about 1 inch in diameter, on slender, glabrous stems, 3-6 inches long.

WINTER-BUDS.—Terminal bud absent; lateral buds ¼-⅜ inch long, conical, blunt, lustrous, pale brown; forming in summer within the petiole of the leaf.

BARK.—Twigs pale green and tomentose, becoming smooth, dark green, finally grayish; thick, red-brown on the trunk and broken into oblong, plate-like scales, separating higher up into thin plates which peel off, exposing the greenish or yellowish inner bark.

WOOD.—Heavy, tough, hard, rather weak, coarse-grained, difficult to split, light red-brown, with thick, darker colored sapwood. See p. 327.

DISTRIBUTION.—Lower Peninsula as far north as Roscommon County.

HABITAT.—Prefers rich bottom-lands along the borders of rivers and lakes.

NOTES.—Rapid of growth. Bears transplanting well. Formerly much planted as a shade and street tree, especially in cities, as it is not injured greatly by dust and smoke, and stands pruning well. Subject to attacks of fungi and insects.

A Sycamore, which has been much planted in this country, is known as the Oriental Plane, *Platanus orientalis* L. It may be distinguished from our native Sycamore by the somewhat longer and narrower lobes of the leaves and by the fruiting heads, which hang in pairs or rarely 3-4-together. According to L. H. Bailey (Manual of Cultivated Plants, 1924.), the name "Oriental Plane" has been misapplied to the London Plane, *Platanus acerifolia* Willd., which is a supposed hybrid between the Oriental Plane and our native species. It does not differ greatly in its characteristics from the species just described, but is somewhat more hardy. The introduced Sycamores are not attacked seriously by insects and fungi, and while they may be killed back slightly in winter in our latitude, the loss is more than made up by their rapid growth.

THE ROSE FAMILY—ROSACEAE

This is one of the largest families of plants and it is comprised of trees, shrubs and a few herbs, which are widely distributed throughout the temperate regions of the world. Of the ninety or more genera, Michigan is represented by four which possess tree-like forms, namely, *Pyrus, Amelanchier, Crataegus* and *Prunus.*

THE APPLES, PEARS AND MOUNTAIN ASHES
—PYRUS

The trees in the genus *Pyrus* are small or only medium-sized. The flowers, which are abundant and showy, are borne in cyme-like clusters, which terminate the leafy branches or spur-like branchlets. They are perfect, with the calyx, corolla and stamens borne on the end of a fleshy receptacle which incloses the ovary. It is largely this ovary and surrounding receptacle which develop later into the fruit or pome. The leaves are arranged alternately and may be either simple or compound.

Only two species of *Pyrus* are native to Michigan, the Sweet or American Crab and the Mountain Ash. Many introduced species have been cultivated since early times, but improved by man from their primitive and often unattractive forms. Among these are our well-known domestic fruit trees, the cultivated Pear, *Pyrus communis,* L., the Apple, *Pyrus malus* L. (*Malus pumila* Mill.) and the Quince, *Pyrus cydonia* L., all having their origin in Europe. Through the work of horticulturists there has been a continuous development of these forms and countless varieties have been originated, which are adapted to a great variety of conditions throughout the temperate regions of the world.

There are a number of Crabs which are widely planted, not for their fruit, but for ornament and especially for their fragrant blooms. Best known among these is Bechtel's Double-flowering Crab, a form of *Pyrus ioensis* (Wood) Bailey [*Malus ioensis,* v. *plena* (Brit.) Rehd.], a medium-sized tree which is covered in early May with large semi-double, fragrant flowers of delicate pink. The Flowering Crab, *Pyrus pulcherrima* Aschers. & Graebn. (*Malus floribunda* Sieb.), is an especially handsome little tree with its very abundant single flowers changing from carmine to white, followed by the small, red fruit. There are a number of others, each with points of merit.

The native Mountain Ash is one of the beautiful trees of the north. Its distribution is limited, and the tree so commonly planted in the southern part of our state is the European Mountain Ash or Rowan Tree, *Pyrus aucuparia* (L.) Ehrh. (*Sorbus Aucuparia* L.). It is a small, rapid-growing tree, usually 20-40 feet in height, with a slender, short trunk which separates a few feet above the ground into stout, spreading branches to form a rounded crown. The leaves are pinnately compound, as in our American tree, but the leaflets are blunt, rounded or short-pointed at the apex and they are more or less pubescent on both sides, whereas those of the native species are acuminate at the apex and glabrous. Other distinguishing features are possessed by the fruit, which is somewhat larger, about ⅓ inch in diameter, and by the winter-twigs and buds. In the European Mountain Ash the twigs are pubescent and the buds are woolly, and they are not gummy. A form with orange-yellow fruit is much planted. Highly ornamental. Should not be planted in rich soil. Liable to sun-scald and somewhat difficult to establish.

SUMMER KEY TO THE SPECIES OF PYRUS

a. Leaves simple; fruit a light green pome an inch or more in diameter; branches contorted, bearing many short, spur-like branchlets .... *P. coronaria*, p. 177

aa. Leaves compound; fruit berry-like, ¼ inch in diameter, bright red; branches not contorted, not bearing many short, spur-like branchlets .... *P. americana*, p. 179

WINTER KEY TO THE SPECIES OF PYRUS

a. Bundle-scars 3 or in 3 compound, but distinct groups; buds ⅛-¼ inch long; branches contorted, bearing many short, spur-like branchlets; fruit a pome an inch or more in diameter, light green .... *P. coronaria*, p. 177

aa. Bundle-scars 4-many in a single U-shaped line, not forming 3 distinct groups; buds about ½ inch long; branches not contorted, not bearing many short, spur-like branchlets; fruit berry-like, ¼ inch in diameter, bright red ....
.... *P. americana*, p. 179

— 175 —

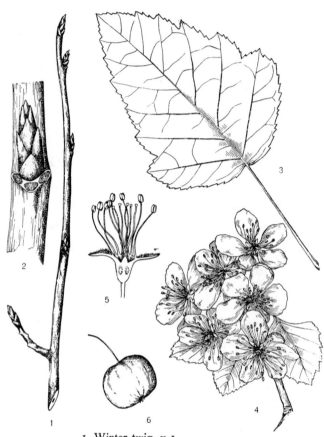

1. Winter twig, x 1.
2. Portion of twig, enlarged.
3. Leaf, x ¾.
4. Flowering branchlet, x ½.
5. Vertical section of flower,
    with petals removed, x ½.
6. Fruit, x ½.

ROSACEAE

Sweet Crab. American Crab
Pyrus coronaria L. [*Malus coronaria* Mill.]

HABIT.—Often a bushy shrub, but frequently a small tree 15-25 feet high, with a trunk 8-12 inches in diameter, forming a broad, rounded crown of rigid, contorted branches bearing many short, spur-like branchlets.

LEAVES.—Alternate, simple, 3-4 inches long, almost as broad; ovate to nearly triangular; sharply and deeply serrate, sometimes lobed; membranaceous; bright green above, paler beneath, glabrous both sides; petioles long, slender, often with two dark glands near the middle.

FLOWERS.—May, after the leaves; perfect; 1½-2 inches across; very fragrant; borne on slender pedicels in 5-6-flowered umbels; calyx urn-shaped, 5-lobed, tomentose; petals 5, rose colored to white; stamens 10-20; ovary hairy; styles 5.

FRUIT.—October; a depressed-globose pome, 1-1½ inches in diameter, pale green, very fragrant, with a waxy surface; flesh very tart; often hanging on the tree until far into the winter; does not rot until following spring.

WINTER-BUDS.—Terminal bud ⅛-¼ inch long, obtuse, bright red; lateral buds smaller.

BARK.—Twigs at first hoary-tomentose, becoming glabrous, red-brown; thin, red-brown, breaking into longitudinal fissures on the trunk.

WOOD.—Heavy, rather soft, close-grained, weak, red-brown, with thick, yellow sapwood.

DISTRIBUTION.—Southern portion of the Lower Peninsula as far north as Roscommon County.

HABITAT.—Rich, moist, but well-drained soil in thickets and along streams.

NOTES.—An excellent ornamental tree or shrub for small gardens and shrubberies. The fruit is sometimes gathered for making preserves and jellies.

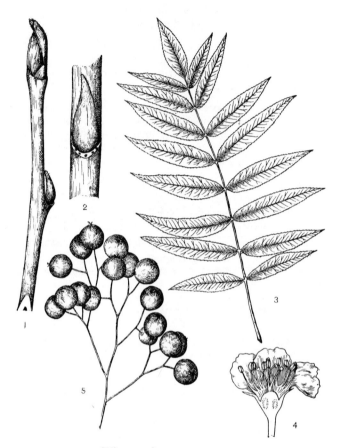

1. Winter twig, x 1.
2. Portion of twig, enlarged.
3. Leaf, x ⅓.
4. Vertical section of flower, enlarged.
5. Portion of a fruiting cyme, x 1.

ROSACEAE
Mountain Ash

Pyrus americana (Marsh.) DC. [*Sorbus americana* Marsh.]

HABIT.—A small tree 15-25 feet high, with a trunk diameter of not over a foot; branches slender, spreading, forming a narrow, rounded crown.

LEAVES.—Alternate, compound, 6-9 inches long. Leaflets 9-17, 2-3 inches long and ½-¾ inch broad; sessile or nearly so, except the terminal; lanceolate to oblong-lanceolate, taper-pointed; finely and sharply serrate above the entire base; membranaceous; glabrous, dark yellow-green above, paler beneath, turning clear yellow in autumn. Petioles slender, grooved, enlarged at the base.

FLOWERS.—May-June, after the leaves; perfect; ⅛ inch across; borne on short, stout pedicels in many-flowered, flat cymes, 3-5 inches across; calyx urn-shaped, 5-lobed, puberulous; petals 5, white; stamens numerous; styles 2-3.

FRUIT.—October, but persistent on the tree throughout the winter; a berry-like pome, subglobose, ¼ inch in diameter, bright red, with thin, acid flesh; eaten by birds in the absence of other food.

WINTER-BUDS.—Terminal bud about ½ inch long, ovoid, acute, with curved apex; lateral buds smaller, appressed; scales rounded on the back, purplish red, more or less pilose above, gummy.

BARK.—Twigs at first red-brown and hairy, becoming glabrous, dark brown; thin, light gray-brown on the trunk, smooth, or slightly roughened on old trees; inner bark fragrant.

WOOD.—Light, soft, close-grained, weak, pale brown, with thick, lighter colored sapwood.

DISTRIBUTION.—Ludington and northward, principally along the shore of Lake Michigan, but common throughout the Upper Peninsula.

HABITAT.—Prefers rich, moist soil on river-banks and on the borders of cold swamps; rocky hillsides and mountains.

NOTES.—More often a shrub. Easily transplanted, but slow of growth. One of the most beautiful trees of our northern forests.

A variety of the Mountain Ash, *decora,* is sometimes planted. It differs from the type in its leaves, which are 4-6 inches long, with red petioles, and in its larger fruit, which is often ½ inch in diameter. See p. 174 for a description of the European Mountain Ash.

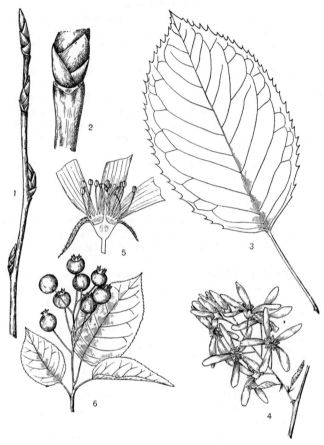

1. Winter twig, x 1.
2. Portion of twig, enlarged.
3. Leaf, x 1.
4. Flowering branchlet, x ½.
5. Vertical section of flower, enlarged.
6. Fruiting branchlet, x ½.

ROSACEAE

Serviceberry. Juneberry. Shad Bush

Amelanchier canadensis (L.) Medic.

HABIT.—A small tree 15-25 feet in height, with a tall trunk 6-12 inches in diameter; forming a narrow, rounded crown of many small limbs and slender branchlets; at times only a large shrub.

LEAVES.—Alternate, simple, 3-4 inches long and about one-half as broad; ovate to obovate; finely and sharply serrate; glabrous, dark green above, paler beneath; petioles slender, about 1 inch long.

FLOWERS.—April-May, when the leaves are about one-third grown; perfect; large, white, borne in erect or lax racemes, 3-5 inches long; calyx 5-cleft, campanulate, villous on the inner surface; petals 5, strap-shaped, white, about 1 inch in length; stamens numerous; styles 5, united below.

FRUIT.—June-August; globular, berry-like pome, ⅓-½ inch long; turning from bright red to dark purple with slight bloom; sweet and edible when ripe.

WINTER-BUDS.—Yellow-brown, narrow-ovoid to conical, sharp-pointed, ¼-½ inch long; bud-scales apiculate, slightly pubescent.

BARK.—Twigs smooth, light green, becoming red-brown; thin, pale red-brown on the trunk, smoothish or divided by shallow fissures into narrow, longitudinal, scaly ridges.

WOOD.—Heavy, very hard, strong, close-grained, dark red-brown, with thick, lighter colored sapwood.

DISTRIBUTION.—Common throughout the state.

HABITAT.—Prefers rich soil of dry, upland woods and hillsides.

NOTES.—Hardy throughout the state. Grows in all soils and situations except in wet lands. The fruits are sought eagerly by birds and other animals. In the spring the tree is a conspicuous object on hillsides, at which time it may be recognized at a distance by the white flowers, which are borne in profusion.

Another small Serviceberry has been added to our arborescent flora, known as *Amelanchier laevis* Wieg. It differs but slightly from *Amelanchier canadensis* and until recently has not been distinguished from it. Its leaves are glabrous from the beginning and purplish up to blossom time. The somewhat larger flowers are borne in loose, drooping racemes, followed by the slightly larger, longer-stalked fruit. It is said to be more northerly in its distribution than *Amelanchier canadensis*.

Dotted Haw

Crataegus punctata Jacq.

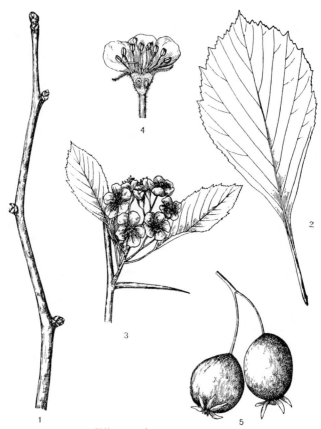

1. Winter twig, x 1.
2. Leaf, x 1.
3. Flowering branchlet, x ½.
4. Vertical section of flower, enlarged.
5. Fruit, x 1.

ROSACEAE

The Haws, Thorns, Hawthorns or Thorn-apples

Crataegus L.

Owing to the complexity of the various forms in this group, the present state of uncertainty as to the value of certain characters and the questionable validity of many of the assigned names, it is thought to be beyond the scope of this bulletin to give more than a general description of the group as a whole, recommending the more ambitious student to the various manuals and botanical journals and papers for more detailed information.

The *Crataegi* are generally low, wide-spreading trees or shrubs, with strong, tortuous branches and more or less zigzag branchlets usually armed with stiff, sharp thorns. The bark varies from dark red to gray and is shallowly fissured or scaly. The leaves are alternate, simple, generally serrate, often lobed, with short or long petioles. The flowers appear in May or June, with or after the leaves, in simple or compound corymbs, whitish or pinkish, perfect. The fruit is a red to yellow, sometimes blue or black pome, subglobose to pear-shaped, with usually dry and mealy flesh and 1-5 seeds. The winter-buds are small, nearly globose, lustrous brown. *Crataegus* produces wood which is heavy, hard, tough, close-grained, red-brown, with thick, pale sapwood. The Haws are trees of the pasture-lands, the roadside, the open woods and the stream-banks, and are more common in the southern than in the northern portions of the state. Some of the species are desirable as ornaments in parks and gardens on account of their beautiful and abundant flowers and showy fruits.

THE PLUMS, CHERRIES AND PEACHES— PRUNUS

The species of *Prunus* number about one hundred and twenty, well distributed over the north temperate zone and occurring locally in the tropics. Some thirty species occur in the United States, eighteen of which are of tree size. Four of them are native to Michigan. They are all small or medium size, with conspicuous pink or white flowers. One of them, the Black Cherry, in more southern latitudes becomes a large tree, sometimes attaining a height of 110 feet, with a diameter of 5 feet. The Plums, Cherries and Peaches are distinguished by their stone fruit and by their astringent bark and leaves.

Among the introduced species which have been cultivated extensively are the Sour Cherry, *Prunus cerasus* L.; the Sweet Cherry, *Prunus avium* L.; the Plum, *Prunus domestica* L.; and the Peach, *Prunus persica* (L.) Stokes. These, like the Apples and Pears, have been subject to continual improvement by man, until there are many varieties and forms adapted to a great range of climate and conditions.

The ornamental Flowering Almond of American gardens is *Prunus triloba* Lindl. It is a small tree not more than 10-15 feet in height, and more often it is shrub-like. Its native home is China, but it has been grown in this country for a long time for its showy blooms, which appear just before the leaves. In the type the flowers are solitary, short-pedicelled, 1-1½ inches across, clear pink or sometimes white. The variety *plena,* with double flowers, is planted more frequently, but the single-flower form is the better. The leaves are broadly ovate or obovate, usually broadest above the middle, abruptly pointed and tending to be 3-lobed at the apex, coarsely doubly serrate, soft-hairy on both sides. It is only fairly hardy.

SUMMER KEY TO THE SPECIES OF PRUNUS

a. Leaves oblong-ovate to obovate, abruptly acuminate at the apex; marginal teeth not incurved.
  b. Margin of leaves sharp-serrate with spreading teeth; leaves not rugose, the veins not prominent; fruit ¼-½ inch in diameter, bright red, racemose, July-August; bark of trunk brown, smooth or only slightly fissured; usually a large shrub .... *P. virginiana*, **p.** 189

bb. Margin of leaves crenate-serrate; leaves more or less rugose, the veins prominent; fruit about 1 inch in diameter, orange-red, clustered, August-September; bark of trunk gray-brown, early splitting off in large, thick plates; a small tree ......
.... *P. nigra,* p. 193
aa. Leaves oval to oblong-lanceolate, taper-pointed at the apex; marginal teeth incurved.
b. Fruit light red, clustered, July-August; twigs usually less than 1/16 inch thick; pith of twigs brown; tree northern ..
..................................*P. pennsylvanica,* p. 191
bb. Fruit black, racemose, August-September; twigs usually more than 1/16 inch thick; pith of twigs white; tree southern
.... *P. serotina,* p. 187

WINTER KEY TO THE SPECIES OF PRUNUS

a. Terminal bud present; bark of young trunks rather smooth.
b. Buds clustered at the tips of all shoots; twigs usually less than 1/16 inch thick; pith of twigs brown...............
....................................*P. pennsylvanica,* p. 191
bb. Buds not clustered, or clustered only on short, spur-like branchlets; twigs usually more than 1/16 inch thick; pith of twigs white.
c. Buds usually 1/4 inch or less in length; bud-scales uniform in color, not grayish on the margins, apiculate at the apex; bark on old trunks blackish, rough-scaly; small to large tree .... *P. serotina,* p. 187
cc. Buds usually 1/4-1/2 inch long; bud-scales grayish on the margins, rounded at the apex; bark on old trunks brown, smooth or only slightly fissured; usually a large shrub
.... *P. virginiana,* p. 189
aa. Terminal bud absent; bark of young trunks early splitting off in large, thick plates.....................*P. nigra,* p. 193

Black Cherry

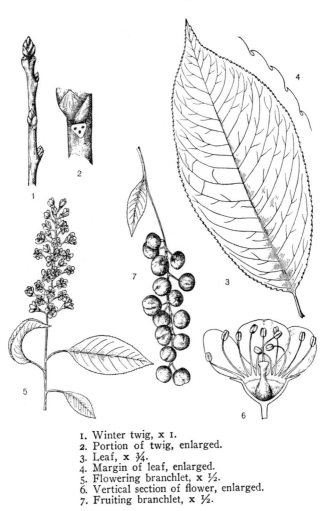

1. Winter twig, x 1.
2. Portion of twig, enlarged.
3. Leaf, x ¾.
4. Margin of leaf, enlarged.
5. Flowering branchlet, x ½.
6. Vertical section of flower, enlarged.
7. Fruiting branchlet, x ½.

ROSACEAE

Black Cherry

Prunus serotina Ehrh. [*Padus serotina* (Ehrh.) Agardh.]

HABIT.—A medium-sized tree 40-50 feet high and 8-36 inches in trunk diameter; branches few, large, tortuous, forming a rather spreading, oblong or rounded crown.

LEAVES.—Alternate, simple, 2-5 inches long, about one-half as broad; oval or oblong to oblong-lanceolate; finely serrate, with teeth incurved; subcoriaceous; dark green and very lustrous above, paler beneath, glabrous both sides; petioles short, slender, usually bearing 2 red glands near the blade.

FLOWERS.—May-June, when the leaves are half grown; perfect; ¼ inch across; borne on slender pedicels in many-flowered, loose racemes, 4-5 inches long; calyx cup-shaped, 5-lobed; petals 5, white; stamens 15-20; stigma thick, club-shaped.

FRUIT.—August-September; a globular drupe, ⅓-½ inch in diameter, nearly black, with dark purple, juicy flesh; slightly bitter, edible.

WINTER-BUDS.—Terminal bud about ¼ inch long, ovoid, blunt to acute; scales keeled on the back, apiculate, light brown.

BARK.—Twigs and branches red to red-brown; young trunks dark red-brown, smooth; blackish on old trunks and rough, broken into thick, irregular plates; bitter, aromatic.

WOOD.—Moderately heavy, rather hard, strong, close- and straight-grained, light brown or red, with thin, yellow sapwood. See p. 329.

DISTRIBUTION.—Frequent in the southern half of the Lower Peninsula, rare in the northern half and the Upper Peninsula.

HABITAT.—Prefers a rich, moist soil, but grows well on dry, gravelly or sandy soils.

NOTES.—Grows very rapidly in youth. Has a long tap root. One of the most valuable timber trees of the forest, rapidly nearing extinction. It deserves to be planted extensively and to be protected carefully where it is growing naturally.

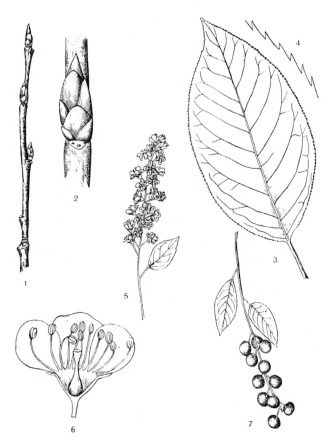

1. Winter twig, x 1.
2. Portion of twig, enlarged.
3. Leaf, x 1.
4. Margin of leaf, enlarged.
5. Flowering branchlet, x ½.
6. Vertical section of flower, enlarged.
7. Fruit, x ½.

ROSACEAE

Choke Cherry

Prunus virginiana L. [*Padus virginiana* (L.) Roemer]

HABIT.—Usually a large shrub, but sometimes a small tree 15-25 feet high, with a crooked, often leaning trunk 5-6 inches in diameter; forming a spreading, somewhat rounded crown.

LEAVES.—Alternate, simple, 2-4 inches long, one-half as broad; obovate to oblong-obovate or oval, abruptly acuminate at the apex; finely and sharply serrate; dull dark green above, paler beneath, glabrous both sides; petioles short, slender, glandular near the blade.

FLOWERS.—May-June, when the leaves are nearly grown; perfect; about ½ inch across; borne on short, slender pedicels in many-flowered racemes, 3-6 inches long; calyx cup-shaped, 5-lobed; petals 5, white; stamens 15-20; stigma broad, on a short style.

FRUIT.—July-August; a globular drupe, ¼-½ inch in diameter, usually bright red, often yellow to almost black, with dark red flesh; astringent, but edible.

WINTER-BUDS.—Terminal bud ¼-½ inch long, conical, acute; scales rounded at the apex, light brown, smooth.

BARK.—Twigs at first light brown or greenish, becoming red-brown, finally dark brown; thin, dark brown on the trunk, slightly fissured.

WOOD.—Heavy, hard, close-grained, weak, light brown, with thick, lighter colored sapwood.

DISTRIBUTION.—Common throughout the entire state.

HABITAT.—Prefers a deep, rich, moist loam, but is common on less favorable sites.

NOTES.—The most widely distributed tree of North America, extending from the arctic circle to Mexico, from the Rocky Mountains to the Atlantic Ocean. The cherry "pits" are dropped by birds along fences and hedge rows, where they germinate and produce extensive thickets which are difficult to eliminate on account of numerous suckers from the roots. Of little commercial importance.

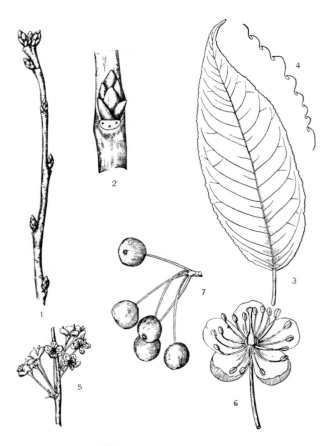

1. Winter twig, x 1.
2. Portion of twig, enlarged.
3. Leaf, x 1.
4. Margin of leaf, enlarged.
5. Flowering branchlet, x ½.
6. Flower, enlarged.
7. Fruit, x 1.

ROSACEAE

Wild Red Cherry. Pin Cherry

Prunus pennsylvanica L. f.

HABIT.—A slender tree, seldom over 30 feet high, with a trunk diameter of 8-10 inches; crown rather open, narrow, rounded, with slender, regular branches.

LEAVES.—Alternate, simple, 3-5 inches long, ¾-1¼ inches broad; oblong-lanceolate; finely and sharply serrate; bright green and shining above, paler beneath; petioles slender, ½-1 inch long, glandular near the blade.

FLOWERS.—May or early June, with the leaves; perfect; about ½ inch across, borne on slender pedicels in 4-5-flowered umbels, generally clustered, 2-3 together; calyx 5-cleft, campanulate; petals 5, white, ¼ inch long; stamens 15-20.

FRUIT.—July-August; a globular drupe, ¼ inch in diameter, light red, with thick skin and sour flesh.

WINTER-BUDS.—Terminal bud ⅛ inch long, broadly ovoid, rather blunt, brownish, smooth.

BARK.—Twigs at first lustrous, red, marked by orange colored lenticels, becoming brownish; red-brown and thin on the trunk, peeling off horizontally into broad, papery plates; bitter, aromatic.

WOOD.—Light, soft, close-grained, light brown, with thin, yellow sapwood.

DISTRIBUTION.—Throughout the northern portion of the state, extending southward to Ionia County.

HABITAT.—Abundant on sand-lands; roadsides; burned-over lands; clearings; hillsides.

NOTES.—Rapid of growth. Short-lived. Furnishes food for birds and wild animals. It springs up abundantly after fires and lumbering operations, protecting the soil and acting as a nurse-tree until larger and better species are established.

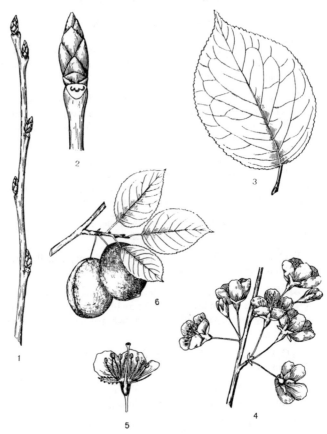

1. Winter twig, x 1.
2. Portion of twig, enlarged.
3. Leaf, x ½.
4. Flowering branchlet, x ½.
5. Vertical section of flower, x 1.
6. Fruiting branchlet, x ½.

ROSACEAE

Canada Plum. Red Plum

Prunus nigra Ait. [*Prunus americana,* v. *nigra* Waugh]

HABIT.—A small tree 20-25 feet high and 5-8 inches in trunk diameter; usually divides 5-6 feet from the ground into a number of stout, upright branches, forming a narrow, rigid crown.

LEAVES.—Alternate, simple, 3-5 inches long and one-half as broad; oblong-ovate to obovate, abruptly acuminate at the apex; doubly crenate-serrate; thick and firm; glabrous, light green above, paler beneath; petioles short, stout, bearing 2 large red glands near the blade.

FLOWERS.—April-May, before the leaves; perfect; slightly fragrant; about 1 inch across; borne on slender, glabrous, red pedicels in 2-3-flowered umbels; calyx 5-lobed, dark red; petals 5, white; stamens 15-20, with purple anthers; ovary 1-celled; style 1; stigma 1.

FRUIT.—August-September; a fleshy drupe, about 1 inch in diameter, oblong-ovoid, with a tough, thick, orange-red skin nearly free from bloom, and yellow flesh adherent to the flat stone. Eaten raw or cooked.

WINTER-BUDS.—Terminal bud absent; lateral buds ⅛-¼ inch long, ovoid, acute, chestnut-brown.

BARK.—Twigs green, marked by numerous pale excrescences, later dark brown; thin, gray-brown and smooth on young trunks, but soon splitting off in large, thick plates, exposing the darker inner bark.

WOOD.—Heavy, hard, strong, close-grained, light red-brown, with thin, lighter colored sapwood.

DISTRIBUTION.—Upper Peninsula and the Lower Peninsula north of Lansing, with occasional occurrences southward.

HABITAT.—Prefers rich, alluvial soil along streams.

NOTES.—Suckers freely, forming low, broad thickets. The fruit is used for preserves and jellies, some trees producing a better quality than others. Attractive ornamentally.

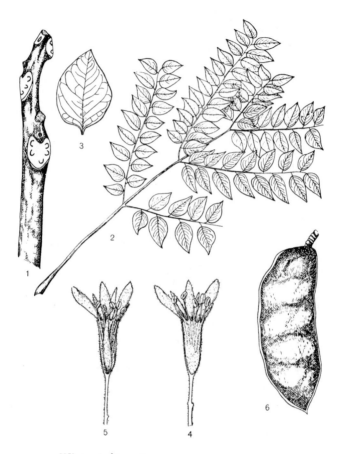

1. Winter twig, x 1.
2. Leaf, x ¼.
3. Leaflet, x ½.
4. Vertical section of staminate flower, enlarged.
5. Vertical section of pistillate flower, enlarged.
6. Fruit, x ¼.

LEGUMINOSAE

Coffeetree. Kentucky Coffeetree

Gymnocladus dioica (L.) Koch [*Gymnocladus canadensis* Lam.]

HABIT.—A slender tree 50-75 feet high, with a trunk diameter of 2-3 feet; divides near the ground into several stems which spread slightly to form a narrow, pyramidal crown; branchlets stout, clumsy, blunt, with conspicuous leaf-scars.

LEAVES.—Alternate, bipinnately compound, 1-3 feet long. Leaflets 40 or more, 2-2½ inches long and one-half as broad; short-stalked; ovate, acute; entire; thin and firm; dark green above, pale yellow-green and glabrous beneath. Petioles stout, terete, glabrous. Appear late in spring.

FLOWERS.—June, after the leaves; dioecious; greenish white; the staminate short-stalked, in racemose corymbs, 3-4 inches long; the pistillate long-stalked, in racemes, 10-12 inches long; calyx tubular, hairy; petals 5, keeled, nearly white; stamens 10; ovary hairy.

FRUIT.—Ripens in autumn, but remains closed until late in winter; short-stalked, red-brown legumes, 6-10 inches long, 1½-2 inches wide, containing 6-9 large, flat seeds.

WINTER-BUDS.—Terminal bud absent; lateral buds minute, depressed, 2 in the axil of each leaf, bronze-brown, silky-pubescent.

BARK.—Twigs coated with short, dense, reddish pubescence, becoming light brown; thick, deeply fissured and scaly on the trunk, dark gray.

WOOD.—Heavy, somewhat soft, strong, coarse-grained, very durable in contact with the soil, light red-brown, with thin, lighter colored sapwood.

DISTRIBUTION.—Southern Michigan as far north as the Grand River. Infrequent.

HABITAT.—Prefers bottom-lands and rich soil.

NOTES.—The seeds in early days were used as a substitute for coffee. Widely planted as an ornamental tree in parks and cemeteries. Requires plenty of light. Will grow in poor soils. Free from insects and disease. Quite hardy.

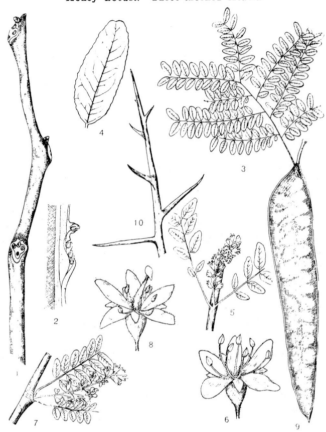

1. Winter twig, x 1.
2. Vertical section through lateral buds, enlarged.
3. Leaf, x ¼.
4. Leaflet, x 1.
5. Staminate flowering branchlet, x ½.
6. Staminate flower, enlarged.
7. Pistillate flowering branchlet, x ½.
8. Pistillate flower, enlarged.
9. Fruit, x ⅓.
10. Spine from trunk, x ½.

LEGUMINOSAE
Honey Locust. Three-thorned Acacia
Gleditsia triacanthos L.

HABIT.—A tree usually 50-75 feet high, with a trunk diameter of 2-3 feet; dividing near the ground into several large, upright branches which divide again into long, slender, horizontal branchlets; both trunk and large branches armed with stout, rigid, simple or branched spines.

LEAVES.—Alternate, pinnately or bipinnately compound, 7-12 inches long. Leaflets 18 or more, ¾-1½ inches long, one-third as broad; lanceolate-oblong; remotely crenulate-serrate; thin; lustrous, dark green above, dull yellow-green beneath. Petioles and rachises pubescent.

FLOWERS.—May-June, when the leaves are nearly full grown; polygamo-dioecious; the staminate in short, many-flowered, pubescent racemes; the pistillate in slender, few-flowered racemes; on shoots of the preceding season; calyx campanulate, hairy, 3-5-lobed; petals 3-5, greenish; stamens 3-10; ovary 1-celled, woolly.

FRUIT.—Autumn, falling in early winter; pendent, flat, twisted, brown legumes, 12-18 inches long, short-stalked in short racemes; seeds 12-14, ovoid, flattened.

WINTER-BUDS.—Terminal bud absent; lateral buds minute, 3 or more superposed, glabrous, brownish.

BARK.—Twigs lustrous, red-brown, becoming gray-brown; thick on the trunk, iron-gray to blackish and deeply fissured into long, narrow ridges roughened by small scales.

WOOD.—Hard, strong, coarse-grained, durable in contact with the soil, red-brown, with thin, pale sapwood.

DISTRIBUTION.—Indigenous to the extreme southern portion of the state, but is planted as far north as Bay City.

HABITAT.—Prefers deep, rich loam, but grows on a variety of soils.

NOTES.—Grows rapidly and is long-lived. Easily transplanted. Remarkably free from fungous and insect enemies. Widely planted as a tall hedge plant. Especially suited to planting in sandy soils, where few other trees will grow. The stiff spines and long pods, which litter the ground, make the tree unsuitable for street or ornamental use.

A variety, *inermis* Pursh., without spines, is more open in its habit, and it is recommended for street planting where the conditions are severe. It resists smoke and gas, but requires full sunlight for its proper development.

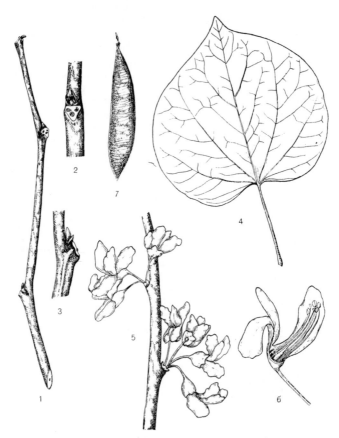

1. Winter twig, x 1.
2. Portion of twig, front view, enlarged.
3. Portion of twig, side view, enlarged.
4. Leaf, x ½.
5. Flowering branchlet, x 1.
6. Vertical section of flower, enlarged.
7. Fruit, x ½.

LEGUMINOSAE

Redbud. Judas-tree

Cercis canadensis L.

HABIT.—A small tree 15-25 feet high, with a trunk diameter of 10-15 inches; divided near the ground into stout, straggling branches to form a broad, flat crown.

LEAVES.—Alternate, simple, 3-5 inches long and broad; heart-shaped or rounded; entire; thick; glabrous, dark green above, paler beneath, turning bright yellow in autumn; petioles slender, terete, enlarged at the base.

FLOWERS.—April-May, before or with the leaves; perfect; ½ inch long; borne on short, jointed pedicels in fascicles of 4-8; calyx campanulate, 5-toothed, dark red; petals 5, rose color; stamens 10, in 2 rows.

FRUIT.—June-July, remaining on the tree until early winter; a short-stalked legume, 2½-3 inches long, pointed at both ends, rose color; seeds 10-12, brownish, ¼ inch long.

WINTER-BUDS.—Terminal bud absent; lateral buds ⅛ inch long, obtuse, somewhat flattened and appressed, brownish.

BARK.—Twigs lustrous, brown, becoming dark or grayish brown; red-brown, deeply fissured, with a scaly surface on old trunks.

WOOD.—Heavy, hard, coarse-grained, weak, dark red-brown, with thin, lighter colored sapwood.

DISTRIBUTION.—Valleys of the Grand and Raisin Rivers and southward.

HABITAT.—Prefers the borders of streams and rich bottom-lands, often in the shade of other trees.

NOTES.—Rapid of growth. Hardy within its range. Can be transplanted with success only when very young. Plants begin to produce flowers freely when 4-5 years old. Much used in landscape gardening.

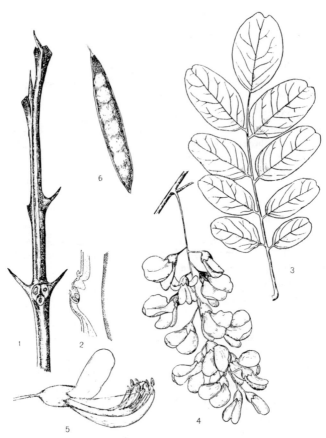

1. Winter twig, x 1.
2. Vertical section through lateral buds, enlarged.
3. Leaf, x ½.
4. Raceme of flowers, x ½.
5. Flower, with part of corolla removed, enlarged.
6. Fruit, x ½.

LEGUMINOSAE

Locust. Black Locust

Robinia pseudo-acacia L.

HABIT.—A tree usually 30-60 feet high, with a trunk diameter of 1-2 feet; forming a narrow, oblong-cylindrical crown of irregular, more or less contorted branches.

LEAVES.—Alternate, compound, 8-14 inches long. Leaflets 7-21, short-petiolate, 1-2 inches long, about one-half as broad; ovate to oblong-oval; entire; very thin; dull dark green above, paler beneath, glabrous both sides. Petioles slender, pubescent.

FLOWERS.—May-June, after the leaves; perfect; showy and abundant; very fragrant; borne on slender pedicels in loose, drooping racemes, 4-5 inches long; about 1 inch long; calyx short, bell-shaped, 5-lobed, hairy; corolla papilionaceous, white, 5-petaled; stamens 10.

FRUIT.—Late autumn, but persistent on the tree through the winter; a smooth, dark brown, flat pod, 3-4 inches long, containing 4-8 small, flattish, brown seeds.

WINTER-BUDS.—Terminal bud absent; lateral buds minute, 3-4 superposed, partially sunken within the leaf-scar, rusty-hairy.

BARK.—Twigs smooth, green, more or less rough-dotted at first, becoming red-brown and armed with prickles; dark red-brown and thick on old trunks, deeply furrowed into firm, sinuous ridges.

WOOD.—Heavy, very strong and hard, close-grained, very durable in contact with the soil, brown, with very thin, pale yellow sapwood.

DISTRIBUTION—Native to the Appalachian Mountains, but much planted in Michigan for ornamental and economic purposes.

HABITAT.—Prefers moist, rich soil, especially on rich bottom-lands and along streams.

NOTES.—Will grow on almost any kind of soil. Very rapid of growth in youth. Short-lived. Subject to the attacks of borers, which burrow in the sapwood and kill the tree or make it unfit for commercial use. Close observers believe that the attacks are abating, and if this is true, the tree should be planted more freely. The wood is very valuable for purposes where strength, freedom from checking and durability are requisite. Spreads by underground shoots. There are many horticultural varieties. See Clammy Locust, p. 277.

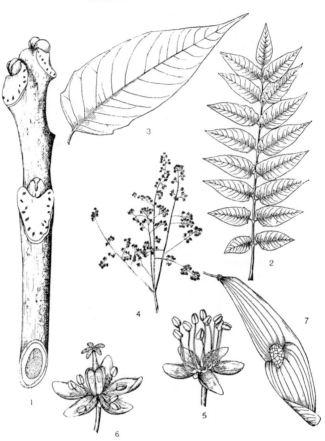

1. Winter twig, x I.
2. Leaf, x ⅛.
3. Leaflet, x ½.
4. Staminate inflorescence, x ¼.
5. Staminate flower, enlarged.
6. Pistillate flower, enlarged.
7. Fruit, x I.

SIMARUBACEAE

Ailanthus. Tree of Heaven

Ailanthus glandulosa Desf. [*Ailanthus altissima* Swingle]

HABIT.—A handsome, rapid-growing, short-lived tree, attaining a height of 40-60 feet and a trunk diameter of 2-4 feet, with a spreading, rather loose, open crown and a coarse, blunt spray.

LEAVES.—Alternate, pinnately compound, 1-3 feet long. Leaflets 11-41 in number, 2-6 inches long and about one-third as broad; ovate-lanceolate; entire with the exception of two or more coarse, glandular teeth at the base; glabrous, dark green above, paler beneath, turning a clear yellow in autumn or falling without change; ill-scented. Petioles smooth, terete, swollen at the base.

FLOWERS.—June, when the leaves are full grown; polygamo-dioecious; small, yellow-green, borne in upright panicles, 6-12 inches or more in length; calyx 5-lobed; petals 5, greenish, hairy; stamens 10. Staminate flowers ill-scented, pistillate almost free from odor.

FRUIT.—October; 1-celled, 1-seeded samaras, spirally twisted, reddish or yellow-green, borne in crowded clusters.

WINTER-BUDS.—Terminal bud absent; lateral buds about ⅛ inch long, subglobose, brownish, downy.

BARK.—Twigs yellowish to red-brown, velvety-downy; thin, grayish and shallowly fissured on old trunks.

WOOD.—Soft, weak, of coarse and open grain, pale yellow, satiny, with thick, lighter colored sapwood.

DISTRIBUTION.—A native of China, but naturalized in the United States and planted frequently in southern Michigan as a foliage tree.

HABITAT.—Tolerates almost any kind of soil, and will grow in dense shade.

NOTES.—Only the pistillate trees should be planted, as these are almost free from the objectionable odor of the staminate trees. The smoke and dust of our large cities have little effect on the foliage, and the tree is perfectly hardy in the southern part of the state. Difficult to eliminate when once established, owing to the habit of producing suckers from the roots.

THE MAPLES—ACER

The Maple family is a large one including a hundred or more species. They are widely distributed over the northern hemisphere, with only one extending south of the equator in Java. Of the thirteen Maples found in North America, Michigan is fortunate in the possession of seven which are native to the state. Several of our species form stately trees, while the others are small or shrub-like. The leaves of the Maples are arranged oppositely, and all are simple except the Boxelder, in which they are compound. The time at which the flowers come into bloom aids considerably in the identification of the different species, and the Maples as a group are distinguished easily from all other trees by their peculiar winged or "key" fruit, which is dispersed chiefly by the wind.

Several introduced Maples are planted so extensively that they would seem almost to be a part of our native flora. Among these are the Norway and Sycamore Maples. A few others, perhaps less well known, are described briefly below.

The Siberian Maple, *Acer ginnala* Maxim., is a dwarf, shrubby tree which is good for grouping or for planting singly on small lawns. It is perfectly hardy and attains a height of 15-20 feet. The 3-lobed leaves are 1-4 inches long and have the terminal lobe much elongated, the margin is doubly serrate to the petiole, and they are glabrous on both sides. In autumn they turn bright red before they fall. The yellow-white flowers are fragrant, followed by paniculate clusters of paired samaras, with their wings nearly parallel.

Another fairly hardy small tree or shrub is the Tatarian Maple, *Acer tataricum* L., native to Europe and Asia. Its leaves are 2-4 inches long, usually not lobed, heart-shaped at the base and acuminate at the apex, nearly glabrous at maturity, turning yellow in autumn. The greenish white flowers are borne in upright panicles in May, followed by the fruit, with nearly parallel wings, turning an attractive red in late summer.

The Japanese Maple, *Acer palmatum* Thunb., a tree or shrub about the size of the others, is somewhat less hardy than they are. In the type the leaves are 2-4 inches broad, deeply 5-9-lobed or-parted, the lobes narrow, acuminate at the apex, and doubly serrate on the margin. The flowers are small, purple, in erect corymbs. The paired samaras are less than an inch in length, with widely spreading wings. There are numerous varieties, exhibiting every possible gradation in shape, dissection and coloration of the leaves. The leaves of the green forms turn bright red in autumn. Introduced from Korea and Japan, and one of the most beautiful of our foreign trees.

The Small-leaved Maple, *Acer campestre* L., common in the fields of Europe, is sometimes planted for ornamental purposes. It is a shrub or small tree seldom more than 20 feet in height, with leaves 1-4 inches long, divided to about the middle into 3-5 obtuse lobes, glabrous above, often pubescent beneath. The fruit is pubescent, with the wings spreading horizontally.

SUMMER KEY TO THE SPECIES OF ACER

a. Leaves simple; twigs usually without whitish bloom.
  b. Leaf-sinuses acute at the base.
    c. Leaf-lobes long and narrow, the sides of the terminal lobe diverging; leaves silvery white beneath; twigs rank-smelling when broken .... *A. saccharinum,* p. 217
    cc. Leaf-lobes short and broad, the sides of the terminal lobe converging; leaves not conspicuously white beneath; twigs not rank-smelling when broken.
      d. Leaves 2-4 inches broad, thin, not pentagonally 5-lobed; wings of fruit ¾-1 inch long.
        e. Leaves distinctly white-downy beneath; twigs appressed-hairy, at least near the tip; fruit hanging in pendulous racemes, persistent on the tree until autumn; seed portion with pit-like depression on one side; usually a shrub or bushy tree .... *A. spicatum,* p. 211
        ee. Leaves not distinctly white-downy beneath; twigs glabrous; fruit hanging in fascicles, falling in early summer; seed portion without pit-like depression on one side; medium-sized tree .... *A. rubrum,* p. 219
      dd. Leaves 4-7 inches broad, thick, pentagonally 5-lobed; wings of fruit 1½ inches long ....
.........................*A. pseudo-platanus,* p. 223
  bb. Leaf-sinuses rounded at the base.
    c. Lower sides of leaves and petioles distinctly downy, the lobes undulate or entire; leaves very thick, drooping at the sides .... *A. saccharum nigrum,* p. 215
    cc. Lower sides of leaves and petioles essentially glabrous, the lobes serrate; leaves not thick, not drooping at the sides.
      d. Leaves coarsely and sparsely toothed or notched; bark not longitudinally white-striped; large trees.
        e. Twigs coarse; petioles exuding a milky juice when cut; wings of fruit diverging by nearly 180°; bark of the trunk closely fissured, not scaly ....
.... *A. platanoides,* p. 221
        ee. Twigs slender; petioles not exuding a milky juice when cut; wings of fruit only somewhat divergent; bark of the trunk deeply furrowed, often cleaving in long, thick plates .... *A. saccharum,* p. 213
      dd. Leaves finely and abundantly toothed; bark longitudinally white-striped; a bushy tree or shrub ....
.... *A. pennsylvanicum,* p. 209
aa. Leaves compound; twigs usually with whitish bloom ....
.... *A. negundo,* p. 225

— 206 —

WINTER KEY TO THE SPECIES OF ACER

a. Terminal buds usually under ¼ inch in length.

  b. Buds white-woolly; twigs usually with a whitish bloom; opposite leaf-scars meeting; fruit often persistent on the tree until spring .... *A. negundo,* p. 225

  bb. Buds not white-woolly; twigs without whitish bloom; opposite leaf-scars not meeting; fruit not persistent on the tree in winter.

    c. Buds reddish or greenish; twigs bright red.

      d. Twigs strictly glabrous; buds glabrous; spherical flower-buds clustered on the sides of the shoot; pith pink; large trees.

        e. Twigs rank-smelling when broken; tip of outer bud-scales often apiculate; tips of branches curving upwards; bark separating into long, thin flakes loose at the ends .... *A. saccharinum,* p. 217

        ee. Twigs not rank-smelling when broken; tip of outer bud-scales rounded; tips of branches not conspicuously curving upwards; bark rough-ridged, but seldom forming loose flakes .... *A. rubrum,* p. 219

      dd. Twigs appressed-hairy, at least near the tip; buds somewhat tomentose; spherical flower-buds absent; pith brown; shrub or bushy tree..........*A. spicatum,* p. 211

    cc. Buds brownish; twigs brownish or grayish.

      d. Buds glabrous, or somewhat pubescent at the apex only; bark dark gray on the trunk ...... *A. saccharum,* p. 213

      dd. Buds hoary-pubescent; bark sometimes almost black on the trunk .... *A. saccharum nigrum,* p. 215

aa. Terminal buds usually ¼-½ inch in length.

  b. Buds reddish; opposite leaf-scars meeting.

    c. Buds conspicuously stalked; bud-scales visible, 1 pair; bark longitudinally white-striped; small tree or large shrub....
.... *A. pennsylvanicum,* p. 209

    cc. Buds not conspicuously stalked; bud-scales visible, 2-3 pairs; bark not white-striped; large tree ....
.... *A. platanoides,* p. 221

  bb. Buds bright green; opposite leaf-scars not meeting ....
...............................*A. pseudo-platanus,* p. 223

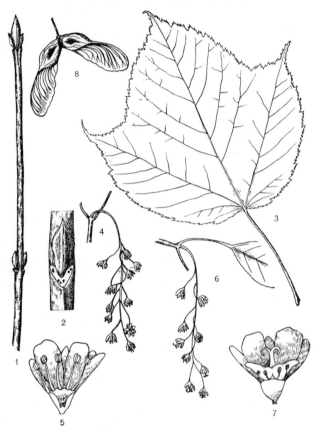

1. Winter twig, x 1.
2. Portion of twig, enlarged.
3. Leaf, x ½.
4. Staminate flowering branchlet, x ½.
5. Vertical section of staminate flower, enlarged.
6. Pistillate flowering branchlet, x ½.
7. Vertical section of pistillate flower, enlarged.
8. Fruit, x ¾.

ACERACEAE

Striped Maple. Moosewood. Whistlewood

Acer pennsylvanicum L.

HABIT.—A small tree at best, more often a large shrub, seldom attaining a height of more than 15-25 feet, with a short trunk 5-8 inches in diameter. The striped, upright branches form a rather compact crown.

LEAVES.—Opposite, simple, 5-6 inches long and nearly as broad; 3-lobed above the middle with short, tapering lobes; palmately 3-nerved; sharply doubly serrate; rounded or heart-shaped at the base; glabrous, yellow-green above, paler beneath, turning pale yellow in autumn; petioles stout, grooved.

FLOWERS.—May-June, when the leaves are nearly full grown; usually monoecious; large, bright yellow, bell-shaped, in slender, drooping racemes, 4-6 inches long; calyx 5-parted; petals 5; stamens 7-8; ovary downy.

FRUIT.—Ripens in autumn; glabrous, paired samaras in long, drooping, racemose clusters, the wings ¾ inch long, widely divergent and marked on one side of each nutlet by a small cavity.

WINTER-BUDS.—Bright red; terminal bud nearly ½ inch long, short-stalked, with bud-scales keeled; lateral buds smaller, appressed.

BARK.—Twigs light green, mottled with black, smooth; trunk and branches red-brown, marked longitudinally by broad, pale stripes.

WOOD.—Light, soft, close-grained, pinkish brown, with thick, lighter colored sapwood.

DISTRIBUTION.—Abundant in the Upper Peninsula, extending southward as far as Roscommon County in the Lower Peninsula.

HABITAT.—Cool, rocky or sandy woods, usually in the shade of other trees.

NOTES.—In the Northwoods the green shoots are browsed by deer and moose. Valued mostly for its aesthetic qualities. Of little or no economic value.

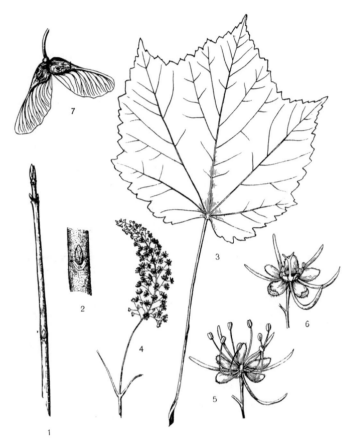

1. Winter twig, x 1.
2. Portion of twig, enlarged.
3. Leaf, x ½.
4. Flowering branchlet, x ½.
5. Staminate flower, enlarged.
6. Pistillate flower, enlarged.
7. Fruit, x 1.

ACERACEAE

Mountain Maple

Acer spicatum Lam.

HABIT.—A bushy tree sometimes 20-30 feet high, with a short trunk 4-8 inches in diameter; small, upright branches form a small, rounded crown. More often a straggling shrub.

LEAVES.—Opposite, simple, 4-5 inches long and two-thirds as broad; 3-lobed above the middle, the lobes coarsely crenate-serrate with pointed teeth, the sinuses usually wide-angled and acute at the base; thin; glabrous, dark green above, covered with a whitish down beneath, turning scarlet and orange in autumn; veining prominent; petioles long, slender, with enlarged base.

FLOWERS.—June, after the leaves are full grown; polygamo-monoecious; small, yellow-green, in erect, slightly compound, many-flowered, long-stemmed, terminal racemes; calyx downy, 5-lobed; petals 5; stamens 7-8; ovary tomentose.

FRUIT.—September; bright red, turning brown in late autumn; small, glabrous, paired samaras, in pendulous, racemose clusters.

WINTER-BUDS.—Small, flattish, acute, bright red, more or less tomentose; the terminal ⅛ inch long, containing the flowers.

BARK.—Twigs reddish, slightly hairy; very thin, red-brown, smooth or slightly furrowed on the trunk.

WOOD.—Light, soft, close-grained, light brown, with thick, lighter colored sapwood.

DISTRIBUTION.—Common in the Upper Peninsula; extends as far south as Saginaw Bay.

HABITAT.—Damp forests; rocky woods; along streams; always in the shade of other trees.

NOTES.—Forms much of the undergrowth of our northern forests. Little used, except for fire-wood. One of the most highly ornamental of the smaller Maples, and worthy of more general cultivation.

1. Winter twig, x 2.
2. Portion of twig, enlarged.
3. Leaf, x ½.
4. Staminate flowering branchlet, x ½.
5. Staminate flower, enlarged.
6. Pistillate flowering branchlet, x ½.
7. Pistillate flower, enlarged.
8. Fruit, x 1.

ACERACEAE

Sugar Maple. Hard Maple. Rock Maple

Acer saccharum Marsh. [*Acer saccharinum* Wang.]

HABIT.—A stately tree 60-100 feet in height, with a trunk diameter of 3-4 feet; in the open forming stout, upright branches near the ground, in forests making remarkably clean trunks to a good height; the crown is a broad, round-topped dome.

LEAVES.—Opposite, simple, 3-5 inches long and broad; usually 5-lobed (sometimes 3-lobed), the lobes sparingly wavy-toothed, the sinuses broad and rounded at the base; thin and firm; opaque, dark green above, lighter and glabrous beneath, turning yellow and red in autumn; petioles long, slender.

FLOWERS.—April-May, with the leaves; polygamo-monoecious or dioecious; on thread-like, hairy pedicels in nearly sessile corymbs; greenish yellow; calyx campanulate, 5-lobed; corolla o; stamens 7-8; ovary hairy.

FRUIT.—September-October, germinating the following spring; paired samaras, glabrous, with somewhat divergent wings about 1 inch long.

WINTER-BUDS.—Small, acute, red-brown, glabrous or somewhat pubescent toward the apex, the terminal hardly ¼ inch long, the lateral smaller, appressed.

BARK.—Twigs smooth, pale brown, becoming gray and smooth on the branches; old trunks dark gray, deeply furrowed, often cleaving at one edge in long, thick plates.

WOOD.—Heavy, hard, strong, close-grained, tough, durable, light brown, with thin, lighter colored sapwood. See p. 329.

DISTRIBUTION.—Found throughout the entire state.

HABITAT.—Prefers moist, rich soil in valleys and uplands and moist, rocky slopes.

NOTES.—The most important hardwood in Michigan. An excellent shade and ornamental tree along country roads and on private estates. Does not thrive in the poor soil and amid the dust and smoke of our large cities. Many trees are tapped in the spring to produce maple syrup and sugar for the market.

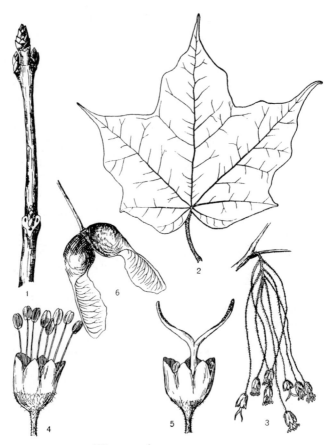

1. Winter twig, x 2.
2. Leaf, x ½.
3. Flowering branchlet, x ½.
4. Staminate flower, enlarged.
5. Pistillate flower, enlarged.
6. Fruit, x 1.

ACERACEAE

Black Maple. Black Sugar Maple

Acer saccharum nigrum (Michx. f.) Britt.
[*Acer nigrum* Michx.]

HABIT.—A stately tree, sometimes reaching a height of 80 feet, with a trunk diameter of 2-3 feet; branches stout, forming a broad, rounded, symmetrical crown.

LEAVES.—Opposite, simple, concave, 5-7 inches across, the breadth usually exceeding the length; usually 5-lobed at maturity, the two lower lobes being small, often reduced to a mere curve in the outline, the pointed lobes undulate or entire and narrowed from the broad, shallow sinuses; thick and firm; glabrous above, downy beneath; petioles stout, usually pendent, tomentose. The sides of the larger leaves often droop, giving to the tree an air of depression.

FLOWERS.—May, with the leaves; monoecious; in nearly sessile, umbel-like corymbs; about ¼ inch long, yellow, on slender, hairy pedicels, 2-3 inches long; calyx campanulate, pilose, 5-lobed; corolla o; stamens 7-8; ovary hairy.

FRUIT.—Ripens in autumn; glabrous, paired samaras, clustered on drooping pedicels; wings set wide apart, but only slightly diverging.

WINTER-BUDS.—Small, ovoid, acute, with dark red-brown, acute scales, hoary-pubescent on the outer surface.

BARK.—Twigs smooth, pale gray; becoming thick, deeply furrowed and sometimes almost black on the trunk.

WOOD.—Hard, heavy, strong, close-grained, creamy white, with thin, lighter colored sapwood.

DISTRIBUTION.—Lower Peninsula, south-eastern portion.

HABITAT.—Prefers low, moist, rich soil of river-bottoms, but does well on gravelly soils and uplands.

NOTES.—Very variable. A very good shade tree because of its dense foliage. It is claimed by some that the finest grades of maple syrup and sugar are made from the sap of this tree.

1. Winter twig, x 1.
2. Portion of twig, enlarged.
3. Leaf, x ½.
4. Staminate flowering branchlet, x 1.
5. Staminate flower, enlarged.
6. Pistillate flowering branchlet, x 1.
7. Pistillate flower, enlarged.
8. Fruit, x ½.

— 216 —

ACERACEAE
Silver Maple. Soft Maple
Acer saccharinum L. [*Acer dasycarpum* Ehrh.]

HABIT.—A beautiful tree, growing to a height of 60-80 feet, with a trunk diameter of 2-4 feet, usually separating near the ground into 3-4 upright stems which are destitute of branches for a considerable distance. Usually the long, slender branches bend downwards, but with their tips ascending in a graceful curve. Crown broad, especially in its upper portion.

LEAVES.—Opposite, simple, 3-6 inches long and nearly as broad; usually 5-lobed by narrow, acute sinuses which extend nearly to the midrib, the lobes often sublobed, sharply toothed; light green above, silvery white beneath, turning pale yellow in autumn; petioles long, slender, drooping.

FLOWERS.—March-April, before the leaves; polygamo-monoecious or dioecious; small, yellow-green, in crowded, sessile umbels; calyx 5-lobed (sometimes each lobe again divided); corolla o; stamens 3-7; ovary hairy.

FRUIT.—May, germinating as soon as it reaches the ground; paired samaras, large, glabrous, curving inwards, one samara often aborted.

WINTER-BUDS.—Dark red, blunt; the terminal about ¼ inch long, with bud-scales often apiculate at the apex; flower-buds clustered on side spurs.

BARK.—Twigs smooth, red-gray, lustrous; young trunks gray, smooth; old trunks dark gray, more or less furrowed, separating into thin, loose scales.

WOOD.—Hard, strong, close-grained, rather brittle, perishable, pale brown, with thick, lighter colored sapwood.

DISTRIBUTION.—Lower Peninsula south of Saginaw Bay.

HABITAT.—Prefers low, rich bottom-lands subject to occasional inundation, but not in swamps.

NOTES.—Rapid of growth, adapting itself to a variety of soils. Does not do well on dry, elevated ground. One of the first trees to blossom in early spring. Once popular as a shade tree on our city streets, but its use for this purpose is to be discouraged. Frequently the weak, brittle branches are broken off during storms, while the roots may enter sewers and drain-pipes, clogging them.

Wier's Maple, also known as the Cut-leaved Maple or Wier's Cut-leaved Maple, *Acer saccharinum*, v. *Wieri* Schwerin (v. *Wieri* Pax), is planted frequently. Its leaves are variable, but they are generally deeply cleft, with the lobes much dissected; and the pendulous branches give to the tree a weeping habit.

—217—

Red Maple. Soft Maple

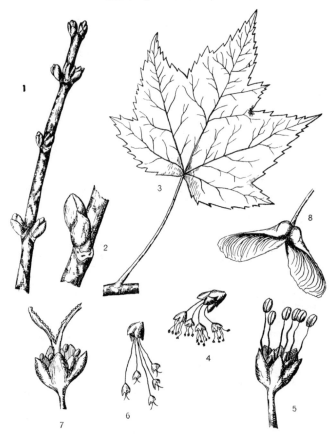

1. Winter twig, x 1.
2. Portion of twig, enlarged.
3. Leaf, x 1.
4. Fascicle of staminate flowers, x 1.
5. Staminate flower, enlarged.
6. Fascicle of pistillate flowers, x 1.
7. Pistillate flower, enlarged.
8. Fruit, x ¾.

— 218 —

ACERACEAE

Red Maple. Soft Maple

Acer rubrum L.

HABIT.—A medium-sized tree 40-50 feet high, occasionally in swamps 60-75 feet; trunk 1-3 feet in diameter; upright branches form a low, rather narrow, rounded crown.

LEAVES.—Opposite, simple, 3-4 inches long and nearly as broad; 3-5-lobed by broad, acute sinuses, the lobes irregularly doubly serrate or toothed; glabrous, green above, whitish and generally glabrous beneath, turning bright scarlet in autumn; petioles long, slender.

FLOWERS.—March-April, before the leaves; polygamo-monoecious or dioecious; in few-flowered fascicles on shoots of the previous year, the pistillate red, the staminate orange; sepals 4-5; petals 4-5; stamens 5-8; ovary smooth.

FRUIT.—May-June, germinating immediately after reaching the ground; samaras small, on drooping pedicels, 2-4 inches long; wings about 1 inch long, diverging at about a right angle.

WINTER-BUDS.—Dark red, blunt; terminal bud about ⅛ inch long, with bud-scales rounded at the apex; flower-buds clustered on side spurs.

BARK.—Twigs bright red, lustrous, becoming smooth and light gray on the branches; old trunks dark gray, ridged, separating into plate-like scales.

WOOD.—Heavy, close-grained, not strong, light brown, with thick, lighter colored sapwood.

DISTRIBUTION.—Throughout the entire state.

HABITAT.—Prefers swamp-lands or banks of streams; rarely found on hillsides.

NOTES.—A valuable shade and ornamental tree for roadside and park planting, but is not sufficiently hardy for city streets, except under favorable conditions. Will tolerate shade. Sugar has been made in small quantities from the sap.

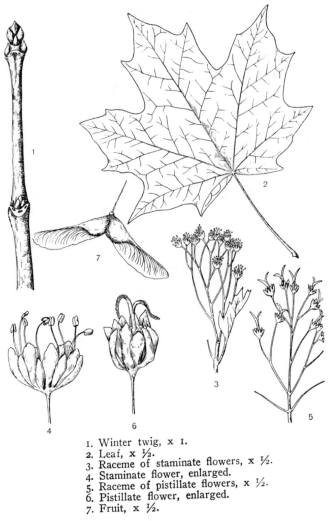

1. Winter twig, x 1.
2. Leaf, x ½.
3. Raceme of staminate flowers, x ½.
4. Staminate flower, enlarged.
5. Raceme of pistillate flowers, x ½.
6. Pistillate flower, enlarged.
7. Fruit, x ½.

ACERACEAE
Norway Maple
Acer platanoides L.

HABIT.—A tall, handsome tree, with a height of 40-60 feet and a trunk diameter of 1-2 feet, having a round, spreading crown of stout branches, resembling *Acer saccharum*. Twigs coarse.

LEAVES.—Opposite, simple, 5-7 inches broad and almost as long; thin; 5-7-lobed at maturity, the lobes remotely coarse-toothed with the teeth drawn out into filamentous points, separated by rounded, scallop-like sinuses; glabrous, bright green both sides, turning pale yellow in autumn; petioles long, slender, exuding a milky juice when cut.

FLOWERS.—May-June, before or with the leaves; dioecious; large, yellow-green, in erect, short, flat racemes; sepals 5; petals 5; stamens 8.

FRUIT.—Ripens in autumn and germinates the following spring; pendent on long stalks; large, glabrous, paired samaras, with wings 2 inches long diverging by nearly 180°.

WINTER-BUDS.—Yellow-green, red or dull red-brown; terminal bud about ¼ inch long, broad, short-stalked, with bud-scales strongly keeled; lateral buds small, appressed; buds exuding a milky juice when cut.

BARK.—Twigs lustrous, light brown to greenish; trunk dark gray, becoming closely fissured, not scaly.

WOOD.—Moderately heavy, hard, close-grained, whitish or brownish, with white sapwood.

DISTRIBUTION.—Introduced from Europe and western Asia; extensively planted in cities for its abundant shade.

HABITAT.—Prefers rich, well-drained soil, but adapts itself to almost any soil and situation.

NOTES.—Rapid of growth and generally long-lived. The best of all Maples for street planting. The roots strike deep and spread laterally, enabling the tree to hold its own in a city environment. It retains its leaves two weeks longer in autumn than do our native Maples. Quite free from insect pests and fungous diseases.

A variety, *Schwedleri* K. Koch, sometimes called the Red-leaved Maple, is much like the parent, except that the new leaves are bright, purplish red, changing later to dull green. Effective for color contrast, if not overplanted.

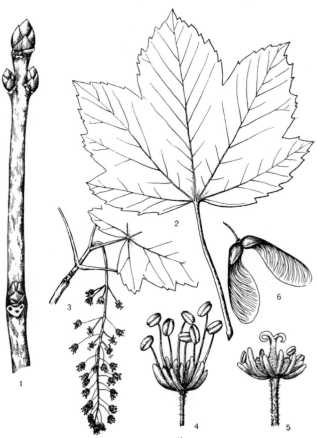

1. Winter twig, x 1.
2. Leaf, x ½.
3. Flowering branchlet, x ½.
4. Staminate flower, enlarged.
5. Perfect flower, enlarged.
6. Fruit, x ½.

ACERACEAE

Sycamore Maple

Acer pseudo-platanus L.

HABIT.—A thrifty tree 50-60 feet high, with a trunk diameter of 2-3 feet; the crown roundish, spreading.

LEAVES.—Opposite, simple, 4-7 inches across, and as long as broad; thick; pentagonally 5-lobed, the lobes more or less ovate, separated by very narrow, acute sinuses extending about half-way to the midrib, the lobes coarsely and irregularly blunt-serrate, crenate-serrate, or slightly lobed; upper surface dark green and shining, somewhat wrinkled, but paler, dull green and glaucous beneath; petioles long, stout.

FLOWERS.—April, before the leaves; polygamo-monoecious; large, greenish yellow, in pendent racemes of umbellate cymes of about three each; sepals 5; petals 5; stamens 8, hairy; ovary hairy.

FRUIT.—Ripens in autumn and germinates the following spring; pendent on long stalks; large, glabrous, paired samaras, with wings 1½ inches long diverging at about a right angle.

WINTER-BUDS.—Bright green; terminal bud ¼-½ inch long, ovoid to subglobose, blunt, with bud-scales more or less keeled; lateral buds small, divergent.

BARK.—Twigs lustrous, brown or gray, becoming slate colored on the branches; trunk gray or brownish, smooth or flaking off in short scales.

WOOD.—Moderately heavy, hard, compact, brownish, with white sapwood.

DISTRIBUTION.—Introduced from Europe and western Asia; frequently planted in our cities, where it is inferior to the Norway Maple.

HABITAT.—Rather intolerant of poor soils, and apparently not well adapted to our climate.

NOTES.—Thrifty, but short-lived. The crown is rather too broad for planting anywhere except on our widest streets, and such use is objectionable except under special conditions. The leaves remain two weeks longer in autumn than do those of our native Maples.

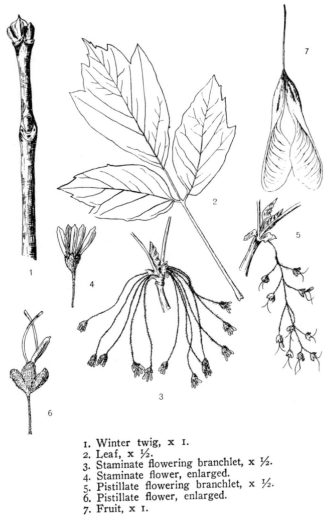

1. Winter twig, x 1.
2. Leaf, x ½.
3. Staminate flowering branchlet, x ½.
4. Staminate flower, enlarged.
5. Pistillate flowering branchlet, x ½.
6. Pistillate flower, enlarged.
7. Fruit, x 1.

ACERACEAE

Boxelder. Ash-leaved Maple

Acer negundo L. [*Negundo aceroides* Moench.]

HABIT.—A sturdy little tree 30-50 feet high, with a trunk diameter of 1-2 feet. Trunk often divides near the ground into several stout, wide-spreading branches, forming a broad, unsymmetrical, open crown.

LEAVES.—Opposite, pinnately compound. Leaflets 3-5 (rarely 7-9) in number, 2-4 inches long, 1½-2½ inches broad; ovate or oval; nearly entire, irregularly and remotely coarse-toothed above the middle, or sometimes 3-lobed (often giving the leaflet a jagged outline); apex acute, base variable; glabrous or somewhat pubescent at maturity, with prominent veins. Petioles slender, 2-3 inches long, the enlarged base leaving prominent crescent-shaped scars partly surrounding the winter-buds.

FLOWERS.—April-May, before or with the leaves; dioecious; small, yellow-green; the staminate in clusters on long, thread-like, hairy pedicels; the pistillate in narrow, drooping racemes; calyx hairy, 5-lobed; corolla o; stamens 4-6; ovary pubescent.

FRUIT.—Early summer, but hanging until late autumn or early spring; narrow, flat, winged samaras, in pairs, clustered in drooping, racemose clusters.

WINTER-BUDS.—Terminal bud ⅛-¼ inch long, acute, inclosed in two dull red scales, often hoary or minutely pubescent; lateral buds obtuse, appressed.

BARK.—Twigs greenish to purple, glaucous; trunk pale gray or light brown, deeply cleft into broad ridges.

WOOD.—Light, soft, close-grained, weak, creamy white, with thick, hardly distinguishable sapwood.

DISTRIBUTION.—Lower Peninsula as far north as Saginaw Bay.

HABITAT.—Banks of streams and borders of swamps. Prefers deep, moist soil.

NOTES.—Accommodates itself to almost any situation. Easily transplanted. Rapid of growth, drought resisting, but short-lived. Much planted for shade and ornament, but it is not a desirable tree for these purposes. Runs into varieties with curled leaflets, leaves spotted or with yellow margins, leaves with broad white margins, and branches purplish with glaucous bloom.

THE BUCKEYES AND HORSE-CHESTNUT— AESCULUS

The members of the genus *Aesculus* are found on every continent in the northern hemisphere, but nowhere are they abundant. Some twenty-five species are known. None are native to Michigan, but the common Horse-chestnut of the Balkans is very widely cultivated, and occasionally the Ohio Buckeye is planted.

The Buckeyes and Horse-chestnut have many distinctive characteristics, but the one which is outstanding is the fruit. It consists of a large brown nut, one or more of which are inclosed in a leathery capsule. No other group of trees produces a fruit like this. Most boys of school age are quite familiar with the nuts, and many a sling has been fashioned from one or more of them and a piece of string, later to "adorn" the branches of another tree or near-by telephone wires. The Buckeyes of the south and west are occasionally planted for their showy flowers and handsome foliage.

The Sweet Buckeye, *Aesculus octandra* Marsh. (*Aesculus flava* Ait.), characteristically has 5 leaflets and yellow flowers; the buds are ovoid, not gummy, dull and dusty in appearance; the fruit is not prickly; and the bark is smooth and firm.

The Red Horse-chestnut, *Aesculus carnea* Hayne (*Aesculus rubicunda* Loisel.), is probably a hybrid between the common Horse-chestnut and the Red Buckeye of the south. The leaflets are usually 5, and the flowers are some shade of red. The fruit has small prickles, and the winter-buds are resinous-sticky.

The Dwarf, Shrubby or Bottlebrush Buckeye, *Aesculus parviflora* Walt., is a spreading shrub which may attain a height of 12 feet. While it is a native of the south, it is quite hardy in the north, where it is especially valuable for lawn clumps. The leaflets vary from 5 to 7, and they are oblong-ovate, finely crenate-serrate, glabrous above and grayish-pubescent beneath. The white flowers are borne in long, cylindrical panicles, and they have a slight fragrance. The period of blooming is prolonged, since the flowers do not all expand at the same time. The buds are not gummy.

SUMMER KEY TO THE SPECIES OF AESCULUS

a. Leaflets usually 5; foliage ill-smelling when bruised; bark broken into thick plates; prickly bur about 1 inch in diameter .... *A. glabra,* p. 231

aa. Leaflets usually 7; foliage not ill-smelling when bruised; bark broken into thin plates; prickly bur about 2 inches in diameter .... *A. hippocastanum,* p. 229

WINTER KEY TO THE SPECIES OF AESCULUS

a. Terminal bud about ⅔ inch long; bud-scales covered with a glaucous bloom, not conspicuously resinous; bark broken into thick plates; prickly bur about 1 inch in diameter .... *A. glabra,* p. 231

aa. Terminal bud 1-1½ inches long; bud-scales conspicuously sticky-resinous, glistening; bark broken into thin plates; prickly bur about 2 inches in diameter ...... *A. hippocastanum,* p. 229

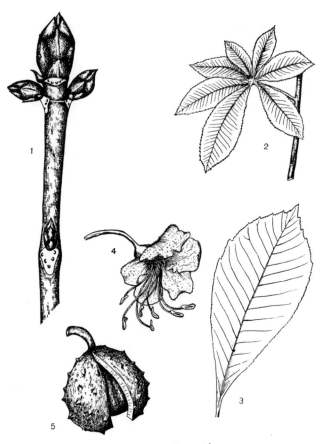

1. Winter twig, x ¾.
2. Leaf, x ⅙.
3. Leaflet, x ½.
4. Flower, x 1.
5. Fruit, x ½.

SAPINDACEAE
Horse-chestnut
Aesculus hippocastanum L.

HABIT.—A handsome tree, with a height of 40-60 feet and a trunk diameter of 1-2 feet, forming a broad, conical crown. The regularly occurring branches ascend from the trunk at first, gradually bend downwards as they lengthen, and end in a coarse, upturning spray.

LEAVES.—Opposite, digitately compound. Leaflets usually 7, rarely 5, 5-7 inches long, 1½-2½ inches broad; obovate, wedge-shaped at the base; irregularly and bluntly serrate; thick; rough, dark green above, paler beneath, turning a rusty yellow in autumn. Petioles long, grooved, swollen at the base.

FLOWERS.—June-July, after the leaves; polygamo-monoecious; large, whitish, in showy, upright, terminal thyrses, 8-12 inches long; pedicels jointed, 4-6-flowered; calyx campanulate, 5-lobed; petals 5, white, spotted with yellow and red, clawed; stamens 7, thread-like, longer than the petals.

FRUIT.—October; a leathery, globular capsule about 2 inches in diameter, roughened with short spines; containing 1-3 large, smooth, lustrous, brown nuts, marked by large, pale scars; not edible.

WINTER-BUDS.—Terminal buds 1-1½ inches long, acute, brownish, covered with glistening, resinous gum; inner scales yellowish, becoming 1½-2 inches long in spring, remaining until the leaves are nearly half grown.

BARK.—Twigs smooth, red-brown; trunk dark brown and broken into thin plates by shallow fissures; rich in tannin, bitter.

WOOD.—Light, soft, close-grained, weak, whitish, with thin, light brown sapwood.

DISTRIBUTION.—Introduced from Greece; extensively cultivated throughout Europe and America, where it is a favorite shade tree.

HABITAT.—Prefers rich, moist soils.

NOTES.—Frequently subject to insect attacks and fungous disease, which weaken the tree seriously and make it somewhat undesirable for general planting. Not suitable for street planting. There are a number of horticultural varieties, including forms with variously cut and lobed leaflets, variegated leaflets and double flowers.

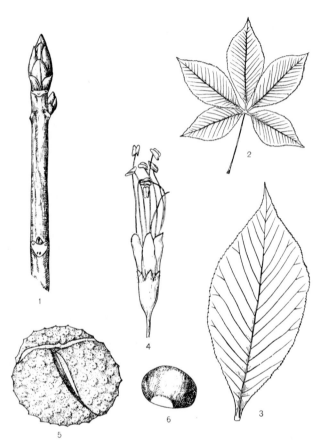

1. Winter twig, x 1.
2. Leaf, x ⅙.
3. Leaflet, x ½.
4. Flower, x 2.
5. Fruit, x ½.
6. Nut, x ½.

SAPINDACEAE

Ohio Buckeye

Aesculus glabra Willd.

HABIT.—A medium-sized tree 30-50 feet in height, with a trunk not over 2 feet in diameter; usually much smaller; slender, spreading branches, forming a broad, rounded crown; twigs coarse.

LEAVES.—Opposite, digitately compound. Leaflets usually 5, rarely 7, 3-6 inches long, 1½-2½ inches broad; ovate or oval, gradually narrowed to the entire base; irregularly and finely serrate; glabrous, yellow-green above, paler beneath, turning yellow in autumn. Petioles 4-6 inches long, slender, enlarged at the base. Foliage ill-smelling when bruised.

FLOWERS.—April-May, after the leaves; polygamo-monoecious; small, yellow-green, in terminal panicles, 5-6 inches long and 2-3 inches broad, more or less downy; pedicels 4-6-flowered; calyx campanulate, 5-lobed; petals 4, pale yellow, hairy, clawed; stamens 7, with long, hairy filaments.

FRUIT.—October; a thick, leathery, prickly capsule about 1 inch in diameter, containing a single large, smooth, lustrous, brown nut, marked by a large pale scar; not edible.

WINTER-BUDS.—Terminal buds ⅔ inch long, acute, resinous, brownish; inner scales yellow-green, becoming 1½-2 inches long in spring and remaining until the leaves are nearly half grown.

BARK.—Twigs smooth, red-brown, becoming ashy gray; old trunks densely furrowed and broken into thick plates; ill-smelling when bruised.

WOOD.—Light, soft, close-grained, weak, whitish, with thin, light brown sapwood.

DISTRIBUTION.—Pennsylvania to Alabama, and westward to Nebraska and Kansas.

HABITAT.—Prefers river-bottoms and the rich, moist soil of river-banks, but will grow in drier situations.

NOTES.—Native trees are becoming quite rare. It is said that many have been cut down, because of the ill-scented bark and foliage. Occasionally planted in southern Michigan for ornamental purposes, but is less popular than the common Horse-chestnut.

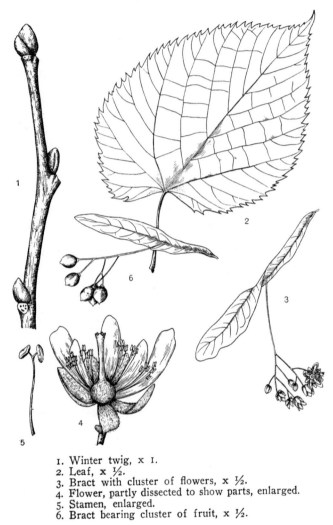

1. Winter twig, x 1.
2. Leaf, x ½.
3. Bract with cluster of flowers, x ½.
4. Flower, partly dissected to show parts, enlarged.
5. Stamen, enlarged.
6. Bract bearing cluster of fruit, x ½.

TILIACEAE

Basswood. Linden

Tilia americana L. [*Tilia glabra* Vent.]

HABIT.—A tree usually 60-70 feet high, with a tall, straight trunk 1-3 feet in diameter; numerous slender branches form a dense, ovoid or rounded crown.

LEAVES.—Alternate, simple, 5-6 inches long, 3-4 inches broad; obliquely heart-shaped; coarsely serrate; thick and firm; glabrous, dull dark green above, paler beneath; petioles slender, 1-2 inches long.

FLOWERS.—June-July, after the leaves; perfect, regular; yellowish white, downy, fragrant; borne on slender pedicels in loose, drooping cymes, the peduncle attached for half its length to a narrow, oblong, yellowish bract; sepals 5, downy; petals 5, creamy white; stamens numerous, in 5 clusters; ovary 5-celled; stigma 5-lobed.

FRUIT.—October; globose, nut-like, woody, gray, tomentose, about the size of a pea; attached to the leafy bract; usually remaining on the tree far into the winter.

WINTER-BUDS.—Terminal bud absent; lateral buds ovoid, acute, often lopsided, smooth, dark red, ¼ inch long.

BARK.—Twigs smooth, reddish gray, becoming dark gray or brown; dark gray and smooth on young stems, on old trunks thick, deeply furrowed into broad, scaly ridges.

WOOD.—Light, soft, close-grained, tough, light red-brown, with thick sapwood of nearly the same color. See p. 331.

DISTRIBUTION.—Common in most parts of the Lower Peninsula, frequent in the Upper Peninsula.

HABITAT.—Prefers rich, well-drained, loamy soils.

NOTES.—Rapid of growth. Easily transplanted. An important timber tree; also used for street and ornamental planting, but is less desirable for these purposes than the European species. For brief descriptions of the latter, see the chapter, Additional Notes On The Species, p. 267.

THE DOGWOODS—CORNUS

The Dogwoods are small trees at best, and most of them are shrubs. Some fifteen or more species occur in North America, of which two, native to Michigan, are described. One of these has its leaves arranged alternately; the other, in common with most of the members of the genus, has its leaves arranged oppositely. They are simple, with entire margins, and the lateral veins are parallel, extending along the margin well toward the apex of the leaves. The Flowering Dogwood is a conspicuous object in May or early June, when the blooms are put forth. The flowers themselves are small, in dense clusters, surrounded by four large, petal-like bracts, which commonly are mistaken for the corolla. A close inspection of the inflorescence, however, will disclose the error. The fruit is a small drupe, with thin flesh inclosing a bony stone. If chewed, it will be found that the Dogwoods have a bitter, astringent bark. While the wood is not obtainable in large sizes, it has some uses, such as for tool-handles, bobbins, engravers' blocks and for turnery. From early times the Dogwoods have been planted around dwellings and in parks and places of recreation, and for such situations they are holding their own in popularity.

A foreign Dogwood, which is a large shrub or small tree 15-20 feet in height, is frequently planted in America, where it is quite hardy. It comes from Europe and the Orient, and is generally known as the Cornelian Cherry, *Cornus mas* L. (*Cornus mascula* Hort.). Not least of its attractive features are the yellowish flowers, which appear in early spring before the leaves unfold. Individually these are small, but the umbel-like clusters are borne in great profusion, clothing the plant with yellow. The leaves are 1½-3½ inches long, with 3-4 pairs of veins, and are more or less appressed-pubescent on both sides. The fruit is an oblong, scarlet drupe, about ½ inch long, ripe in autumn, sweet and edible. The twigs are appressed-hairy, greenish yellow, later turning brown. The lateral buds are very divergent, and the branchlets into which they develop are often short and nearly at right angles to the branch.

SUMMER KEY TO THE SPECIES OF CORNUS

a. Leaves mostly alternate; branches usually greenish; flowers not surrounded by large petal-like bracts; fruit globular, blue, borne many in loose clusters.....*C. alternifolia,* p. 239

aa. Leaves opposite; branches usually reddish or yellowish; flowers surrounded by large petal-like bracts; fruit ovoid, scarlet, borne in close clusters of 3-4.........*C. florida,* p. 237

WINTER KEY TO THE SPECIES OF CORNUS

a. Leaf-scars mostly alternate; buds light brown; branches usually greenish ....*C. alternifolia,* p. 239

aa. Leaf-scars opposite; buds greenish; branches usually reddish or yellowish ....*C. florida,* p. 237

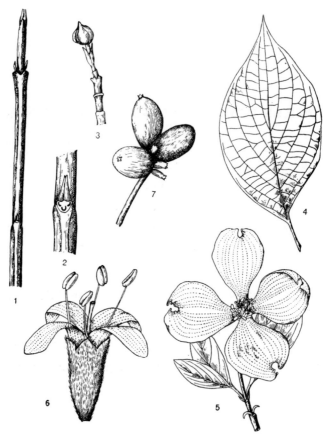

1. Winter twig, with leaf buds, x 1.
2. Portion of twig, enlarged.
3. Winter twig, with flower bud, x 1.
4. Leaf, x ½.
5. Flowering branchlet, x ½.
6. Flower, enlarged.
7. Fruit, x 1.

CORNACEAE

Flowering Dogwood. Dogwood. Boxwood

Cornus florida L.

HABIT.—A bushy tree with a height of 15-30 feet and a short trunk 6-12 inches in diameter; slender, spreading branches form a flat-topped crown.

LEAVES.—Opposite, closely clustered at the ends of the branches, simple, 3-5 inches long, 2-3 inches broad; ovate to elliptical; entire or obscurely wavy-toothed; thick and firm; bright green, covered with minute, appressed hairs above, pale and more or less pubescent beneath, turning bright scarlet in autumn; petioles short, grooved.

FLOWERS.—May or early June, with the leaves; perfect; greenish; in dense clusters surrounded by 4 large, white or pinkish, petal-like bracts (often mistaken for the corolla), borne on short, stout peduncles; calyx 4-lobed, light green; petals 4, yellow-green; stamens 4, alternate with the petals; ovary 2-celled.

FRUIT.—October; an ovoid, scarlet drupe, borne in close clusters of 3-4; flesh bitter.

WINTER-BUDS.—Leaf-buds narrow-conical, acute, greenish; flower-buds spherical or vertically flattened, grayish.

BARK.—Twigs pale green, becoming red or yellow-green their first winter, later becoming light brown or red-gray; red-brown or blackish on the trunk, often separating into quadrangular, plate-like scales.

WOOD.—Heavy, hard, strong, tough, close-grained, brownish, with thick, lighter colored sapwood.

DISTRIBUTION.—Southern Michigan as far north as the Grand-Saginaw Valley.

HABITAT.—Prefers rich, well-drained soil, usually under the shade of other trees.

NOTES.—A valuable species for ornamental purposes. Rather slow of growth. A form with bright red floral bracts, v. *rubra* West., is extensively cultivated.

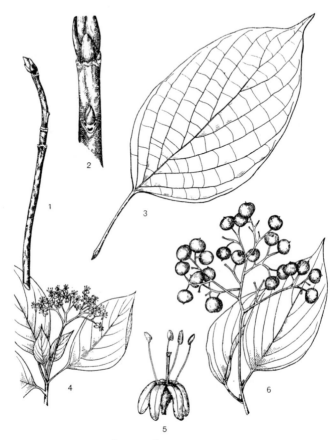

1. Winter twig, x 1.
2. Portion of twig, enlarged.
3. Leaf, x ¾.
4. Flowering branchlet, x ½.
5. Flower, enlarged.
6. Fruiting branchlet, x ½.

CORNACEAE

Blue Dogwood. Alternate-leaved Dogwood

Cornus alternifolia L. f.

HABIT.—A small tree or large shrub reaching a height of 25-30 feet and a trunk diameter of 6-8 inches; more often smaller than this. The long, slender branches are arranged in irregular whorls, forming flat, horizontal tiers, giving the tree a storied effect.

LEAVES.—Mostly alternate and clustered at the ends of the branchlets; simple, 3-5 inches long, 2½-3 inches broad; oval or ovate, long-pointed, wedge-shaped at the base; entire or obscurely wavy-toothed; thin; dark green, nearly glabrous above, paler and covered with appressed hairs beneath, turning yellow and scarlet in autumn; petioles slender, grooved, hairy, with clasping bases.

FLOWERS.—May-June, after the leaves; perfect; borne on slender pedicels in many-flowered, irregular, open cymes from the season's shoots; calyx cup-shaped, obscurely 4-toothed, covered with fine, silky, white hairs; petals 4, cream colored; stamens 4; ovary 2-celled.

FRUIT.—October; a globular, blue-black drupe, borne in loose, red-stemmed clusters; flesh bitter.

WINTER-BUDS.—Leaf-buds small, acute, light brown; flower-buds spherical or vertically flattened.

BARK.—Twigs greenish or reddish, becoming smooth, dark green; thin, dark red-brown and shallowly fissured on the trunk.

WOOD.—Heavy, hard, close-grained, red-brown, with thick, lighter colored sapwood.

DISTRIBUTION.—Scattered throughout both peninsulas.

HABITAT.—Prefers moist, well-drained soil on the borders of streams and swamps, often in the shade of other trees.

NOTES.—Hardy throughout the state. Easily transplanted. The only *Cornus* with alternate leaves and branches.

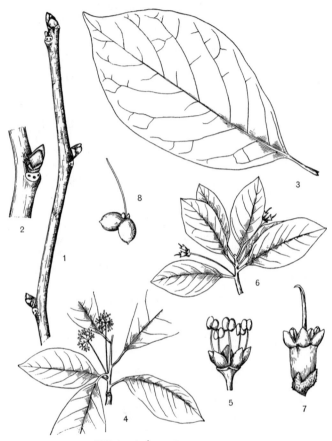

1. Winter twig, x 1.
2. Portion of twig, enlarged.
3. Leaf, x ¾.
4. Staminate flowering branchlet, x ½.
5. Staminate flower, enlarged.
6. Pistillate flowering branchlet, x ½.
7. Pistillate flower, enlarged.
8. Fruit, x ½.

CORNACEAE

Black Gum. Pepperidge

Nyssa sylvatica Marsh. [*Nyssa multiflora* Wang.]

HABIT.—A medium-sized tree 40-60 feet high, with a trunk diameter of 1-2 feet, forming a rounded to cylindrical crown of slender, spreading, pendulous branches and a stiff, flat spray.

LEAVES.—Alternate, simple, 2-5 inches long, one-half as broad; oblong-obovate to oval; entire, or sometimes wavy-margined; thick and firm; very lustrous and dark green above, pale and often hairy beneath, turning bright scarlet in autumn on the upper surface only; petioles short.

FLOWERS.—May-June, with the leaves; polygamo-dioecious; greenish; borne on slender, downy peduncles; the staminate slender-pedicelled, in many-flowered heads; the pistillate sessile, in several-flowered clusters; calyx cup-shaped, 5-toothed; petals 5; stamens 5-10; stigma stout, terete, recurved.

FRUIT.—October; fleshy drupes, ovoid, blue-black, about ½ inch long, sour, in clusters of 1-3.

WINTER-BUDS.—⅛-¼ inch long, ovoid, obtuse, dark red.

BARK.—Twigs greenish or light brown, smooth or often downy, becoming smooth, dark red-brown; thick, red-brown on old trunks, deeply furrowed.

WOOD.—Heavy, soft, strong, very tough, difficult to split, not durable in contact with the soil, pale yellow, with thick, whitish sapwood.

DISTRIBUTION.—Frequent in the southern half of the Lower Peninsula. Has been reported as far north as Manistee.

HABITAT.—Prefers the borders of swamps and low, wet lands. Rarely flourishes in exposed situations.

NOTES.—Of great ornamental value. In winter habit the tree is most picturesque. Not easily transplanted. Pith of twigs with thin, transverse partitions.

THE ASHES—FRAXINUS

The Olive family takes its name from the Olive tree of Asia. The only representatives among our native trees are the Ashes; but several of the commonly planted ornamental shrubs, the Lilacs, Privets and the beautiful Forsythia, belong to this family. The genus *Fraxinus* includes about forty species distributed throughout the northern hemisphere and also in Cuba and Java. Sixteen species occur in North America, five of which, including one variety, are native to the state of Michigan. Of these, the White Ash is the most beautiful and it yields by far the most useful wood.

Possessing oppositely arranged, compound leaves, the Ashes are not likely to be confused with many other trees. Within the genus, it may be more difficult to distinguish the several kinds, although each is rather well marked in its characteristics. The individual flowers of the Ashes are small; but coming as they do before the leaves and appearing in crowded clusters, they are quite conspicuous. In all but one species the flowers are of two kinds, the pollen-producing and the pistil-bearing being on separate trees. The Ashes, like the Maples, have prominently winged fruits, but those of the Ash hang singly, whereas the Maple "keys" are always in pairs. Both wind and water are agencies in their distribution.

The European Ash, *Fraxinus excelsior* L., has been planted to some extent in parks and on private estates. In many of its characteristics it resembles our native White Ash. Since it possesses no merits of superiority over our native tree, its planting has not been extensive and is not to be recommended except for scientific purposes.

SUMMER KEY TO THE SPECIES OF FRAXINUS

a. Lateral leaflets sessile......................*F. nigra*, p. 253
aa. Lateral leaflets petioluled.
  b. Twigs, petioles and lower sides of leaves pubescent........
    ....*F. pennsylvanica*, p. 247
  bb. Twigs, petioles and lower sides of leaves essentially glabrous.
    c. Twigs prominently 4-angled......*F. quadrangulata*, p. 251
    cc. Twigs terete.
      d. Lower sides of leaves essentially of the same color as
        the upper; leaflet-margins rather finely sharp-serrate...
        ....*F. pennsylvanica lanceolata*, p. 249
      dd. Lower sides of leaves paler than the upper; leaflet-
        margins entire or obscurely serrate...................
        ....*F. americana*, p. 245

WINTER KEY TO THE SPECIES OF FRAXINUS

a. Twigs prominently 4-angled; fruit falling in early autumn...
  ....*F. quadrangulata*, p. 251
aa. Twigs terete; fruit often persistent on the tree until midwinter or the following spring.
  b. Buds rusty-tomentose; twigs more or less downy.........
    ....*F. pennsylvanica*, p. 247
  bb. Buds not tomentose; twigs not downy.
    c. Terminal bud black or nearly so, showing 3 pairs of
      scales in cross-section; bud-scales apiculate at the apex;
      samaras with broad wings, the seed portion flattish; bark
      flaky, rubbing off on the hand...........*F. nigra*, p. 253
    cc. Terminal bud brownish, showing 4 pairs of scales in
      cross-section; bud-scales rounded at the apex; samaras
      with narrow wings, the seed portion terete; bark ridged,
      not flaky nor rubbing off on the hand.
      d. Upper margin of leaf-scars deeply concave...........
        ....*F. americana*, p. 245
      dd. Upper margin of leaf-scars not concave, but straight
        across or projecting upward..........................
        ....*F. pennsylvanica lanceolata*, p. 249

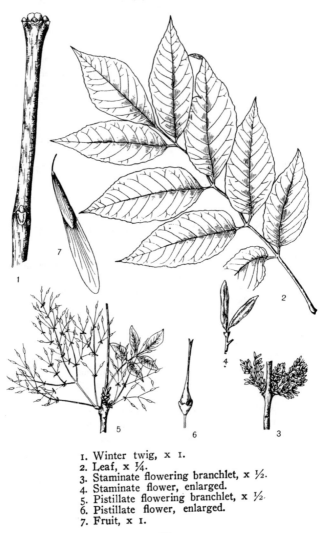

1. Winter twig, x 1.
2. Leaf, x ¼.
3. Staminate flowering branchlet, x ½.
4. Staminate flower, enlarged.
5. Pistillate flowering branchlet, x ½.
6. Pistillate flower, enlarged.
7. Fruit, x 1.

OLEACEAE

White Ash

Fraxinus americana L.

HABIT.—A large tree 50-75 feet high, with a trunk diameter of 2-3 feet; forming an open, pyramidal crown of long, slender, lateral branches and a stout, rather sparse spray.

LEAVES.—Opposite, pinnately compound, 8-12 inches long. Leaflets usually 7-9, 3-5 inches long, 1-2 inches broad; short-stalked; ovate to oblong-lanceolate; entire or obscurely serrate; thick and firm; glabrous, dark green above, paler beneath. Petioles glabrous, stout, grooved.

FLOWERS.—May, before the leaves; dioecious; borne in loose panicles on shoots of the previous season; calyx campanulate, 4-lobed; corolla o; stamens 2, rarely 3; ovary 2-celled.

FRUIT.—August-September, persistent on the branches until midwinter or the following spring; samaras 1-2 inches long, in crowded, drooping, paniculate clusters, 6-8 inches long.

WINTER-BUDS.—Short, rather obtuse; bud-scales apiculate keeled, 4 pairs, rusty-brown.

BARK.—Twigs at first dark green, becoming gray or light brown, often covered with a glaucous bloom; gray, deeply furrowed into firm, narrow, flattened ridges on the trunk.

WOOD.—Heavy, hard, strong, close-grained, tough, brown with thick, lighter colored sapwood. See p. 331.

DISTRIBUTION.—Of common occurrence throughout the state.

HABITAT.—Prefers a rich, moist, loamy soil, but grows in any well-drained situation; common along stream-beds.

NOTES.—Grows rapidly. Easily transplanted. Fairly free from disease. Leaves appear late in spring. The best of our native Ashes for street planting. Forms a shallow root-system.

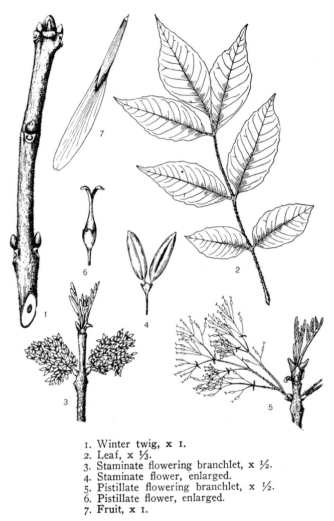

1. Winter twig, **x** 1.
2. Leaf, **x** ⅓.
3. Staminate flowering branchlet, **x** ½.
4. Staminate flower, enlarged.
5. Pistillate flowering branchlet, **x** ½.
6. Pistillate flower, enlarged.
7. Fruit, **x** 1.

OLEACEAE

Red Ash

Fraxinus pennsylvanica Marsh. [*Fraxinus pubescens* Lam.]

HABIT.—A medium-sized tree 30-50 feet high, with a trunk diameter of 1-2 feet; stout, upright branches and slender branchlets form a compact, irregular crown.

LEAVES.—Opposite, pinnately compound, 10-12 inches long. Leaflets 7-9, 3-5 inches long, 1-1½ inches broad; short-stalked; oblong-lanceolate to ovate; slightly serrate or entire; thin and firm; glabrous, yellow-green above, pale and silky-downy beneath. Petioles stout, pubescent.

FLOWERS.—May, before or with the leaves; dioecious; borne in compact, downy panicles on shoots of the previous season; calyx cup-shaped, 4-toothed; corolla 0; stamens 2, rarely 3; ovary 2-celled.

FRUIT.—Early autumn, persistent on the branches throughout the winter; samaras 1-2 inches long, in open, paniculate clusters.

WINTER-BUDS.—Small, rounded; bud-scales rounded on the back, 3 pairs, rusty brown, tomentose.

BARK.—Twigs pale-pubescent at first, lasting 2-3 years or often disappearing during the first summer, finally ashy gray or brownish and often covered with a glaucous bloom; brown or dark gray on the trunk, with many longitudinal, shallow furrows; somewhat scaly.

WOOD.—Heavy, hard, strong, brittle, coarse-grained, light brown, with thick, yellow-streaked sapwood.

DISTRIBUTION.—Not a common tree. Most frequent in the southern half of the Lower Peninsula, but has been reported further north—i. e., Drummond's Island and Luce and Keweenaw Counties, Upper Peninsula.

HABITAT.—Prefers wet or moist, rich loam; river-banks; swampy lowlands.

NOTES.—Rapid of growth in youth. Fairly immune from insect and fungous diseases.

Green Ash

1. Winter twig, x 1.
2. Leaf, x 1/3.
3. Staminate flowering branchlet, x 1/2.
4. Staminate flower, enlarged.
5. Pistillate flowering branchlet, x 1/2.
6. Pistillate flower, enlarged.
7. Fruit, x 1.

OLEACEAE

Green Ash

Fraxinus pennsylvanica lanceolata (Borkh.) *Sarg.* [*Fraxinus lanceolata,* Borkh.] [*Fraxinus viridis* Michx. f.]

Considered by some authors to be a distinct species, and by others a variety of *Fraxinus pennsylvanica* Marsh., which it resembles. The main points of difference are:

The usual absence of pubescence from the branchlets, the underside of the leaflets and the petioles.

The rather narrower, shorter and more sharply serrate leaflets.

The color of the leaves, which is bright green on both sides.

A very hardy tree, of rapid growth and desirable habit, making it useful for ornamental and street planting. Easily transplanted.

Of rare occurrence in Michigan, but has been reported from several localities.

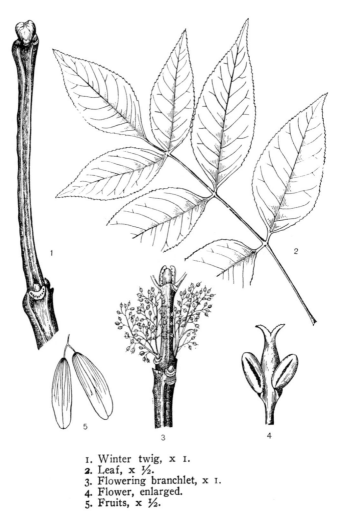

1. Winter twig, x 1.
2. Leaf, x ½.
3. Flowering branchlet, x 1.
4. Flower, enlarged.
5. Fruits, x ½.

OLEACEAE

Blue Ash

Fraxinus quadrangulata Michx.

HABIT.—A medium-sized tree 40-50 feet high, with a trunk diameter of 1-3 feet; small, spreading branches and stout, 4-angled, more or less 4-winged branchlets form a narrow crown.

LEAVES.—Opposite, pinnately compound, 8-12 inches long. Leaflets 5-9, usually 7, 3-5 inches long, 1-2 inches broad; short-stalked; ovate-oblong to lanceolate, long-pointed; coarsely serrate; thick and firm; yellow-green above, paler beneath, glabrous. Petioles slender, glabrous.

FLOWERS.—April, before the leaves; perfect; borne in loose panicles on shoots of the previous season; calyx reduced to a ring; corolla o; stamens 2; ovary 2-celled.

FRUIT.—September-October, falling soon after; samaras 1-2 inches long, in long, loose, paniculate clusters.

WINTER-BUDS.—Short, rather obtuse; bud-scales rounded on the back, 3 pairs, dark red-brown, somewhat pubescent.

BARK.—Twigs orange, rusty-pubescent, becoming brownish or grayish; on the trunk light gray tinged with red, irregularly divided into large, plate-like scales, often with the shaggy appearance of a Shagbark Hickory.

WOOD.—Heavy, hard, close-grained, brittle, light yellow streaked with brown, with thick, light yellow sapwood.

DISTRIBUTION.—Occasionally in the southern half of the Lower Peninsula. Nowhere abundant.

HABITAT.—Prefers rich, limestone hills, but grows well in fertile bottom-lands.

NOTES.—Hardy and grows rapidly. Formerly a blue dye was made by mascerating the inner bark in water. Well adapted to street and park planting.

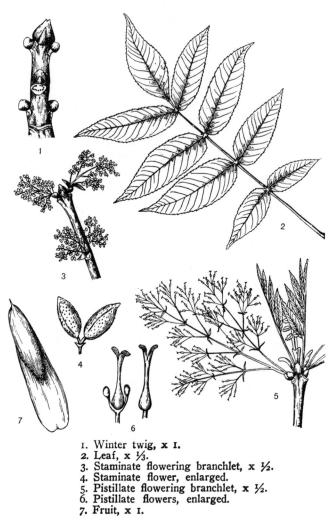

1. Winter twig, **x 1**.
2. Leaf, **x 1/3**.
3. Staminate flowering branchlet, **x 1/2**.
4. Staminate flower, enlarged.
5. Pistillate flowering branchlet, **x 1/2**.
6. Pistillate flowers, enlarged.
7. Fruit, **x 1**.

OLEACEAE

Black Ash

Fraxinus nigra Marsh. [*Fraxinus sambucifolia* Lam.]

HABIT.—A medium-sized tree 40-70 feet high, with a trunk diameter of 1-2 feet; slender, upright branches form in the forest a narrow crown, in the open a rounded, ovoid crown.

LEAVES.—Opposite, pinnately compound, 12-16 inches long. Leaflets 7-11, 3-5 inches long, 1-2 inches broad; sessile, except the terminal; oblong to oblong-lanceolate, long-pointed; remotely, but sharply serrate; thin and firm; dark green above, paler beneath, glabrous. Petioles stout, grooved, glabrous.

FLOWERS.—May, before the leaves; polygamo-dioecious; borne in loose panicles on shoots of the preceding season; calyx o; corolla o; stamens 2; ovary 2-celled.

FRUIT.—August-September, falling early, or sometimes hanging on the tree until the following spring; samaras, 1-1½ inches long, in open, paniculate clusters 8-10 inches long.

WINTER-BUDS.—Ovoid, pointed; bud-scales rounded on the back, 3 pairs, almost black.

BARK.—Twigs at first dark green, becoming ashy gray or orange, finally dark gray and warted; thin, soft ash-gray and scaly on the trunk. Bark flakes off on rubbing with the hand.

WOOD.—Heavy, tough, coarse-grained, weak, rather soft, dark brown, with thin, lighter colored sapwood.

DISTRIBUTION.—Common throughout most portions of Michigan.

HABITAT.—Prefers deep, cold swamps and low river-banks, but grows in any good soil.

NOTES.—Hardy throughout the state. Not easily transplanted. Foliage falls early in autumn.

THE CATALPAS—CATALPA

The Catalpas are trees of rapid growth with stout, pithy branchlets. The leaves are large, simple, usually entire, oppositely arranged or whorled, mostly ill-smelling when bruised. Very showy flowers, in large, terminal panicles, appear in profusion after the leaves are fully grown. They are followed by long, cylindrical pods or capsules filled with small-winged seeds, and the trees in some parts of our country are known as Cigar Trees, from these distinctive fruits, which hang on the trees all winter.

Most of the Catalpas belong to the tropics and they are therefore not particularly hardy. The two species described here have become naturalized in Michigan, where they are hardy in the southern portion.

Of other cultivated forms, the Umbrella Catalpa, *Catalpa bignonioides,* v. *nana* Bur., is best known. It is produced by grafting, at a height of about six feet from the ground, on a hardy stem, where it grows into a bushy, umbrella-shaped head without pruning. It is planted only for very formal effect, especially where very little ground is available. It is very showy when in bloom.

The Manchurian Catalpa, *Catalpa bungei* C. A. Meyer, is beginning to be cultivated. Horticultural catalogs commonly list *Catalpa bungei* as the Umbrella Catalpa, but this is an error, and the Manchurian Catalpa is a different and distinct species. This small tree comes from northern China, and is apparently quite hardy. The leaves are 3-6 inches long, narrowly triangular-ovate, long-acuminate at the apex, more or less truncate at the base, entire or with a few pointed teeth near the base, and have purple spots in the axils of the veins beneath. It has white flowers, spotted with purple inside.

Another Chinese tree, which is hardier than the American species, is *Catalpa ovata* Don (*Catalpa Kaempferi* Sieb.). It is a small tree, 20-30 feet in height, or smaller in northern latitudes, with spreading branches. The leaves are 5-8 inches long, broadly ovate, frequently somewhat 3-5-lobed, abruptly acuminate at the apex, mostly cordate at the base, with reddish spots in the axils of the veins beneath. The fragrant flowers are yellow, striped with orange and spotted with dark violet inside.

The Hybrid or Teas Catalpa, *Catalpa hybrida* Spaeth, should prove to be a valuable addition to our ornamental trees. It was originated in Indiana, and is a cross between *Catalpa bignonioides* and *Catalpa ovata.* Accordingly it has characteristics common to both the parents. It flowers profusely, is of rapid growth, and is hardy. The flowers resemble those of *Catalpa bignonioides,* but they are smaller, although the panicle is about twice as long. The leaves are like those of *Catalpa ovata,* but are much larger, and they are purple when they first unfold.

SUMMER KEY TO THE SPECIES OF CATALPA

a. Leaves 5-8 inches long, thick; flowers 1½ inches across, prominently yellow-spotted; seeds with *pointed,* fringed wings at each end; branches rather crooked and straggling; bark thin, separating into thin scales on the trunk ....
....*C. bignonioides,* p. 259

aa. Leaves 8-12 inches long, thin; flowers 2½ inches across, not prominently spotted; seeds with *rounded,* wide-fringed wings at each end; branches neither crooked nor straggling; bark thick, separating into thick scales on the trunk ....
....*C. speciosa,* p. 257

WINTER KEY TO THE SPECIES OF CATALPA

a. Fruiting capsules about ¼ inch in diameter; seeds with *pointed,* fringed wings at each end; branches rather crooked and straggling; bark thin, separating into thin scales on the trunk.
.... *C. bignonioides,* p. 259

aa. Fruiting capsules about ½ inch in diameter; seeds with *rounded,* wide-fringed wings at each end; branches neither crooked nor straggling; bark thick, separating into thick scales on the trunk .... *C. speciosa,* p. 257

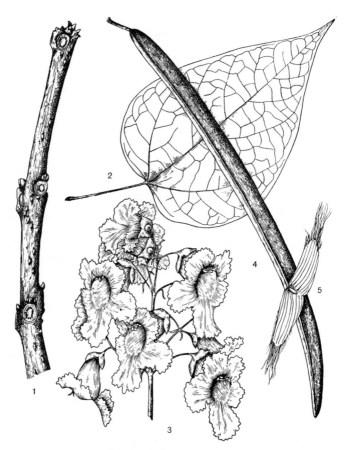

1. Winter twig, x 1.
2. Leaf, x ¼.
3. Panicle of flowers, x ⅜.
4. Fruit, x ½.
5. Seed, x 1.

BIGNONIACEAE
Hardy Catalpa
Catalpa speciosa Warder

HABIT.—A tree 50-60 feet high, with a short, often crooked trunk and a broad, rounded crown of slender, spreading branches and thick branchlets.

LEAVES.—Opposite or whorled, simple, 8-12 inches long, 6-8 inches broad; heart-shaped; entire or sometimes slightly lobed; thick and firm; glabrous, dark green above, downy beneath, with clusters of dark, nectariferous glands in the axils of the primary veins, turning black and falling with the first severe frost; petioles long, stout, terete.

FLOWERS.—June-July, after the leaves are full grown; perfect; borne on slender, purplish pedicels in open, few-flowered panicles, 5-6 inches long; calyx 2-lobed, purple; corolla white with inconspicuous yellow spots, campanulate, 5-lobed, 2½ inches across; stamens 2, staminodia 3; ovary 2-celled.

FRUIT.—Ripens in early autumn; slender, 2-celled, cylindrical capsule, 10-20 inches long and about ½ inch in diameter; hangs on tree all winter, opening in spring before falling; seeds light brown, 1 inch long, with rounded, wide-fringed wings at each end.

WINTER-BUDS.—Terminal bud absent; lateral buds brownish, globose, inconspicuous.

BARK.—Twigs greenish, often with purple tinge, becoming orange or red-brown and covered with a slight bloom the first winter, finally darker with age; thick, red-brown, broken into thick scales on the trunk.

WOOD.—Light, soft, weak, coarse-grained, light brown, with very thin, almost white sapwood; very durable in contact with the soil.

DISTRIBUTION.—A native of Illinois, Indiana and the states adjoining on the south, but much planted in Michigan as a shade and ornamental tree, and naturalized here.

HABITAT.—Prefers rich, moist soils along streams and on bottom-lands, but will grow in drier situations; prefers shade.

NOTES.—Closely resembles *Catalpa bignonioides*, but is a larger and hardier tree. Should not be used for street planting. It is known also as the Western Catalpa.

Catalpa

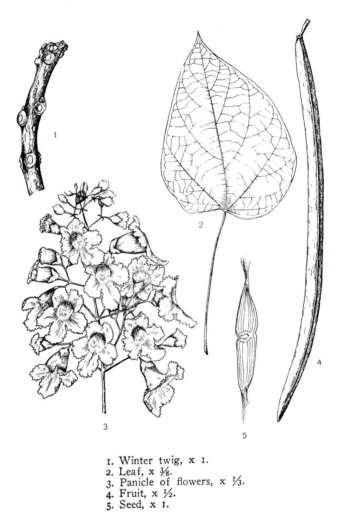

1. Winter twig, x 1.
2. Leaf, x ⅜.
3. Panicle of flowers, x ⅓.
4. Fruit, x ½.
5. Seed, x 1.

BIGNONIACEAE

Catalpa

Catalpa bignonioides Walt. [*Catalpa catalpa* (L.) Karst.]

HABIT.—A tree 40-50 feet high, with a short, thick trunk and a broad, irregular crown of long, crooked branches and coarse, upright branchlets.

LEAVES.—Opposite or whorled, simple, 5-8 inches long, 4-5 inches broad; heart-shaped; entire or sometimes slightly lobed; thin and firm; glabrous, light green above, downy beneath, with dark, nectariferous glands in the axils of the primary veins, turning black and falling with the first severe frost; petioles long, stout, terete.

FLOWERS.—June-July, after the leaves are full grown; perfect; borne on slender, hairy pedicels in compact, many-flowered panicles, 8-10 inches long; calyx 2-lobed, green or purple; corolla white with yellow spots, campanulate, 5-lobed, 1½ inches across; stamens 2, staminodia 3; ovary 2-celled.

FRUIT.—Ripens in early autumn; slender, 2-celled, cylindrical capsule, 8-20 inches long and about ¼ inch in diameter; hangs on tree all winter, opening in spring before falling; seeds silvery gray, 1 inch long, with pointed, fringed wings at each end.

WINTER-BUDS.—Terminal bud absent; lateral buds brownish, globose, inconspicuous.

BARK.—Twigs greenish purple, becoming red-brown and marked by a network of thin, flat ridges; thin, red-brown on the trunk, separating into large, thin, irregular scales.

WOOD.—Light, soft, weak, coarse-grained, light brown, with very thin, whitish sapwood; very durable in contact with the soil.

DISTRIBUTION.—A native of the Lower Mississippi River Basin, but naturalized in southern Michigan, where it is a popular shade and ornamental tree.

HABITAT.—Prefers rich, moist soils along streams and on bottom-lands, but will grow in drier situations; prefers shade.

NOTES.—The foliage appears very tardily in spring. A smaller tree than *Catalpa speciosa,* and less hardy. Should not be used for street planting. Several varieties are in cultivation.

Sheepberry. Nannyberry

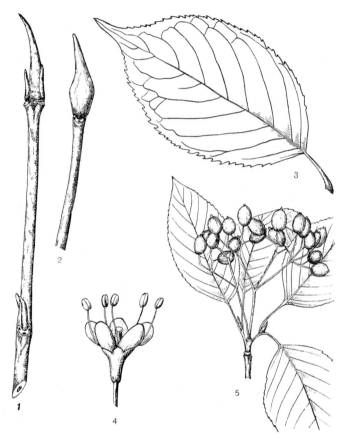

1. Winter twig, with leaf buds, x 1.
2. Winter twig, with flower bud, x 1.
3. Leaf, x ¾.
4. Flower, enlarged.
5. Fruiting branchlet, x ½.

CAPRIFOLIACEAE
Sheepberry. Nannyberry
Viburnum lentago L.

HABIT.—A low tree or shrub 15-25 feet high, with a short trunk 6-10 inches in diameter; numerous tortuous branches form a wide, compact, rounded crown.

LEAVES.—Opposite, simple, 2-4 inches long, one-half as broad; ovate to suborbicular; finely and sharply serrate; thick and firm; lustrous, bright green above, pale and marked with tiny black dots beneath; petioles broad, grooved, more or less winged, about 1 inch long.

FLOWERS.—May-June, after the leaves; perfect; small; cream-white, borne in stout-branched, scurfy, flat, terminal cymes, 3-5 inches across; calyx tubular, 5-toothed; corolla 5-lobed, cream color or white, ¼ inch across; stamens 5, with yellow anthers; ovary 1-celled, with short, thick, green style and broad stigma.

FRUIT.—September; a fleshy drupe, ½ inch long, ovoid, flattened, blue-black, borne in few-fruited, red-stemmed clusters; stone oval, flat, rough; flesh sweet, edible.

WINTER-BUDS.—Leaf-buds narrow, acute, red, scurfy-pubescent, ½ inch long; flower-buds swollen at the base, with spire-like apex, grayish with scurfy pubescence, ¾ inch long.

BARK.—Twigs at first light green, rusty-pubescent, becoming dark red-brown; red-brown on old trunks and broken into small, thick plates.

WOOD.—Heavy, hard, close-grained, ill-smelling, dark orange-brown, with thin, whitish sapwood.

DISTRIBUTION.—Frequent throughout the state.

HABITAT.—Prefers rich, moist soil along the borders of forests; roadsides; river-banks.

NOTES.—Too small for street use. Propagated from seed or by cuttings. One of the most attractive of our small ornamental trees.

The Black Haw or Stagbush, *Viburnum prunifolium* L., is of rare occurrence in its wild state, but has been reported from several localities in southern Michigan. It deserves to be planted more extensively for ornamental purposes. Usually it is a shrub or small tree, seldom over 15 feet in height. It resembles the Sheepberry, from which it may be distinguished by its blunt-pointed leaves, which do not possess wings on the petioles, and by the buds, which are short-pointed and rusty-pubescent. For other Viburnums, see pp. 271-272.

ADDITIONAL NOTES ON THE SPECIES

The distinction between a tree and a shrub is purely a matter of arbitrary definition, the application of which is not always possible. Many times the plant which one wishes to identify is small, and it is difficult to tell whether it may be tree-like, when fully developed, or shrub-like. Some plants, shrubby with us, may become tree-like in more favorable latitudes or environments. Without question these smaller, woody plants, although they may remain shrub-like, form an important and characteristic under-story in our woods and forests. To meet the need for more complete information concerning our woody plants, there will be found here brief descriptions of species which are less frequently seen or are of minor importance, and especially of those which are more often seen as large shrubs and perhaps only occasionally as trees. No attempt has been made to make this list complete, but it does include those species, native and introduced, which might under any circumstances be considered tree-like. To aid in readily locating the name of a plant under observation, the descriptive matter has been arranged in the form of a simple key, of the same sort as has been employed throughout the manual.

a. *Leaves simple.*

　b. *Leaves needle-shaped, awl-shaped, strap-shaped or scale-like.*

　　c. *Leaves evergreen.*

Japanese Yew
Taxus cuspidata Sieb. & Zucc.

A very hardy evergreen, seldom over 15-20 feet high with us, but in its native country forming a tree 40-50 feet in height. The spreading or upright branches are reddish brown, as is the older bark. Linear leaves, ¾-1 inch long, are dull dark green above, with 2 broad, yellow bands beneath; they are contracted into a distinct, yellowish petiole, and they stand in 2 ranks, often upright and forming a V-shaped trough. The fruit is an edible, scarlet, berry-like, pulpy cup, open at the apex and surrounding a nut-like seed. An evergreen of unsurpassed beauty, but difficult to propagate. There are dwarf forms and varieties with yellow leaves. Japanese Yew is closely related to the native American

Yew or Ground Hemlock, *Taxus canadensis* Marsh., which is a low, straggling bush found along the Great Lakes on the east and west, becoming more abundant in the northern part of the state. The leaves of the latter are ½-¾ of an inch long, and are not yellow-banded beneath. The Yews are proverbially long-lived, growing more beautiful year by year.

Chinese Juniper
Juniperus chinensis L.

This very hardy evergreen forms a small, pyramidal tree, or sometimes it is a procumbent shrub. It has leaves of 2 kinds: (1) scale-like, obtuse, closely appressed; (2) needle-shaped, sharp-pointed, spreading, with 2 white bands above. The berry-like, brownish yellow strobile is coated with a thick, mealy bloom; it ripens in the second year, and is attractive throughout the winter months. The species runs into many garden forms, differing in color and habit. Of these, the variety, *Pfitzeriana* Spaeth, a low form with horizontally spreading branches, is one of the most important decorative Junipers.

Sawara Cypress
Chamaecyparis pisifera Endl. [*Retinispora pisifera* Sieb. & Zucc.]

A small tree with red-brown, rather smooth bark, which peels off in thin strips, spreading branches forming a narrow-pyramidal crown, and flattened branchlets, somewhat pendulous at the ends. The leaves are opposite, scale-like, with mucronate tips, appressed, obscurely glandular, lustrous, dark green above, with whitish lines beneath. The fruit is an erect, globose cone, about ¼ inch in diameter, brown, maturing the first season. Introduced from Japan. There are many varieties, of which the following, perfectly hardy in our latitude, are planted extensively. The variety, *filifera* Beiss., is a medium-sized, pyramidal tree of graceful outline, with elongated, pendulous, thread-like branches and few short, lateral branchlets. The variety, *plumosa* Beiss., is of dense, conical habit, with the branches ascending and bearing frond-like, feathery branchlets. Both the species and its varieties should be planted more extensively. Propagated from cuttings or grafted. Should be planted in good, moist soil, in situations protected from the sweep of the prevailing cold winds.

cc. *Leaves deciduous.*

Tamarisk
Tamarix L.

The Tamarisks are deciduous shrubs or small trees, with very slender, erect, terete branches. The leaves are alternate, minute. sessile, scale-like, often sheathing. The flowers are likewise small, usually pink, in dense, lateral racemes or in terminal panicles. The fruit is a small, dehiscent capsule, containing many minute, densely-bearded seeds. Leaf-scars lacking, since the foliar shoots are deciduous in their entirety in autumn. While there are no native woody plants resembling the Tamarisks, the species within the genus are very much alike and difficult to distinguish. The Tamarisks are natives of the Mediterranean region, eastern Asia and India. Perhaps among the hardiest are *Tamarix pentandra* Pall. and *Tamarix gallica* L. Both of these bear their flowers in large, terminal panicles, appearing in summer. In *Tamarix parviflora* DC., which is fairly hardy, the flowers appear in spring in lateral racemes on branches of the previous year. The Tamarisks have been cultivated from ancient times for their attractive feathery foliage and their profuse pink blooms. They thrive in either wet or dry situations.

bb. *Leaves broad and flat.*

c. *Leaves alternate or clustered, never opposite nor whorled.*

d. *Margin of leaves entire or only slightly undulate.*

e. *Leaves and branchlets decidedly silvery-scaly.*

Oleaster. Russian Olive
Elaeagnus angustifolia L.

Usually a tree 20-30 feet high, erect or commonly leaning or twisted and distorted, branching low to form a number of erect or pendulous, often spiny branches. The young branchlets are silvery-hairy, becoming glabrous, lustrous brown. The lanceolate or oblong-lanceolate leaves are 2-3 inches long, light green above and silvery-scaly beneath, with short petioles. The small, perfect flowers appear in June, in the axils of the leaves; they are silvery gray outside, yellow within, and are very fragrant and rich in honey. An olive-shaped, inedible, silver-gray drupe, not quite ½ inch long, follows the flowers, and this persists on the branches into late autumn or the next spring. The leaf-scars are semicircular, minute, more or less raised, with 1 bundle-scar. The native home of the Oleaster is Europe and western Asia, indicating a tree of great hardiness. It makes an excellent low windbreak and is useful to bind shifting sand and to prevent erosion, besides being very attractive ornamentally. Propagated either from seed or by cuttings. Rapid of growth under favorable soil and moisture conditions.

ee. *Leaves and branchlets not silvery-scaly.*

Papaw
Asimina triloba Dunal

A low tree not over 10 feet in height with us, usually lower or shrub-like. It is common in the valleys of the Grand and Maple Rivers and southward, often growing in dense thickets in the shade of other trees. The bark of the slender stems is thin and close, dark brown, with whitish blotches and small, wart-like protuberances. It has slender twigs, soon glabrous, enlarged at the nodes. The winter-buds are naked, rusty brown and tomentose. Leaf-scars broadly crescent-shaped, with 5 (or 7) bundle-scars, sometimes compound. Obovate-lanceolate leaves, gradually tapering to the base, are 4-12 inches long, light green above, paler beneath, glabrous both sides, with a short, stout petiole. Reddish purple, perfect flowers appear in late May and June, with the leaves, but usually below them on the twigs; they are 1½-2 inches across, on short, stout, hairy pedicels. The fruit is ripe in September or October, and resembles a stubby banana, 3-5 inches long. At first it is green, but later it becomes dark brown or blackish. The pulp is edible, although not relished by some people, and imbedded in it are many large, dark brown, lustrous, flattened seeds. The fruit should not be eaten before the blackening appears and the pulp becomes mellow. It finds its way to the markets in localities where the tree abounds, but is not grown commercially.

Smoke Tree
Rhus cotinus L. [*Cotinus Coggygria* Scop.]
[*Cotinus Cotinus* Sarg.]

One of the most striking small trees or bushy shrubs of our lawns and gardens. Although belonging among the Sumacs, it does not resemble them very closely, because of its slender branchlets and simple leaves. The latter are oval to obovate, 1½-3½ fnches long, glabrous, with slender petioles of about the same length. The flowers are tiny, usually yellowish, borne in large, terminal, densely plumose panicles in June or July. Later these become billowy masses of green, yellow and red, suggesting a puff of smoke, from which peculiarity the name Smoke Tree is derived. Leaf-scars are crescent-shaped, raised, with 3 bundle-scars. Introduced from Europe and Asia, and long-cultivated. Perfectly hardy. There are pendulous forms and a variety with purplish hairs on the panicles.

Alder Buckthorn
Rhamnus frangula L.

A tall shrub or small tree, widely planted for ornament. It has been introduced from Europe, western Asia and northern Africa. The young branchlets are pubescent. The leaves are obovate to obovate-oblong, 1-2½ inches long, dark lustrous green above, lighter and often slightly pubescent beneath. The inconspicuous pale yellow flowers are borne in May and June in axillary clusters, followed by globose drupes about ¼ inch in diameter, changing from red to black, inclosing 2-3 nut-like stones. The winter-buds are naked (see *Rhamnus cathartica*), and the leaf-scars are half-elliptical, small, somewhat raised, with 3 bundle-scars. Makes an excellent tall hedge. Will thrive in almost any kind of soil.

dd. *Margin of leaves serrate, toothed or lobed.*

Common Buckthorn
Rhamnus cathartica L.

Resembles the Alder Buckthorn in some of its characteristics, and may be distinguished from it by the branchlets, which are often tipped with stout spines, and by the crenate-serrate leaves, which often have a tendency to oppositeness. They remain green and persist on the branches until very late in autumn. The winter-buds are scaly (see *Rhamnus frangula*); the leaf-scars are crescent-shaped, with 3 bundle-scars. The Common Buckthorn makes an excellent hedge plant, is perfectly hardy, never suckers, is free from insect attacks, stands shearing and is thorny. The fruit of both the Buckthorns is nauseous, and has been used medicinally; while the sap is capable of producing dyes.

European Basswoods
Tilia (Tourn.) L.

Besides the native Basswood, described on p. 233, the following European species may be planted:

The **Small-leaved Linden,** *Tilia cordata* Mill. [*Tilia parvifolia* Ehrh.], may be recognized by its leaves, which are nearly orbicular, 1½-2½ inches long, rather finely serrate, whitish or blue-green beneath. The twigs are slender, glabrous at maturity, and the winter-buds are small. The fruit is rusty-tomentose, with a thin, fragile shell.

The **Large-leaved Linden** or **Lime,** *Tilia platyphyllos* Scop. [*Tilia grandifolia* Ehrh.], has orbicular-ovate leaves, 3-4½ inches long, sharply serrate, usually pubescent beneath. The twigs are slender, somewhat loosely hairy, and the winter-buds are small. The fruit is about ⅛ inch long, pear-shaped, strongly ribbed, with thick shell.

The **Crimean Linden,** *Tilia euchlora* K. Koch [*Tilia dasystyla* Kirchn.], has thick, leathery leaves, which are 2-3 inches long, serrate with slender-pointed teeth, lustrous, dark green above, and glabrous except for tufts of brown hairs in the axils of the veins beneath. The branchlets are slender, often slightly pendulous, yellowish, glabrous; and the fruit is small, slightly ribbed and tomentose. The best Linden for street planting.

The **European Linden,** *Tilia vulgaris* Hayne, is also planted. In most of its characteristics it more nearly resembles our native Basswood. It is a hardy, moisture-loving tree, but it will grow in a variety of soils. Makes a good street tree where proper soil conditions are available, and should be more generally planted.

Alder
Alnus (Tourn.) Hill

This genus belongs to the Birch family. In common with the Birches, the Alders bear their flowers early in spring, before the leaves appear; and they are unisexual, in catkins, the two kinds occurring on the same plant. Unlike the Birches, both kinds of catkins develop from naked buds formed during the preceding season. The fruit, as in the other members of the family, is a persistent cone or strobile, bearing small, narrow-winged nuts. The Alders may be distinguished from the Birches by their buds.

which are produced early and which are borne on long stalks. The leaf-scars are half-round, somewhat raised, with bundle-scars 3 or in 3 groups. The Alders prefer wet situations, and are commonly found along our streams and lake-shores, where they serve a very useful purpose in preventing erosion.

Two species of Alders are native to Michigan, of which the **Speckled** or **Hoary Alder**, *Alnus incana* (L.) Moench., is the prevailing species in the center of the state and throughout the Upper Peninsula. It is a shrub or small tree with smooth, light gray bark, branchlets which at first are pubescent and dotted with orange lenticels, and reddish-downy winter-buds. The leaves are broadly ovate, 1½-4 inches long, doubly serrate, dull dark green above, whitish and more or less pubescent beneath. Both staminate and pistillate catkins droop, the fruiting cones are pendent, and the winged nutlets are orbicular or nearly so.

The **Smooth Alder**, *Alnus rugosa* (DuRoi) Spreng., is rather rare or only locally abundant in the southern half of the Lower Peninsula. It may be distinguished by its obovate leaves, which are finely serrate on the margin, by the pistillate catkins which are set at right angles to the staminate catkins, by its erect fruiting cones, and by the winged nutlets, which are ovate.

The **Black Alder** of Europe, *Alnus vulgaris* Hill [*Alnus glutinosa* Gaertn.], is sometimes cultivated. It may be distinguished by its coarsely dentate and glutinous leaves, as well as by its glutinous twigs; it tends, also, to be more tree-like than our native species.

Witch-hazel
Hamamelis virginiana L.

One of our commonest under-shrubs or small trees and occurs abundantly throughout the state. It has several characteristics which unmistakably identify it. In summer it may be known by its oval leaves, which are 4-6 inches in length, short-petioled, and sinuate-dentate on the margin. It has the distinction of being our only woody plant which blossoms in late autumn, sometimes after the first snowfall. The flowers have strap-like, yellow petals. The fruit is a yellow-brown, woody pod, with 2 cells in which shiny black seeds are produced. A year is required for its development, so that it is not unusual to find flowers and fully developed fruits from the previous season occurring together on the same plant.

The woody pods burst open when ripe, throwing the seeds for a considerable distance. In winter the old seed pods may be found, and these, with the distinctly stalked, naked, tomentose buds, make the identification simple.

Dwarf Chestnut Oak. Scrub Chestnut Oak
Quercus prinoides Willd.

Reported from several localities in southern Michigan. It is usually a small shrub, but may attain a height of 9-15 feet. Frequently it occurs in clumps or forms small thickets. In general it resembles *Quercus muhlenbergii,* except in the matter of size. The leaves are smaller than in the larger tree, with more undulate margins and shorter petioles; also the cup of the acorn is somewhat deeper and the scales are more swollen. It is not unusual to find this little Oak literally loaded down with acorns.

    cc. *Leaves opposite or whorled.*
      d. *Margin of leaves entire.*

Common Lilac
Syringa vulgaris L.

A native of Europe, long cultivated in America, and not rarely found growing in a wild state. There is no need to describe this universally-known favorite. It is a tall, upright shrub, frequently growing in dense clumps; sometimes it is a small tree. The Common Lilac has 2 end buds, both of which flower. There are varieties of many colors, double-flowered varieties and one with variegated leaves.

The **Himalaya Lilac,** *Syringa villosa* Vahl., comes into bloom somewhat later than the Common Lilac. In this species there is only 1 end bud, and the flowers are pale lilac or pinkish white, strongly scented. It has broadly oblong leaves, often 7 inches long, short-pointed at both ends, glabrous except for a pubescence on the veins beneath.

The **Persian Lilac,** *Syringa persica* L., is also much grown. It has lanceolate leaves, acuminate at the apex, 1½-3 inches long. The tree-like **Japanese Lilac,** *Syringa japonica* Decne., and the **Amur Lilac,** *Syringa amurensis* Rupr., are also seen. The last named, coming from northern China and Manchuria, is extremely hardy.

Fringe-tree

Chionanthus virginica L.

Closely related to the Lilacs. Its native home ranges from Pennsylvania to Florida and Texas, but it has wandered far from these confines. It forms a large shrub or slender tree 20-30 feet in height. The trunk is rather short, bearing numerous stout, ascending branches, to form a narrow crown. The leaves are ovate, 4-8 inches long, wedge-shaped at the base, lustrous, dark green above and lighter beneath; they unfold late in spring and fall early in autumn. The white flowers appear in May or June, in drooping panicles, 4-6 inches long; long, narrow petals give a distinctly fringe-like appearance, hence the name Fringe-tree. The fruit is berry-like, dark blue, ½-¾ inch long. A very ornamental tree, which has a place in gardens and parks and on our lawns. It is not entirely hardy until it is well established, for which reason it should be planted in sheltered situations. It can be grafted upon our common species of Ashes, enabling it to grow in somewhat dry situations.

Buffalo-berry

Shepherdia argentea Nutt.

An upright, thorny shrub, 12-18 feet in height, or sometimes nearly tree-like. The young growth is silvery-tomentose. Its leaves are oblong to oblong-lanceolate, 1-2 inches long, and silvery on both sides. Small, nearly sessile, yellowish flowers appear in April or May, followed by the drupe-like, ovoid, scarlet fruits, which are edible, but sour. The winter-buds are rather small, stalked; leaf-scars half-round, minute, with 1 bundle-scar. Very resistant to drought and winter-killing. To insure the production of fruit, it should never be planted singly, but always in groups of both sexes, since the plant is dioecious. A cool soil is desirable, and shade is beneficial. Splendid for the banks of streams, but seldom planted there. Good for the border and makes an excellent hedge-plant. Its native home is Kansas to Minnesota, extending westward and northward.

dd. *Margin of leaves serrate, toothed or lobed.*

Hydrangea
Hydrangea paniculata Sieb.

This plant appears to have no common name, except the Latin genus name. Usually a strong-growing shrub, it may become tree-like, with a height of 25-30 feet. It comes to us from Japan and China, and is very hardy. The branchlets are stout, pubescent, oppositely arranged, like the leaves. The latter are elliptic or ovate, abruptly acuminate at the apex, narrowed or rounded at the base, and short-petioled. They are 2½-5 inches long, serrate on the margin, sparingly pubescent above and usually bristly-hairy on the veins beneath. The common garden form is variety *grandiflora* Sieb., in which the large, persistent, white flowers are nearly all sterile. They are borne in terminal, showy panicles, which may be nearly a foot in length. The blooms appear in late July or August and remain until frost-time, when they are tinged with pink. Long-cultivated and popular everywhere. The blooms are often used for interior decorating for winter, after they have been frosted.

Wayfaring Tree
Viburnum lantana L.

This is one of a long list of species, mostly shrubs, many of which are native to the state or are commonly planted, introduced forms. It is an upright shrub, sometimes 15-20 feet in height, often tree-like. The leaves are ovate to oblong-ovate, 2-4 inches long, blunt-pointed, heart-shaped or rounded at the base, minutely toothed, sparingly stellate-pubescent and wrinkled above, stellate-tomentose beneath. The white flowers appear in late May or June, in flat-topped cymes, which are 2-3 inches across. Bright red fruits, which are 1-seeded drupes, about ⅓ inch long, succeed the flowers, ultimately becoming black. The winter-buds are naked, stellate-scurfy like the twigs; leaf-scars narrow, crescent-shaped, with 3 bundle-scars. The fruits are very attractive throughout late summer and autumn. Introduced from Europe and western Asia. Absolutely hardy and adapted to a wide range of conditions.

The **European Cranberry-bush,** *Viburnum opulus* L., is very commonly planted. It may be distinguished by its usually 3-lobed leaves, which are 2-4 inches long, with the lobes coarsely and irregularly toothed, and by its rather ill-scented, red fruit, which hangs on the plant all winter. A variety of this, *roseum* L. (*sterile* DC.), known as the **Common Snowball**, is cultivated for its large, globose heads of sterile flowers; its leaves turn deep red in autumn.

The **High-bush Cranberry**, *Viburnum opulus*, v. *americanum* (Mill.) Ait., is a native, low form, common throughout the state, where it frequents the borders of streams and swamps. Its bright red, translucent fruits are quite acid, and they are frequently gathered for use as a substitute for cranberries.

Wahoo. Burning Bush

Evonymus atropurpureus Jacq.

Common in the central and south portions of our state, the Wahoo is nowhere abundant. It is a tree-like shrub, with oval-oblong, finely serrate leaves, which are 1½-4½ inches long, pubescent beneath. The perfect flowers are borne in small, axillary cymes; they are about ½ inch across, have their parts in fours, and are purple in color. It is in the autumn that the Wahoo comes into full glory. At this time the plant has the appearance of being on fire, from the profuse crimson fruits, which droop on long peduncles, whence the name of Burning Bush. These are more or less lobed, fleshy capsules, which open eventually to discharge the brownish seeds. The leaf-scars are half-elliptical, rather small, with 1 bundle-scar. Very ornamental; sometimes planted; prefers lowlands and river-banks. It is one of the few woody plants with 4-sided branchlets.

The **European Spindle-tree**, *Evonymus europaeus* L., is frequently planted. It resembles our native species, but has less numerous, yellow-green flowers. The **Japanese** or **Winged Spindle-tree**, *Evonymus alata* Regel, of smaller form, is also much cultivated. It may be distinguished from the others by its conspicuously corky-winged branches, its yellowish flowers and purplish fruits, which open to expose the orange-red interior.

aa. *Leaves compound.*
  b. *Leaves alternate.*
    c. *Leaflets 3.*

Hop-tree. Wafer Ash

Ptelea trifoliata L.

Native to the southern half of the Lower Peninsula, and is more abundant near the shores of the Great Lakes. It is a shrub with distinctly tree-like habit, sometimes growing to a height of 25 feet. It is easily identified by its trifoliate leaves, with the leaflets nearly sessile, entire or crenulate on the margin, dotted with transparent glands. The small, greenish white, polygamous flowers are borne in corymbs, appearing in June. The fruit is a 2-celled, 2-seeded, orbicular samara, from which character the name Wafer Ash is derived. It ripens in late autumn and remains on the branches through the winter. The winter-buds are very low-conical, closely superposed in pairs, breaking through the leaf-scars, not distinctly scaly, whitish-hairy; the leaf-scars are rather large, horseshoe-shaped when torn by the buds, with 3 bundle-scars. Sometimes planted in parks and gardens for ornament. Several varieties are in cultivation. Also known as the **Quinine-tree**.

cc. *Leaflets usually 5-many.*
  d. *Stems armed with sharp prickles.*

Northern Prickly Ash. Toothache-tree

Zanthoxylum americanum Mill.

Belongs to the same family as the Hop-tree. It is a native plant, found throughout the Lower Peninsula, along streams and on low ground. It is a prickly (usually in pairs) shrub or low tree, with twigs at first pubescent, and usually 5-9 leaflets. The leaflets are 1-2 inches long, sessile or nearly so, entire or finely crenate-serrate, dotted with oil glands. The small, yellow-green flowers appear in April or May, before or with the leaves, in axillary clusters on the last year's branchlets. The fruit is an ellipsoid capsule, thick and fleshy, containing 1-2 shiny, black seeds. The winter-buds are moderate, superposed, globose, red-woolly and indistinctly scaly; the leaf-scars are broadly triangular or 3-lobed, with 3 bundle-scars. All parts of the plant are pungent and aromatic, with a strong lemon-like odor, especially if bruised. Sometimes cultivated.

Hercules' Club. Angelica-tree
Aralia spinosa L.

A shrub, or more often a small tree, 20-35 feet in height, with a trunk diameter of 4-8 inches; the crown is flat-topped, consisting of a few stout, club-like, spreading branches; the trunk is usually branchless; the stems are armed with stout, irregularly scattered prickles. The leaves are tropical-like in size, being 2-4 feet long and 2-2½ feet wide, and once-, twice- or thrice-compound. The leaflets are arranged oppositely, and are short-stalked, 2-3 inches long, broadly ovate to lanceolate, finely serrate, dark green and glabrous above, paler, glabrous, or somewhat pubescent and often with prickles on the midribs beneath; the veins curve upward before reaching the margin. The petioles have enlarged, clasping bases. The flowers appear in late July and August; each flower is tiny, usually perfect, cream-white; many of them are grouped together in panicled umbels, which occur solitary or in groups, often 3-4 feet long. The fruit is an ovoid, 5-angled, juicy, black berry, about ¼ inch in diameter, ripening in late August and September. The leaf-scars are narrow, nearly encircling the twig, with about 20 bundle-scars arranged in a single, curved line. Hercules' Club is native from southern New York to Florida, and west to Missouri and Texas, where it frequents rich, moist bottom-lands and moist, fertile woodland slopes. Not quite hardy north. Of rapid growth, but short-lived. Extensively planted south for its grotesque habit and handsome foliage.

The **Chinese Angelica-tree**, *Aralia chinensis* L. [*Aralia japonica* Hort.], is hardier than our American species and may be planted with some protection in the southern part of our state. It may be distinguished from it by the leaves, which are without spines; and the leaflets are larger, 3-6 inches long, sessile, closely and finely serrate, with the veins dividing before reaching the margin and ending in the teeth, pubescent on the veins beneath and sometimes above. Less prickly than *Aralia spinosa*. Will grow in somewhat dry and rocky or clayey soil.

The **Japanese Angelica-tree**, *Aralia elata* Seem., is the hardiest of the Angelica-trees. It greatly resembles *Aralia chinensis*, differing from it principally in the character of the inflorescence. In the Japanese tree this consists of a short main axis, from which arise subumbellate, spreading, secondary axes; while in the

Chinese tree the inflorescence has a long main axis, forming an elongated panicle, 10-16 inches in height. Another difference exists in the leaves; in *Aralia elata* the leaflets are rather coarsely or remotely serrate, while in *Aralia chinensis* they are rather closely and finely serrate.

dd. *Stems not armed.*

Sumac
Rhus L.

There are six native Sumacs with rather wide distribution in Michigan. Two of these are to many persons poisonous to the touch, and it is quite important to the well-being of these to know their characteristics and danger.

Poison Ivy or **Poison Oak**, *Rhus toxicodendron* L., is easily recognized by its trifoliate leaves, with the leaflets 1-4 inches long, entire or sparingly and coarsely dentate or sinuate, usually more or less wrinkled, and by the whitish fruits, about the size of small peas, borne in loose, paniculate clusters. It is a suberect or bushy, woody plant which scrambles over the ground and over walls and fences, or climbs high into trees by means of clinging rootlets. It is found abundantly throughout the state.

Poison Sumac, also known as **Dogwood** or **Poison Dogwood,** *Rhus vernix* L., is an upright shrub or small tree, sometimes 15-20 feet in height. It is common in lowlands and swamps in the southern half of the Lower Peninsula. More poisonous even than its smaller brother, it is fortunately identified by its pinnately compound, lustrous, dark green leaves, with 7-13 entire leaflets, 3-4 inches long, with scarlet midribs. The flowers and fruit are much like those of Poison Ivy; the berries remain on the branches far into the winter. A beautiful plant in its native habitat, but it should not be planted for ornamentation, because of its highly poisonous properties.

Symptoms of poisoning are acute irritation of the skin, accompanied by itching, swelling and the formation of watery blisters. Susceptible persons who have come into contact with either of the poisonous Sumacs may counteract the effects of the poison by bathing the parts with rubbing alcohol as soon after exposure as possible. Soap and water, with vigorous scrubbing, may be resorted to, but this treatment is less effective. If the eruption has already appeared, bathing the parts with lead acetate or baking soda in water will alleviate the discomfort, help to prevent the spread of the eruption and hasten the drying-up.

The **Fragrant Sumac,** *Rhus canadensis* Marsh., is seldom over 3 feet in height. Like the Poison Ivy, the leaves are trifoliate but it may be distinguished from it by the smaller leaflets, which are 1-2 inches long, rather regularly crenate-serrate, pleasantly fragrant when bruised, and by the fruit, which is produced sparingly and consists of a red-downy, globose drupe.

The three other common Sumacs are distinguished from the preceding species by the inflorescence and fruits. The flowers are densely clustered in compact, terminal panicles, followed by compact, paniculate clusters of globular fruits, each clothed with acid crimson hairs.

The **Smooth Sumac,** *Rhus glabra* L., has glabrous, glaucous branches. The leaflets vary from 11-31, are serrate and whitened beneath. It is common throughout the state. The **Dwarf Cut-leaf Sumac,** *Rhus glabra,* v. *laciniata* Carr., with pinnately dissected leaflets and distinctly reddish veins, is very ornamental and frequently planted. It is small, usually 3-5 feet in height.

The **Staghorn Sumac,** *Rhus typhina* L., is less common in the state. Its branches, twigs and leaf-petioles are densely velvety hairy. The leaflets, as in the preceding species, are 11-31 in number, serrate. The wood is orange colored and brittle. The **Fern-leaf Sumac,** *Rhus typhina,* v. *dissecta* Rehd., is frequently planted. In it the leaflets are deeply and delicately cut, almost fern-like. Grows to a height of 12-15 feet.

The **Dwarf Sumac,** *Rhus copallina* L., is common in the Lower Peninsula as far north as Roscommon County, and is especially abundant in the Pine region. It has red-pubescent branchlets; the leaves have 9-21, mostly entire leaflets, very lustrous above, and the rachis is provided with winged extensions on either side. The latest of the Sumacs to bloom, the flowers appearing in July and August. The foliage turns brilliant reddish purple in autumn.

Pea-tree
Caragana arborescens Lam.

A shrub, which eventually becomes a tree 10-20 feet in height. Coming, as it does, from Siberia and Manchuria, it is extremely hardy. A rather sparse foliage is offset by the attractive yellow-green twigs with prominent lenticels. The leaves have 4-6 pairs of small, entire leaflets. It blossoms in May or June; the small, yellow, pea-like flowers are borne singly on slender, downy pedicels, several from each of the enlarged, scaly buds on shoots of the previous year. The fruit is a pod, 1½-2 inches long, on a slender stalk of about the same length, containing several pea-like seeds. Frequently cultivated for ornamental purposes. Should be planted in a sunny situation if possible.

Clammy Locust
Robinia viscosa Vent.

A small, rough-barked tree native to the southern Appalachian Mountains, but frequently planted in the north. It derives its name from the characteristic of the dark red-brown branchlets, the fruit pod, and usually the leaf-petioles and flower-peduncles being densely glandular-viscid. It differs further from the Black Locust in having 13-25 leaflets, which are usually pubescent beneath, and in the flowers being pink and borne in dense, rather upright racemes.

China-tree
Koelreuteria paniculata Laxm.

A small tree from China, Korea and Japan. The leaves may be as much as 14 inches long, with 7-15 ovate to oblong-ovate leaflets, which are coarsely and irregularly crenate-serrate, often lobed or deeply cut into secondary leaflets at the base. Chiefly valued ornamentally for its many-flowered, broad panicles of yellow blossoms which appear in July and August. The flowers have the calyx deeply divided into 5 unequal lobes; petals 4, lanceolate, clawed, with 2 upturned appendages at the base; stamens 8, sometimes less, with long filaments. The fruit is a bladdery, dehiscent capsule, 1½-2 inches long, with papery walls, containing 3 roundish, black seeds. The winter-buds are small, with 2 outer scales; the leaf-scars are rather large, shield-shaped, with 3 compound bundle-scars, forming a single, jagged, irregular series. Not particular as to soil, but prefers a sunny situation. Probably short-lived. Occasionally killed back in severe winters. Also, but incorrectly, called the **Varnish-tree** and **Pride of India.**

bb. *Leaves opposite.*

Bladder Nut
Staphylea trifolia I.

Seldom tree-like, but it does form an upright shrub to a height of 15 feet. It occurs throughout the state, but is more common in the Lower Peninsula, where it frequents river-banks. Several characteristics readily serve to distinguish it. The bark is a greenish gray, with linear, white fissures. The leaves are trifoliate, as in the Hop-tree, but the leaflets are finely serrate, pubescent beneath, and they are not glandular-dotted. Also, the flowers come earlier, in April or May, and they are perfect, white, bell-shaped, and hang in drooping, compound racemes. The fruit is altogether unlike that of the Hop-tree, being a bladder-like, membranous capsule, 1-1½ inches long, 2-3-lobed, containing a few bony, brown, shining seeds, which break loose when mature and rattle about when the pod is shaken. The winter-buds are ovoid, glabrous, with 4 blunt scales; the leaf-scars are half-round, with 3 (or 5-7) bundle-scars. Sometimes planted for ornamental purposes, when it improves greatly under cultivation, growing more luxuriantly and flowering more profusely.

Elder
Sambucus (Tourn.) L.

The Elders are thrifty shrubs, 5-15 feet in height, which are readily distinguished by their 5-11 leaflets, which are serrate on the margin, and by their stout, pithy branches, which are swollen at the nodes and are more or less warty. Two species are native to the state.

The **Common Elder,** *Sambucus canadensis* L., occurs throughout the state, following settlements, and is abundant on the borders of streams, in moist places generally and along fences, often growing in large numbers in a place.

The **Red-berried Elder,** *Sambucus racemosa* L., is more northern in its range, occupies the drier situations and frequents the shade of other plants.

The two species may be distinguished as follows. The Common Elder has usually 7 leaflets; the flowers appear from June until August in great profusion, in flat, spreading, compound cymes, 5-8 inches across; the berry-like drupes are blue to black, with crimson flesh and pleasant taste; the pith is white; and the winter-buds are small, conical, greenish or brown. The Red-berried Elder has usually 5 leaflets; the flowers appear in April and May, in narrow, pyramidal cymes; the drupes are bright red, with yellow flesh and unpleasant taste; the pith is orange to red-brown; and the winter-buds are large, ovoid, purplish. The Common Elder, when in full bloom, is a sight to behold. Its fruit is eagerly sought by the birds, and it is esteemed for pies, generally mixed with some other acid fruit; both flowers and fruit are employed in making wine. A golden-leaved variety, *aurea* Cowell, is frequently seen in cultivation. A variety of the Red-berried Elder, *Sambucus racemosa*, v. *laciniata* Koch, with regularly and deeply dissected leaves, is seen in Clare County, and perhaps elsewhere.

THE STRUCTURE AND IDENTIFICATION OF OUR COMMON WOODS

Common as wood is in its varied forms and uses, comparatively few people are able to distinguish our familiar trees when sawed into lumber and fashioned into houses, furniture and other manufactured products. Yet each wood has characteristics of color, odor, graining, weight, hardness, strength and minute structure peculiar to itself which distinguish it from other woods.

The value of each kind of wood for building purposes and every other use is determined to a large extent by its characteristics. These, taken in connection with the available supply of any particular timber in the country, govern the value or cost of that timber in the lumber market. So certain trees, like oak and cedar, because of their durability in contact with the soil, make admirable fence posts; spruce and the broad-leaved white birch and cottonwood possess structural qualities adapting them to the manufacture of paper pulp; hickory, very strong, tough and straight-grained, has long been valued for carriage- and wagon-stock and tool-handles. Many examples might here be cited to show how various woods are peculiarly adapted to certain uses to a greater extent than are others. Again, some species, on account of our wasteful methods of lumbering, failure to provide means of reproduction and lack of restriction as to particular uses, have become so scarce that substitutes are offered in the markets to take their places. To such an extent has this become true that methods are in use to imitate the grain and color of some of the more depleted but valuable woods. Thus birch enters very largely into the composition of a great deal of so-called modern mahogany furniture, and cheap woods are often grained to imitate quarter-sawed white oak.

With the great variety of useful woods to be found in any lumber yard, it is important that consumers of wood in any form should be able to identify the different kinds offered so that they may choose those woods best suited to their particular needs and that they may obtain them and not lumber similar in appearance but otherwise of inferior qualifications.

that some are hard and some soft and that some season rapidly and without injury while others have a tendency to check and split. The wide medullary rays of the oak explain the pleasing effect of the wood when quarter-sawed and polished to bring out the grain. The peculiar undulations of the growth rings sometimes found in the maple produce the "bird's-eye" markings which make the lumber so prized in the manufacture of furniture. It is our purpose to consider briefly the structure of a tree trunk and the various elements of the woody tissues.

If we should go into a forest where felling operations are in progress or into a sawmill where there are unsawed logs, we would have an opportunity to examine the smooth-cut end of a mature log. We would note that it exhibits several well-defined areas or layers. The first layer on the outside is probably rough externally and dark-colored. This is the bark, (*a,* fig. VIII), a protective covering to the inner woody tissues. The outer portion of the bark of a forest tree is dead tissue which is stretched and fissured as the tree grows in diameter, while the inner portion is live tissue, serving to conduct food materials up and down the trunk. In some kinds of trees the bark is quite thick, in others very thin. This factor, together with color and external appearance, makes the bark, when present, of considerable value in the determination of woods. At the center of the log is a small cylinder of loose tissue less than one-fourth of an inch in diameter, the pith (*g,* fig. VIII). Lying between the bark and the pith is the wood. In some kinds of trees, like the balsam fir and the hemlock, the wood is all of one color. In others, it consists of two parts distinct from each other in color. The outer portion is called sapwood (*b,* fig. VIII). It is recently formed wood and serves chiefly in the living tree to conduct the sap, or water which is taken up by the roots, to the leaves. The width of the sapwood varies with different species and with different individuals of the same species. In very young trees all the wood is sapwood. As the sapwood grows older, the tissue composing it becomes choked so as to prevent the further passage of sap. This choking of the water-conducting elements is usually followed by the death of the tissues, which thenceforth serve only as a support to the rest of the tree, holding up its great weight and making it rigid enough to resist strong winds. Accompanying this change there is frequently a darkening of the elements, the tissues become dry and are then called heartwood (*c*, fig. VIII). Since only a portion of the sapwood, the older part, is thus modified, there is always the younger portion left to conduct the sap. The sapwood and heartwood differ not only in color, but also in durability. In some species only the heartwood is suitable for sawing into lumber, being, as a rule, harder, heavier and drier than sapwood. In other cases where pliability or elasticity is required, as, for example,

IX. TYPICAL WOOD ELEMENTS, DIAGRAMMATIC

GREATLY ENLARGED

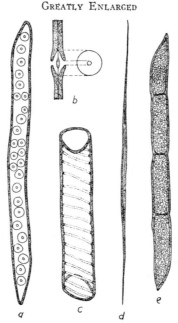

a. Tracheid, showing bordered pits.
b. Scheme of bordered pit in section and surface views.
c. Segment or single cell of a vessel, showing spiral thickenings.
d. Wood or bast fiber.
e. Group of wood-parenchyma cells.

in hickory and ash which are used in making baskets or for handles of rakes, hoes and golf clubs, the sapwood is more valuable than the heartwood.

Separating the wood from the bark is a very thin layer, the cambium. From this layer is added new wood on the outside of that already formed and new bark on the inside of the old bark. It is by this process that the trunk grows in diameter. Each year the cambium adds a new layer of wood, sapwood, to the circumference of the tree. These layers appear on the end of the log as concentric rings. They are called annual, yearly or growth rings (*h,* fig. VIII). In maple, birch, white pine and many other woods there is no sharp distinction between the wood formed in the spring and that formed in summer. In other cases the wood which is formed in the spring, when growth is most rapid, differs in nature from the harder and denser wood formed later in the season. The oaks, elms and hickories present clearly defined layers. The two layers are called early or spring wood and late or summer wood. The presence or absence of well-defined spring and summer wood is an important factor in distinguishing and naming the different woods; in fact, the grain or figure of some kinds of lumber depends entirely upon the difference between spring and summer wood.

Radiating from the center of the trunk toward the bark, like the spokes of a wheel, are slender but more or less distinct lines. These are the medullary rays (*i,* fig. VIII). Medullary rays serve two functions; they are paths for the conduction of food materials between bark and wood or wood and bark, and they bind the trunk together from pith to bark. Woods differ in the size and number of medullary rays present, the rays being inconspicuous in some and very prominent in others. If an oak log be cut along any of its many radii, i.e., parallel to one of the lines of the medullary rays, the beautiful "flakes" of the quarter-sawed oak are exposed to view. In other trees, like the maples, the medullary rays may be so small as to escape notice. But whether prominent or inconspicuous, the medullary rays help greatly to make up the pattern which often readily and surely distinguishes one wood from another.

We have learned from our superficial inspection that a tree is not a simple structure, but a complex organism composed of several kinds of tissues, each having its particular function in the life of the tree. In order to continue our study further, it is necessary that we use a magnifier or a compound microscope. If we examine the smoothly cut end of a piece of wood, or, better, a very thin shaving, we find that it is seemingly made up of a network of holes or pores held together by chains of solid tissue, in appearance resembling the chambers of a honeycomb. All trees, all tissues composing trees, are made up of millions of these units, just as a wall is built of bricks and mortar. These units making up the bodies of trees are called cells (fig. IX). A cell may be considered to be of the nature of a box, but so small is it that it is usually indistinguishable to the unaided eye. The walls of the box or cell are composed for the most part of a woody substance called cellulose; we call them cell-walls. In young cells, such as we find in the actively growing parts of trees, the whole cavity of the cell is filled with a slimy substance called protoplasm. The protoplasm is the living substance of the tree; where there is protoplasm, there is life and growth. As the cells grow older and larger, the protoplasm does not continue to fill the whole cavity within the cell-walls, but forms only a thin lining around the walls. Finally it disappears altogether, leaving the dead cell-walls intact, making the substance called wood. The cells composing wood are not all the same shape or size, but vary greatly according to the function which they serve in the life of the tree. Because of the great variety of the cells composing it, wood takes on various characters of structure, graining and coloring, which are distinctive for each kind of wood and which greatly aid in distinguishing the various kinds from one another.

The wood of conifers is very regular and simple, consisting mainly of cells of one sort. It is this uniformity of structure which makes the wood of conifers valuable for so many purposes. These cells are called tracheids (a, fig. IX). They are vertical, elongated, tapering tubes, one-twentieth to one-fifth of an inch in length, with closed ends and a relatively large cavity. The pointed ends of the tracheids overlap one another in a dovetailed fashion, breaking the joints and making the wood much stronger than it would be otherwise. They are further identified by the presence of pits or pores in their walls which serve as waterways between the tubes. These pits (b, fig. IX) appear as if made up of two circles, and they are for this reason called bordered pits. The other cells making up the wood of conifers are the ray cells. These extend horizontally, and in a radial-section appear as tiers of regular, brick-shaped cells. The cells communciate with one another by numerous pits in the walls. In certain genera the medullary rays are bordered by tracheids similar to the ordinary wood tracheids, but designated as ray tracheids. In one of the pines the ray tracheids have teeth-like projections from the walls, which are useful in identifying this species. Scattered here and there on the cross-section of some coniferous woods are to be seen irregular grayish or brownish dots. These are resin ducts and are especially well-represented in the pines. Resin ducts are openings between cells containing resin, which is manufactured by certain trees. If one cuts a limb from a pine tree, the cut surface will very quickly become sticky with the resin which oozes from these ducts. On a warm day in the pine woods the resin is quite apparent by its fragrant odor. Some woods have present also certain cells or groups of cells which produce resin, which gives them a distinctive appearance, and therefore they are called resin cells. Their presence or absence aids in the determination of certain woods.

The wood of broad-leaved trees is much more complex in structure than the wood of conifers. Instead of being made up essentially of one kind of cells, tracheids, as is the case in the coniferous woods just mentioned, the wood of broad-leaved trees is composed of several kinds of cells. If we examine the cut end of a red oak branch we notice that the spring wood contains many comparatively large openings which are visible even to the unaided eye. These openings are called pores; they are cross-sections of open tubes or vessels or tracheae which run up and down the trunk of the tree and out into the branches and twigs. In the beginning they resemble the tracheids of conifers, i.e., they are made up of separate and distinct cells. Later, the end walls of the cells which meet endwise are absorbed, leaving a continuous series of connected cells or a tube (c, fig. IX). These tubes or vessels serve in the living tree as water-carriers. For the sidewise conduction of fluids, the vessels are usually abundantly pitted with bordered pits, but the pits are somewhat smaller than those commonly found in the tracheids of coniferous woods. Furthermore, it is very common for vessels, especially the smaller ones, to be marked with spiral thickenings on their interior walls. The scalariform perforations present in the end partitions of the vessels of a few woods, as seen in radial-section, are sometimes confused with the true spiral thickenings just mentioned. This point may be definitely determined by an inspection of tangential- as well as radial-sections. Tyloses also occur in the vessels of many of the broad-leaved woods, sometimes being visible to the unaided eye. Tyloses are usually rather thin-walled cells which protrude into the cavities of the vessels, where they divide rapidly and grow, sometimes filling the entire cavity and plugging the vessels so as to prevent further conduction of fluids. The value of white oak for cooperage is increased by tyloses, which are especially abundant in the vessels of this wood. They are also well-represented in the locust, in this instance being rather thick-walled.

It is convenient to divide broad-leaved woods into two groups, which are characterized by the size and arrangement of the vessels. In some species of wood the vessels which are formed later in the season are much smaller than those formed earlier. A wood of this kind, with its large pores collected into a row or band in each growth ring, is spoken of as ring-porous. In other woods, the pores are more nearly uniform in size in both spring and summer wood. They are designated as diffuse-porous woods. The wood of the maple is of this character. In many of the diffuse-porous woods the pores are too small to be seen with the unaided eye, and in some cases they may even be indistinct when viewed with a magnifier. They should not, however, because of this, be confused with the non-porous coniferous woods, which they may resemble.

Tracheids in the wood of broad-leaved trees are subordinate elements. They are much smaller and less uniform in size and shape than in conifers and are more abundant in the vicinity of the tubes or vessels. As in conifers, the tracheids have numerous bordered pits in their walls. In some cases, as in the wood of the ash, tracheids are absent.

Strength, hardness and toughness are given to broad-leaved woods principally by the wood fibers. These are slender, spindle-shaped, sharp-pointed cells with thick walls and narrow cavities (d, fig. IX). Usually they are provided with oblique, slit-like, simple pits. The wood fibers for the most part lie vertically side by side and parallel to one another, but in some woods, like the sycamore, they are more or less interwoven. This makes the wood cross-grained, difficult to work and hard to split.

While the medullary rays of coniferous woods are uniformly small and inconspicuous, they are often broad and prominent in broad-leaved woods. They are largest in the oak, where they may become twenty-five to seventy-five cells wide and several hundred cells high; between these broad rays are numerous smaller ones, mostly uniseriate and from one to twenty cells high. In the sycamore all the rays are broad, while in the beech only a portion of the rays are broad. Ray cells are usually elongated in the radial or horizontal direction and are then termed procumbent. Not infrequently, however, the marginal cells, as in the willow, are elongated vertically; cells of this kind are said to be upright. These differences in the character of the medullary rays are important means of identification.

Another kind of tissue which is more or less prominent in broad-leaved woods is wood parenchyma. Wood parenchyma consists of vertical groups of short cells, the end ones of each group tapering to a point (e, fig. IX). The cells of wood parenchyma resemble the cells of the medullary rays; the walls are invariably pitted with rounded, simple pits. The function of the wood parenchyma is the distribution and storage of the food products manufactured by the leaves. The occurrence of wood parenchyma on the cross-sections of different species is subject to more or less variation, making this feature of considerable importance in classifying woods. Commonly wood parenchyma is grouped around the pores or vessels. In the basswood it occurs in somewhat broken, tangential lines, forming, with the wood fibers, a tier-like arrangement of the wood elements. In the hickory it forms numerous, fine, concentric lines which are as distinct as the rays. In other woods it may be confined to several rows of cells at the outer limit of the growth ring.

As a final feature having some value in the identification of certain of the woods the so-called "pith flecks" are to be mentioned. They are common in many of our native woods, appearing as crescent-shaped, discolored patches on the cross-section and as brownish streaks running up and down the stem in longitudinal-section. Pith flecks are not a special kind of tissue, but are tunnels made by the larvae of a two-winged insect which lives in the cambium during the growing season. These pith flecks have been found to occur in only five families of trees in the United States, namely, the willow, birch, rose, maple and linden families. They are by no means constant in their occurrence; some stems have numerous pith flecks, while other stems of the same species from the same vicinity do not have them. Taken in conjunction with other characters, however, the presence of pith flecks in considerable numbers may aid in the identification of woods.

The subject of wood structure is one of absorbing interest to one who will but take a little trouble to go beneath the surface. Facts will be revealed which have hitherto lain hidden because of our usual cursory method of handling wood. Some practise may be necessary at first, a little patience may be needed at times, but success will be the reward of honest effort. In all identification work a very sharp knife or razor blade is necessary. Surfaces must be cut cleanly and smoothly, keeping always in mind that a bruised and broken surface reveals but little of the structure of the wood. Large pieces are not essential; even small cuts along the edge will often suffice. Twigs cut easier than seasoned boards and are frequently as instructive as the more mature wood. Wetting the cut surface will usually make the structural features more prominent. Instructive sections may be made with a very sharp knife or razor, or even with a plane, by cutting very thin pieces and mounting them in water or glycerin between two thin pieces of glass. The sections may even be colored to advantage by soaking them for a time in a dye, thus making certain features more evident. Transparent water colors such as are used in coloring photographs and prints are generally available and will be found to serve as well as the usual laboratory stains. The mounts may be examined with a magnifier by holding them between the eye and the light, or they may be viewed with a compound microscope. If the latter is employed, the sections of wood must be cut very thin and the customary thin cover-glass must be used between the wood-section and the microscope lens.

In the key to the woods which follows, it will be noticed that two large divisions have been made, one the porous woods, being the great mass of broad-leaved woods, the other the non-porous or coniferous woods. Porous woods have again been divided into

KEY TO THE WOODS*

In the following key, the Roman type calls attention to characters which may be readily distinguished by the unaided eye or by the use of a pocket magnifier, and should not be interpreted as indicating more important characters. The italics represent characters which can be studied only with a compound microscope.

The word in parenthesis indicates the section, cross-, radial-, tangential- or longitudinal-, which shows the point in question to greatest advantage.

For emphasis, the genus name is printed in capitals, as in the summer and winter keys to the genera, while the species name, when given, is printed in small letters.

Except for a few species too small to be lumbered or which are otherwise commercially unimportant, the key contains all of the woods native to Michigan; and in addition there have been added some half-dozen woods which are not native, but which are in common use by wood-working industries of the state.

  a. Pores (cross-) visible and conspicuous, at least with magnifier, i.e., *wood composed of three to six kinds of cells, which are not uniform in structure and usually not arranged in definite radial rows;* resin ducts and resin cells (cross-) absent; rays (cross-) for the most part conspicuous. (For aa, see p. 303)
    b. Growth rings (cross-) defined by zones of large pores in the spring wood alternating with the denser summer wood; pores (cross-) in summer wood small, or few and scattered. (For bb, see p. 297)
      c. Rays (cross-), or part of them, broad, easily distinguishable by the unaided eye at 3 feet distance; on close inspection, rays of two kinds, broad and fine.
        d. Pores (cross-) of summer wood arranged in radial rows or patches, frequently branched or fan-like; wood parenchyma (cross-) forming fine, concentric lines, usually visible with magnifier; *tyloses (longitudinal-) usually present, gum absent.*

---

*See page 18.

e. Pores (cross-) in summer wood individually distinct with magnifier, arranged chiefly in single, radial rows; pores (cross-) in spring wood usually crowded in a broad zone and becoming smaller outward, usually open....QUERCUS (RED-OAK GROUP)*, p. 323

ee. Pores (cross-) in summer wood not individually distinct with magnifier, arranged chiefly in fan-like patches; pores (cross-) in spring wood in a narrow zone of 1-3 rows, the transition to small pores of summer wood abrupt. usually closed *with tyloses*....
.....QUERCUS (WHITE-OAK GROUP)*, p. 323

dd. Pores (cross-) of summer wood not arranged in radial rows or patches, but joined, forming short or more or less extended, tangential lines; wood parenchyma (cross-) not forming fine concentric lines; *tyloses (longitudinal-) absent, gum present.*

e. Heartwood red-brown; wood heavy and hard........
.... GLEDITSIA triacanthos

ee. Heartwood pale yellow; wood light and soft........
........................AILANTHUS glandulosa

cc. Rays (cross-) not broad, indistinguishable by the unaided eye at 3 feet distance; on close inspection, rays of one kind, all fine.

d. Pores (cross-) of summer wood small and inconspicuous, or when visible single, grouped, or forming short, broken lines, but never forming extended radial or tangential lines.

e. Rays (cross-) clearly distinct to the unaided eye at 6-12 inches distance; growth rings for the most part wide to very wide (variable in *Gymnocladus*); rays (radial-) mostly high and prominent.

f. Pores (cross-) of late summer wood in large groups *of 6-many, joined tangentially by wood parenchyma,* often forming tangential lines plainly visible to the

*The woods of the species belonging to this group are so similar that they are not readily distinguishable, and in the present key it is impracticable to attempt more than a group classification.

unaided eye at a distance of 6-12 inches; *tyloses* (*longitudinal-*) *very abundant, densely plugging the vessels* .... ROBINIA pseudo-acacia

ff. Pores (cross-) of late summer wood single, or in small groups *of 3-6, not joined tangentially by wood parenchyma,* never forming tangential lines which are plainly visible to the unaided eye at a distance of 6-12 inches; *tyloses* (*longitudinal-*) *absent or only fairly abundant, never plugging the vessels.*

    g. Heartwood orange-yellow to brown, becoming russet-brown upon exposure; rays (cross-) in heartwood light brown, the thicker ones visible to the unaided eye at a distance of 2 feet; *tyloses* (*longitudinal-*) *present* .... MORUS rubra

    gg. Heartwood bright cherry red to reddish brown; rays (cross-) in heartwood white, not visible to the unaided eye at a distance of 2 feet; *tyloses* (*longitudinal-*) *absent or rare, but gummy substance present in vessels.....................* ....GYMNOCLADUS dioica

ee. Rays (cross-) not clearly distinct to the unaided eye at 6-12 inches distance, inconspicuous to microscopic; growth rings (cross-) for the most part narrow; rays (radial-) not high and prominent.

    f. Pores (cross-) of summer wood *solitary, rarely grouped,* not forming short, tangential lines; wood parenchyma (cross-) forming more or less continuous, tangential lines as distinct, or nearly so, as the rays..........................CARYA*, p. 319

    ff. Pores (cross-) of summer wood *usually grouped,* for the most part forming short, tangential lines; wood parenchyma (cross-) not forming continuous, tangential lines.

---

*Identification of the species of *Carya* from wood characters alone is ordinarily not possible.

g. Rays (cross-) distinct without magnifier; wood light and soft, with spicy odor and taste; *tyloses (longitudinal-) common*......................
.....................SASSAFRAS variifolium

gg. Rays (cross-) indistinct without magnifier; wood mostly heavy and hard, without characteristic odor or taste; *tyloses (longitudinal-) absent.*

   h. Pores (cross-) of spring wood 1-2 rows deep, forming a narrow zone not over one-fourth the width of the growth ring.................
.........FRAXINUS pennsylvanica lanceolata

   hh. Pores (cross-) of spring wood 3-5 rows deep, forming a broad zone one-third to one-half the width of the growth ring.

     i. Pores (cross-) of summer wood *joined by wood parenchyma,* forming short or more or less extended, tangential lines; wood hard and strong.

      j. Lines of pores and wood parenchyma (cross-) in summer wood short and broken, mostly near the periphery of the growth ring (occasionally absent *or very indistinct*)
..........FRAXINUS americana, p. 331

      jj. Lines of pores and wood parenchyma (cross-) in summer wood long, more or less extended, usually well distributed through the growth ring......................
..............FRAXINUS pennsylvanica
..............FRAXINUS quadrangulata

     ii. Pores (cross-) of summer wood *not joined by wood parenchyma,* rarely forming tangential lines; wood soft and weak.................
.....................FRAXINUS nigra

dd. Pores (cross-) of summer wood small, but distinct, grouped or more or less confluent, or joined by wood parenchyma, to form wavy or branching, more or less extended, radial or tangential lines.

   e. Rays (cross-) clearly distinct to the unaided eye at 6-12 inches distance.

— 294 —

f. Rays (cross-), or some of them, and pores (cross-) of spring wood distinct at a distance of 3 feet; *tyloses (longitudinal-) absent*.....................
.....................AILANTHUS glandulosa

ff. Rays (cross-) and pores (cross-) of spring wood not distinct at a distance of 3 feet; *tyloses (longitudinal-) common to abundant.*

g. Heartwood yellowish or grayish; pores (cross-) in summer wood arranged in more or less continuous, wavy, tangential lines..............
.....................CELTIS occidentalis

gg. Heartwood yellow-brown to brown; pores (cross-) in summer wood usually not arranged in continuous lines, but grouped to form short, wavy bands.

h. Rays (cross-) clearly visible to the unaided eye at a distance of 6-12 inches; wood not yielding a yellow stain when rubbed with a wet, white handkerchief.

i. Wood extremely hard, like horn; *all pores (cross-) of the heartwood completely filled with tyloses* ...... ROBINIA pseudo-acacia

ii. Wood not extremely hard, not like horn; *pores (cross-) of heartwood only partially filled with tyloses*...........MORUS rubra

hh. Rays (cross-) barely visible without magnifier; wood yielding a yellow stain when rubbed with a wet, white handkerchief...................
.....................MACLURA pomifera

ee. Rays (cross-) not clearly distinct to the unaided eye at 6-12 inches distance, barely visible without magnifier.

f. Pores (cross-) of summer wood arranged in radial, branching lines (when very crowded, radial arrangement somewhat obscured); pores (cross-) of spring wood plainly visible to the unaided eye at a distance of 2 feet, *strongly oval or elliptical,* occupying nearly half the growth ring.....................
.....................CASTANEA dentata, p. 327

— 295 —

ff. Pores (cross-) of summer wood arranged, *or joined by wood parenchyma*, to form short, wavy or branching, tangential lines; pores (cross-) of spring wood not plainly visible to the unaided eye at a distance of 2 feet, *not strongly oval nor elliptical,* not occupying nearly half the growth ring.

g. Wood light and soft; pores (cross-) of spring wood in several rows, forming a broad-porous ring; tangential lines of pores (cross-) in summer wood short, confined mostly to the outer portion of the growth ring; large pores (cross-) containing glistening tyloses....CATALPA speciosa ....CATALPA bignonioides

gg. Wood fairly heavy and hard; pores (cross-) of spring wood mostly in a single row (or 3-many in *Ulmus fulva*), forming usually a narrow ring; tangential lines of pores (cross-) in summer wood long and conspicuous, throughout the summer wood; large pores (cross-) not containing glistening tyloses.

h. Pores (cross-) of spring wood in 3-many rows; pores (cross-) of summer wood small, forming thin, rather broken and disconnected, tangential lines, not strongly wavy; heartwood chocolate-brown....................... ULMUS fulva

hh. Pores (cross-) of spring wood usually in a single row, or nearly so; pores (cross-) of summer wood large, forming broad, mostly connected, tangential lines, strongly wavy; heartwood light brown or red.

i. Pores (cross-) of spring wood large, plainly visible to the unaided eye at a distance of 6-9 inches, forming a continuous row; texture coarse; wood hard to split................. ....ULMUS americana, p. 325

ii. Pores (cross-) of spring wood small, not visible to the unaided eye at a distance of 6-9 inches, not forming a continuous row, but the

larger ones few and rather widely separated; texture medium; wood fairly easy to split.
....................ULMUS racemosa

bb. Growth rings (cross-) not defined by zones of large pores in the spring wood, but pores all the same size, or nearly so, scattered more or less evenly through the growth ring, or occasionally more numerous and very often somewhat larger in the spring wood.

c. Rays (cross-) usually plainly visible to the unaided eye at a distance of 6-9 inches.

d. Rays (cross-) uniform, all of them more or less equal in size. (*Pyrus coronaria* and the genus *Crataegus* apparently belong here; but the woods vary so greatly and are of so little importance commercially that no attempt has been made to incorporate them within the key.)

e. Wood parenchyma (cross-) forming continuous or somewhat broken, tangential lines or bands, scarcely visible with magnifier; wood, for the most part, light and soft (exception, *Cornus*).

f. Heartwood with distinct greenish tinge; wood elements (cross-) not alternating with parenchyma elements in a tier-like arrangement, *but confined to 2-4 rows of flattened cells at the outer limit of the growth ring; tyloses (longitudinal-) present*.......
...............LIRIODENDRON tulipifera, p. 325

ff. Heartwood without distinct greenish tinge; wood elements (cross-) alternating with parenchyma elements in a tier-like arrangement; *tyloses (longitudinal-) absent.*

g. Wood light and soft; growth rings (cross-) regular; heartwood light brown to nearly white; rays barely visible to the unaided eye at a distance of 6 inches; *vessels (tangential-) with spirals*...
....................TILIA americana, p. 331

gg. Wood very heavy and hard; growth rings (cross-) somewhat sinuous; heartwood red-brown to brown; rays distinctly visible to the unaided

eye at a distance of 6 inches; *vessels* (*tangential-*)
without spirals ....CORNUS florida
.... CORNUS alternifolia

ee. Wood parenchyma (cross-) not forming tangential
lines nor bands; wood moderately heavy and hard.

f. Heartwood rich red-brown or wine color; rays
(radial-) for the most part lighter in color than
background; *ray cells* (*radial-*) *about as long as
high; vessels* (*longitudinal-*) *plugged at intervals
with dark red gum.*

g. Rays (cross-) distinct to the unaided eye; pith
flecks (cross-) usually absent; pores (cross-)
large and conspicuous with magnifier.

h. Pores (cross-) of the spring wood larger and
more numerous than those of the summer wood;
rays (radial-) darker than background; *larger
rays* (*tangential-*) *3-4-seriate;* wood rather
soft........................PRUNUS nigra

hh. Pores (cross-) of the spring wood neither
noticeably larger nor more numerous than those
of the summer wood; rays (radial-) lighter
than background; *larger rays* (*tangential-*)
6-8-seriate; wood rather hard................
...................PRUNUS serotina, p. 329

gg. Rays (cross-) barely visible to the unaided eye;
pith flecks (cross-) usually present, often prominent; pores (cross-) rather small and inconspicuous, even with magnifier......................
......................PRUNUS pennsylvanica

ff. Heartwood light brown to reddish; rays (radial-)
for the most part darker in color than background
(exception, *Acer negundo*); *ray cells* (*radial-*)
about twice as long as high; vessels (*longitudinal-*)
not plugged at intervals with dark red gum.

g. Heartwood cream-white, with reddish tinge;
rays (radial-) lighter than background; growth
rings (cross-) usually very wide..............
..............................ACER negundo

gg. Heartwood light red-brown to decidedly reddish;
rays (radial-) darker than background; growth
rings (cross-) usually moderately wide to narrow.

h. Larger rays (*tangential-*) *4-6-seriate,* for the
most part broader than the pores (cross-);
pith flecks absent or rare; growth rings more
or less distinct; wood very heavy and hard....
.....................ACER saccharum, p. 329
....................ACER saccharum nigrum

hh. Larger rays (*tangential-*) *2-3-,* or *occasionally*
4-seriate, mostly narrower than the pores
(cross-); pith flecks present, often abundant;
growth rings for the most part indistinct; wood
rather light and soft.

i. Pith flecks (cross-) usually rather large,
more or less abundant and generally conspicuous........................ACER rubrum
....................ACER pennsylvanicum

ii. Pith flecks (cross-) usually small, neither
abundant nor conspicuous (sometimes abundant) .... ACER saccharinum

dd. Rays (cross-) not uniform, but some of them conspicuously broad.

e. Growth rings (cross-) strongly sinuous; heartwood
white, not showing (longitudinal-) marked graining;
broad rays (cross-) confined to short radii of the
concave portions of the growth rings..............
.........................CARPINUS caroliniana

ee. Growth rings (cross-) regular, not strongly sinuous;
heartwood brownish to reddish, showing (longitud-
inal-) marked graining; broad rays (cross-) uniformly
distributed, not confined to short radii.

f. Rays (cross-) mostly all broad; *vessels (longitud-*
inal-) with spirals; rays (tangential-) between
broad rays rarely or never uniseriate; wood cross-
grained, difficult to split.......................
................PLATANUS occidentalis, p. 327

— 299 —

ff. Rays (cross-) only part of them broad; *vessels (longitudinal-) without spirals; rays (tangential-) between broad rays mostly uniseriate;* wood mostly straight-grained, easy to split....................
......................FAGUS grandifolia, p. 321

cc. Rays (cross-)' mostly not plainly visible to the unaided eye at a distance of 6-9 inches, indistinct to microscopic.

d. Pores (cross-), or some of them, plainly visible to the unaided eye at a distance of a foot, mostly conspicuous in the spring wood, and for this reason often approaching characteristics of ring-porous wood; *tyloses (longitudinal-) abundant.*

e. Heartwood chocolate-brown, heavy and hard, with mild odor, especially when wet; *squarish crystals in cells of wood parenchyma (longitudinal-) common...*
..........................JUGLANS nigra, p. 318

ee. Heartwood light chestnut-brown, light and soft, without pronounced odor, even when wet; *crystals not present in wood parenchyma.*

f. *Rays (tangential-) mostly uniseriate, slender-tapering;* wood odorless............JUGLANS cinerea

ff. *Rays (tangential-) mostly 2-3-seriate, blunt-tapering;* wood sometimes with slight odor like kerosene .... CATALPA

dd. Pores (cross-) not visible to the unaided eye at a distance of a foot, mostly well-distributed throughout growth ring; *tyloses (longitudinal-) absent to few or common, but not abundant.*

e. *Vessels (longitudinal-) with spirals.* (Note: If this character is unknown, proceed on the assumption that the wood may be under either e or ee, and seek it by elimination through the use of other characters.)

f. Heartwood pale yellow to whitish; wood light and soft; *rays (tangential-) all alike, uniseriate throughout, or nearly so; tyloses (longitudinal-) few*.................AESCULUS hippocastanum

— 300 —

ff. Heartwood brownish, reddish or dark red-brown; wood heavy and hard (exception, *Pyrus americana*); *rays (tangential-) not all alike, 1-6-seriate; tyloses (longitudinal-) absent.*

    g. Pores (cross-) abundant or fairly abundant, rather evenly distributed; growth rings (cross-) not sinuous; pith flecks (cross-) usually present; wood parenchyma (cross-) not forming distinct, tangential markings.

        h. Growth rings narrow; cross-section with curious, sinuous-mottled appearance; sapwood whitish...................PYRUS americana

        hh. Growth rings rather wide; cross-section without sinuous-mottled appearance; sapwood yellow to light brown.

            i. Wood heavy and very hard; sapwood light brown........AMELANCHIER canadensis

            ii. Wood light and soft; sapwood yellow......
..................PRUNUS pennsylvanica

    gg. Pores (cross-) not abundant, scattered singly or in remote, radial lines; growth rings (cross-) sinuous; pith flecks (cross-) usually absent; wood parenchyma (cross-) forming distinct, tangential markings..................OSTRYA virginiana

ee. *Vessels (longitudinal-) without spirals.* (See note under e.)

    f. Rays (tangential-) all alike, *uniseriate throughout or nearly so;* wood for the most part light and soft.

        g. Pores (cross-) of summer wood markedly smaller and fewer in number than pores of spring wood, often arranged in irregular, tangential lines; wood (radial-) without silky luster; *rays (radial-) with both upright and procumbent cells*
.... SALIX

        gg. Pores (cross-) of summer wood not markedly smaller and fewer in number than pores of spring wood, not arranged in tangential lines; wood (radial-) with silky luster; *rays (radial-) with procumbent cells only*.......POPULUS*, p. 317

ff. Rays (tangential-) not all alike, or if so, *not uniseriate, but all or some of them 2-6-seriate;* wood mostly heavy and hard.

g. Growth rings (cross-) indistinct, or when present not indicative of annual seasons of growth.

h. Growth rings (cross-) very narrow and crowded together; pores (cross-) minute; rays (cross-) indistinct; *tyloses (longitudinal-) present;* heartwood pale yellow to gray-brown.....
........................NYSSA sylvatica

hh. Growth rings (cross-) wide, not crowded together; pores (cross-), or some of them, readily visible to the unaided eye at a distance of 6 inches; rays (cross-) fine, but distinct; *tyloses (longitudinal-) absent;* heartwood rich red-brown ....
..SWIETENIA mahogani (Mahogany), p. 333

gg. Growth rings (cross-) more or less distinct, indicating annual seasons of growth.

h. Rays (cross-) just visible to the unaided eye with close scrutiny; pores (cross-) more or less uniformly distributed, neither larger nor more numerous in the spring wood; wood heavy and hard.

i. Wood mostly cross-grained, difficult to split..
...................PYRUS malus (Apple)

ii. Wood mostly straight-grained, easy to split.

j. *Larger rays (tangential-) 3-5-seriate;* pores (cross-) hardly visible to the unaided eye with close scrutiny....BETULA lenta

*The woods of the Poplars are so similar that no attempt is made here to separate the different species.

jj. *Larger rays (tangential-) 1-2-, sometimes 3-seriate;* pores (cross-) visible to the unaided eye with close scrutiny..........
................BETULA lutea, p. 320

hh. Rays (cross-) not visible to the unaided eye with close scrutiny; pores (cross-) not uniformly distributed, but more numerous and somewhat larger in the spring wood; wood light and soft .... BETULA alba papyrifera

aa. Pores (cross-) neither visible nor conspicuous, even with magnifier, i.e., *wood composed mostly of one kind of cells (tracheids), which are uniform in structure and arranged in definite, radial rows;* resin ducts and resin cells (cross-) often present, especially in the summer wood; rays (cross-) never conspicuous.

b. Resin ducts or resin cells or both (cross-) present, the former usually visible to the unaided eye, the latter for the most part prominent and more or less confluent, often forming conspicuous, tangential lines; *fusiform rays (tangential-) present* (absent in *Juniperus* and *Taxodium*).

c. Resin ducts and resin cells (cross-) scattered, singly or in groups, but never forming tangential lines; *fusiform rays (tangential-) present; rays (radial-) with tracheids.*

d. Heartwood distinct in color from sapwood; resin ducts (cross-) conspicuous, because of size or color; *fusiform rays (tangential-) broad and prominent, usually with 1-several large resin ducts.*

e. Resin ducts (cross-) few, widely scattered, inconspicuous to microscopic, *without tyloses;* wood without noticeable. resinous odor; heartwood light brown; *tracheids (longitudinal-) rarely with spirals*........
.........................LARIX laricina, p. 311

ee. Resin ducts (cross-) numerous, evenly scattered through the growth rings, more or less conspicuous, *with prominent tyloses;* wood with noticeable resinous odor; heartwood whitish, orange to reddish; *tracheids (longitudinal-) wholly without spirals.*

— 303 —

f. Transition (cross-) from spring wood to summer wood gradual, the growth rings distinguished by narrow lines of darker colored summer wood; wood light and soft, slightly resinous..................
..........................PINUS strobus, p. 309

ff. Transition (cross-) from spring wood to summer wood more or less abrupt, the growth rings distinguished by broad bands of darker colored summer wood; wood medium heavy and hard, strongly resinous.

g. Wood relatively light and soft, not highly resinous.

h. Resin ducts (cross-) large, the openings usually visible to the unaided eye, confined to the outer half of the growth rings; wood obtainable in large dimensions...........................
....PINUS ponderosa (Western Yellow Pine)

hh. Resin ducts (cross-) small, the openings not visible to the unaided eye, most numerous in the spring wood or in a wide band occupying the center of the growth rings; wood not obtainable in large dimensions......PINUS banksiana

gg. Wood relatively heavy and hard, mildly to strongly resinous.

h. Growth rings (cross-) narrow; summer wood (cross-) wide, occupying about half of the growth ring; resin ducts (cross-) large, the openings usually visible to the unaided eye; wood heavy and hard, strongly resinous ......
...........PINUS palustris (Longleaf Pine, Georgia Pine)

hh. Growth rings (cross-) fairly wide; summer wood (cross-) narrow, occupying less than half of the growth ring; resin ducts (cross-) small, the openings not visible to the unaided eye; wood rather light and soft, not strongly resinous..................PINUS resinosa, p. 309

dd. Heartwood not distinct in color from sapwood; resin ducts (cross-) not conspicuous, small or of same color as surrounding wood; *fusiform rays (tangential-) not prominent, but narrow, with only 1 small resin duct.*
  e. Resin ducts (cross-) scattered through both spring and summer wood, *with tyloses usually absent; pits (radial-) on the tangential walls of the summer wood chiefly confined to the outermost tracheid wall* ......
    ....PICEA canadensis, p. 311
  ee. Resin ducts (cross-) confined chiefly to the summer wood, *with tyloses present; pits (radial-) on the tangential walls of the summer wood not confined to the outermost wall, but usually numerous*............
    ....PICEA mariana
cc. Resin ducts (normally absent) and resin cells (cross-) not scattered, but more or less confluent, forming tangential lines; *fusiform rays (tangential-) absent; rays (radial-) chiefly or wholly without tracheids.*
  d. Wood with aromatic odor, especially when wet; resin cells inconspicuous; heartwood brown or red-brown to purplish, neither greasy nor waxy to the touch.
    e. Wood firm and compact, cutting smoothly across the grain; transition between spring wood and summer wood gradual; wood usually knotty, except in very small sizes, often streaked with white............
      ....JUNIPERUS virginiana, p. 315
    ee. Wood soft and more or less spongy, difficult to cut smoothly across the grain; transition between spring wood and summer wood abrupt; wood not knotty, not streaked with white...............................
      ....THUJA plicata (Western Red Cedar, Shinglewood)
  dd. Wood without aromatic odor; resin cells (to the eye in mass) conspicuous; heartwood dull yellow- to gray-brown, greasy or waxy to the touch.................
    TAXODIUM distichum (Bald Cypress, Cypress), p. 317
bb. Resin ducts (cross-) or resin cells (cross-) absent or few, if present not conspicuous, usually not forming tangential lines; *fusiform rays (tangential-) absent.*

c. Wood with mild odor like cedar oil, especially when wet; growth rings (cross-) wavy; wood spongy, difficult to cut smoothly across the grain; heartwood distinct in shade from the sapwood; *ray tracheids (radial-) wholly absent..* ....THUJA occidentalis, p. 315

cc. Wood without odor of cedar oil; growth rings (cross-) not wavy; wood not spongy, easy to cut smoothly across the grain; heartwood not distinct in shade from the sapwood (exception, *Sequoia*); *ray tracheids (radial-) present* (occasional only in *Sequoia*).

  d. Heartwood deep red-brown, with whitish sapwood; resin cells (cross-) numerous, readily visible with magnifier; transition (cross-) from spring wood to summer wood rather abrupt.....................................
.................SEQUOIA sempervirens (Redwood)

  dd. Heartwood pale brown to whitish, with sapwood of about the same color; resin cells (cross-) absent or few, not conspicuous even with magnifier; transition (cross-) from spring wood to summer wood rather gradual (exception, *Tsuga canadensis*).

    e. Transition (cross-) from spring wood to summer wood abrupt; wood with rancid odor, especially when wet, slivery (tangential-) and hard to work, inclined to split apart between growth rings.................
........................TSUGA canadensis, p. 313

    ee. Transition (cross-) from spring wood to summer wood rather gradual; wood without rancid odor, not splintery (tangential-) and fairly easy to work, not inclined to split apart between growth rings.

      f. Abnormal resin passages often present, forming tangential lines in the summer wood; *ray tracheids (radial-) prominent;* small black checks common...
........TSUGA heterophylla (Western Hemlock)

      ff. Abnormal resin passages usually not present; *ray tracheids (radial-) not prominent, occasional;* small black checks not present....ABIES balsamea, p. 313

WOOD STUDIES

(Descriptions and Illustrations of Selected Types)

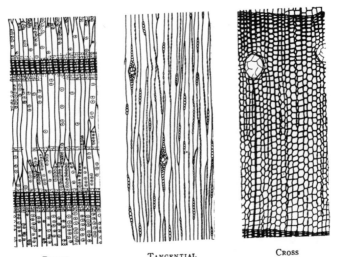

RADIAL   TANGENTIAL   CROSS

Sections of wood of Pinus strobus, x 33

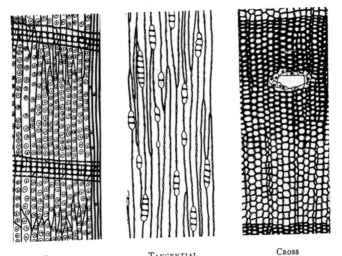

RADIAL   TANGENTIAL   CROSS

Sections of wood of Pinus resinosa, x 82

White Pine

Pinus strobus L.

CHARACTERISTICS.—Bark thick, dark gray, shallowly fissured into broad, scaly ridges; sapwood thin, whitish; heartwood clear yellow to light brown, turning red on exposure to the atmosphere; non-porous; growth rings wide, distinct; transition from spring wood to summer wood gradual; rays very faint without resin ducts, the fusiform rays few; resin ducts numerous evenly scattered through the growth rings, with prominent tyloses resin cells wholly absent; tracheids wholly without spirals.

QUALITIES.—Very light in weight, 27 pounds per cubic foot, seasoned; soft; rather weak; warps very little; moderately durable when exposed; very close- and straight-grained; easily worked; splits readily, but nails well.

USES.—Doors, window-sashes, interior finish and other carpentry, patterns, cabinetwork, matches, boxes, etc.; the most generally useful of all American woods.

Red Pine. Norway Pine

Pinus resinosa Ait.

CHARACTERISTICS.—Bark thick, red-brown, shallowly fissured into broad, flat ridges; sapwood thin, yellow to white heartwood pale red; non-porous; growth rings fairly wide and distinct; transition from spring wood to summer wood more or less abrupt; rays numerous, faintly distinct, with fusiform rays few and these chiefly rather low and broad; resin ducts numerous evenly scattered through the rings, with prominent tyloses; resin cells absent; tracheids without spirals.

QUALITIES.—Rather light in weight, 31 pounds per cubic foot, seasoned; fairly soft; fairly strong; warps moderately; not durable when exposed; straight- and very close-grained; easily worked; splits readily, but nails well.

USES.—Piles, flooring, sheathing, freight cars, poles, masts etc.

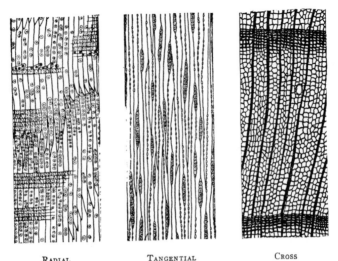

RADIAL   TANGENTIAL   CROSS

Sections of wood of Larix laricina, x 53.

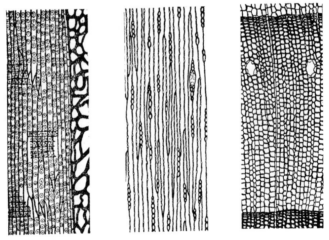

RADIAL   TANGENTIAL   CROSS

Sections of wood of Picea canadensis, x 70.

Tamarack

Larix laricina (DuRoi) Koch

CHARACTERISTICS.—Bark red-brown, scaly, without ridges; sapwood thin, nearly white; heartwood light brown; non-porous; growth rings rather broad and uniform, distinct; transition from spring wood to summer wood more or less abrupt; rays inconspicuous, many of them broadly fusiform, prominent and containing resin ducts; resin ducts few, widely scattered, without tyloses; resin cells present near outer limit of summer wood; tracheids mostly without spirals.

QUALITIES.—Of medium weight, 39 pounds per cubic foot, seasoned; hard; rather strong; warps but little; rather coarse-grained; very durable in contact with the soil; easy to work; splits readily.

USES.—Ship and boat timbers, telegraph poles, fence posts, railroad ties, etc.

White Spruce

Picea canadensis (Mill.) BSP.

CHARACTERISTICS.—Bark thin, light gray-brown, separating into thin, plate-like scales; sapwood scarcely distinguishable from the light yellow heartwood; non-porous; growth rings moderately wide to wide, distinct; transition from spring wood to the narrow summer wood somewhat gradual to rather abrupt; rays crowded, fine, fairly distinct with magnifier; resin ducts widely scattered or in small tangential groups, through both spring and summer wood, appearing as small whitish dots hardly visible without magnifier, usually without tyloses; resin cells absent; tracheids without spirals.

QUALITIES.—Light in weight, 25 pounds per cubic foot, seasoned; soft; weak; straight-grained; warps little; fairly durable when exposed; easy to plane and tolerably easy to saw; splits easily in nailing.

USES.—A principal source of paper pulp, boats and canoes, oars and paddles, ship timbers, building construction, silos, sounding boards, ladders, etc.

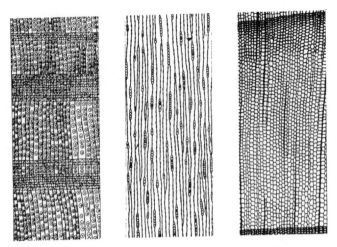

RADIAL   TANGENTIAL   CROSS

Sections of wood of Abies balsamea, x 36.

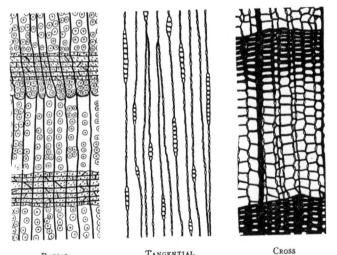

RADIAL   TANGENTIAL   CROSS

Sections of wood of Tsuga canadensis, x 74.

Balsam Fir

Abies balsamea (L.) Mill.

CHARACTERISTICS.—Bark pale gray-brown and marked by swollen resin chambers, becoming red-brown and somewhat roughened by small, scaly plates; sapwood thick, whitish; heartwood yellow-white to pale brown; non-porous; growth rings wide, indistinct; transition from spring wood to summer wood rather gradual; rays inconspicuous, never fusiform and mostly without resin ducts; both resin ducts and resin cells absent; tracheids without spirals.

QUALITIES.—Very light in weight, 23 pounds per cubic foot, seasoned; very soft; weak; warps little; coarse-grained; not durable in contact with the soil; works easily; splits readily.

USES.—Cut, sold and used with spruce and pine, boxes, crates, packing cases, sheathing, etc.

Hemlock

Tsuga canadensis (L.) Carr.

CHARACTERISTICS.—Bark thick, red-brown or grayish, deeply divided into narrow, rounded, scaly ridges; heartwood light red-brown, ill-smelling, with thin, darker colored sapwood; non-porous; growth rings rather wide, distinct; transition from spring wood to summer wood abrupt; rays numerous, obscure, none of them fusiform; resin ducts absent; resin cells few in number, but prominent; tracheids without spirals.

QUALITIES.—Rather light in weight, 26 pounds per cubic foot, seasoned; soft; fairly strong; warps little; checks badly; not durable when exposed; coarse- and crooked-grained; difficult to work, because brittle and splintery; splits easily, but holds nails well.

USES.—Dimension materials, timbers, joints, rafters, plank walks, laths, etc.

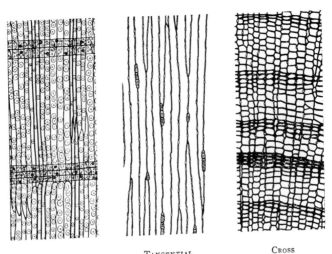

RADIAL   TANGENTIAL   CROSS

Sections of wood of Thuja occidentalis, x 113.

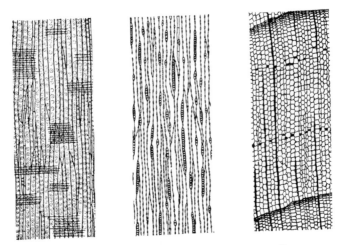

RADIAL   TANGENTIAL   CROSS

Sections of wood of Juniperus virginiana, x 42.

Arborvitae. White Cedar

Thuja occidentalis L.

CHARACTERISTICS.—Bark thin, light red-brown, slightly furrowed or deciduous in ragged strips; sapwood thin, whitish; heartwood pale yellow-brown; wood with mild odor like cedar oil; non-porous; growth rings narrow to wide, rather irregular and wavy, made fairly distinct by the narrow, denser summer wood; transition from spring wood to summer wood more or less abrupt; rays very faint, microscopic; resin ducts absent and resin cells few and usually widely scattered; tracheids wholly without spirals.

QUALITIES.—Very light in weight, 19 pounds per cubic foot, seasoned; very soft; very weak; shrinks and checks but little; warps little; rather coarse-grained; brittle; very durable in contact with the soil; easily worked; splits easily, but nails well.

USES.—Posts, railroad ties, shingles, etc.

Red Juniper. Red Cedar

Juniperus virginiana L.

CHARACTERISTICS.—Bark thin, light red-brown, exfoliating lengthwise into long, narrow, persistent strips, exposing the smooth, brown inner bark, frequently somewhat spirally twisted; sapwood thin, nearly white; heartwood dull red to purplish, soon becoming dull brown upon exposure to sunlight, often streaked with white; non-porous; growth rings moderate, but often very irregular in width and outline, frequently eccentric; transition from spring wood to summer wood gradual; rays indistinct with magnifier, in the heartwood deep red or purplish; resin cells very numerous, deeply colored, mostly in concentric lines, visible with magnifier and often to the unaided eye.

QUALITIES.—Light in weight, 30 pounds per cubic foot, seasoned; soft; weak; brittle; easily worked; very durable in contact with the soil; highly fragrant; usually knotty, except in very small sizes.

USES.—Lead pencils, moth-proof chests and closets, cabinet-making, interior finish, pails and woodenware, fence posts, sills, railroad ties.

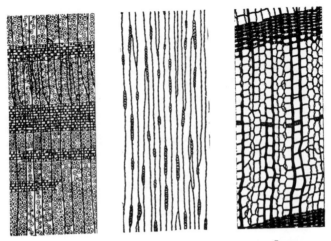

RADIAL   TANGENTIAL   CROSS

Sections of wood of Taxodium distichum, x 39.

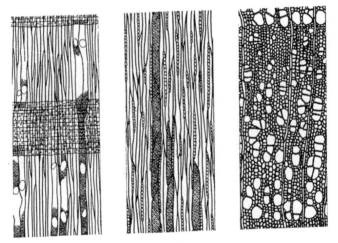

RADIAL   TANGENTIAL   CROSS

Sections of wood of Populus tremuloides, x 65.

Bald Cypress. Cypress

Taxodium distichum (L.) Richard

CHARACTERISTICS.—Bark light red, shallowly fissured into broad, flat plates and peeling into fibrous strips; sapwood thin, nearly white; heartwood dull yellow- to gray-brown or sometimes blackish, greasy or waxy to the touch; non-porous; growth rings usually very broad and well-marked by the dense and conspicuous summer wood; transition from spring wood to summer wood somewhat gradual; rays very obscure, none of them fusiform; resin ducts absent; resin cells numerous, large, more or less confluent and forming tangential lines on the cross-section; tracheids wholly without spirals.

QUALITIES.—Fairly light in weight, 29 pounds per cubic foot, seasoned; soft; rather weak; warps but little, although liable to check; close-grained; very durable in contact with the soil; easy to work; nails well; frequently "peggy" or "pecky" from a fungous disease.

USES.—Shingles, posts, interior finish, boats, cooperage greenhouse construction, etc.

Aspen

Populus tremuloides Michx.

CHARACTERISTICS.—Bark thin, yellowish or greenish and smooth, often roughened with darker, horizontal bands or wart-like excrescences; sapwood thin, whitish; heartwood light brown; diffuse-porous; growth rings very wide, not well-defined; pores more or less uniform in size, but rather more crowded in the spring wood; rays very fine and indistinct; vessels without spirals

QUALITIES.—Very light, 25 pounds per cubic foot, seasoned; soft; weak; shrinks moderately; warps considerably to excessively, but checks little; close-grained; not durable when exposed; works easily.

USES.—Paper pulp, boxes, crates, excelsior, woodenware, etc

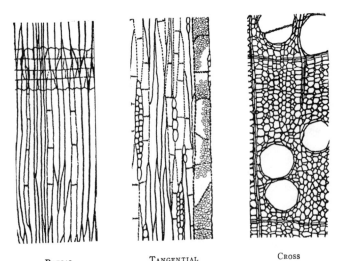

RADIAL   TANGENTIAL   CROSS

Sections of wood of Juglans nigra, x 105.

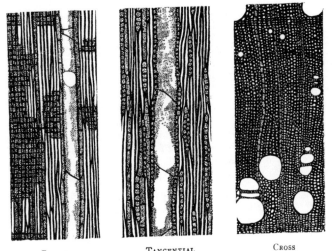

RADIAL   TANGENTIAL   CROSS

Sections of wood of Carya ovata, x 82.

Black Walnut

Juglans nigra L.

CHARACTERISTICS.—Bark thick, brownish or blackish, deeply furrowed by broad, rounded ridges; heartwood rich dark brown, with thin, lighter colored sapwood; odor mild, but characteristic; diffuse-porous; growth rings narrow, terminated by narrow bands of very thick-walled, flattened wood fibers; pores somewhat larger and more conspicuous in the spring wood, and for this reason often approaching characteristics of ring-porous wood; tyloses abundant; wood parenchyma in numerous, very fine, concentric lines, independent of the pores; rays indistinct to microscopic; vessels without spirals.

QUALITIES.—Heavy, 38 pounds per cubic foot, seasoned; hard; strong; rather coarse-grained; easily worked; susceptible to high polish; splits easily; takes glue well; durable in contact with the soil.

USES.—Furniture, cabinetmaking, interior finish, gun stocks, etc.

Shagbark Hickory. Shellbark Hickory

Carya ovata (Mill.) K. Koch

CHARACTERISTICS.—Bark thick and grayish, separating into thick strips 1-3 feet long, free at one or both ends, giving the log a shaggy appearance; sapwood thin, whitish; heartwood light brown; ring-porous; growth rings narrow, but distinctly marked by the one or more rows of relatively large pores in the spring wood; pores of the summer wood small and inconspicuous; rays numerous, but inconspicuous to microscopic; wood parenchyma forming more or less continuous, tangential lines as distinct, or nearly so, as the rays; vessels without spirals, but containing tyloses.

QUALITIES.—Very heavy, 51 pounds per cubic foot, seasoned; very hard; very strong; warps badly; straight- and close-grained; not durable when exposed; hard to split and very difficult to nail; very tough and hard to work.

USES.—Agricultural implements, handles, wagon- and carriage-stock, automobile wheels, sled runners, fuel, etc.

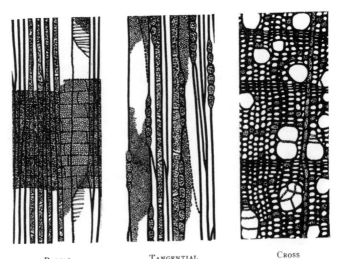

RADIAL   TANGENTIAL   CROSS

Sections of wood of Betula lutea, x 132.

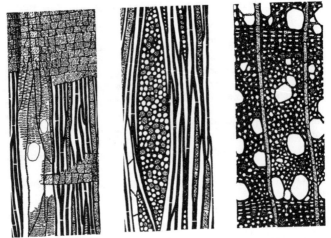

RADIAL   TANGENTIAL   CROSS

Sections of wood of Fagus grandifolia, x 128.

Yellow Birch. Gray Birch

Betula lutea Michx. f.

CHARACTERISTICS.—Bark silvery yellow-gray and breaking into strips more or less curled at the edges, or blackish and deeply and irregularly fissured into large, thin plates; sapwood thin, whitish; heartwood light brown tinged with red; diffuse-porous; growth rings fairly distinct; pores more or less uniform in size, not crowded, inconspicuous; rays numerous, indistinct; vessels without spirals.

QUALITIES.—Heavy, 40 pounds per cubic foot, seasoned; moderately hard; very strong; warps little; close-grained and compact; not durable when exposed; difficult to split and holds nails well; rather hard to work, but polishes well.

USES.—Furniture, spools, flooring, shoe lasts and pegs, handles, etc.

Beech. White Beech

Fagus grandifolia Ehrh.

CHARACTERISTICS.—Bark close, smooth, steel-gray, often mottled by darker blotches and bands; sapwood thin, whitish; heartwood light or dark red; diffuse-porous; growth rings obscure; pores largest in spring wood, gradually diminishing in size toward outer limit of summer wood; rays of two kinds, partly very broad and partly very narrow; vessels without spirals.

QUALITIES.—Heavy, 42 pounds per cubic foot, seasoned; rather hard; strong; warps and checks during seasoning; straight- and very close-grained; not durable when exposed; moderately difficult to split; tough; hard to work; difficult to nail.

USES.—Ship timbers, flooring, tool-handles, furniture, fuel, etc.

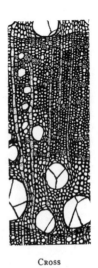

RADIAL   TANGENTIAL   CROSS

Sections of wood of Quercus alba, x 81.

RADIAL   TANGENTIAL   CROSS

Sections of wood of Quercus rubra, x 50.

White Oak
Quercus alba L.

CHARACTERISTICS.—Bark thick, light gray or whitish on old trunks, shallowly fissured into broad, flat ridges; heartwood light brown, with thin, lighter colored sapwood; ring-porous; growth rings moderately wide to narrow, marked by a narrow zone of large pores in the spring wood; transition to small pores of summer wood abrupt, the pores arranged chiefly in fan-like patches and usually too small to be distinguished by the unaided eye; wood parenchyma forming light-colored tangential lines and also surrounding the pores of the summer wood; rays of two kinds, some broad and conspicuous, some narrow and indistinct; vessels without spirals.

QUALITIES.—Heavy, 46-50 pounds per cubic foot, seasoned; hard; tough; strong; liable to check unless seasoned with care; usually straight- and close-grained; durable in contact with the soil; will take a high polish.

USES.—Ship-building, cooperage, furniture, interior finish, agricultural implements, railroad ties, fuel, etc.; one of the most generally useful timbers where a hard wood is required.

Red Oak
Quercus rubra L.

CHARACTERISTICS.—Bark gray-brown, smooth or shallowly fissured into thin, firm, broad ridges; sapwood thin, lighter than the pale red-brown heartwood; ring-porous; growth rings rather wide, distinctly marked by several rows of very large pores in the spring wood; pores of summer wood arranged in radial, branching lines, diminishing in size toward outer limits of the summer wood; wood parenchyma grouped irregularly around the pores; rays few, but mostly broad and conspicuous; vessels without spirals.

QUALITIES.—Rather heavy, 45 pounds per cubic foot, seasoned; fairly hard; rather strong; warps and checks badly; coarse-grained; moderately durable in contact with the soil; splits readily and nails badly.

USES.—Furniture, interior finish, cooperage, agricultural implements, fuel, etc.

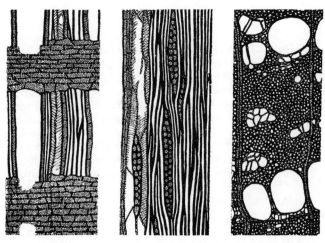

RADIAL   TANGENTIAL   CROSS

Sections of wood of Ulmus americana, x 113.

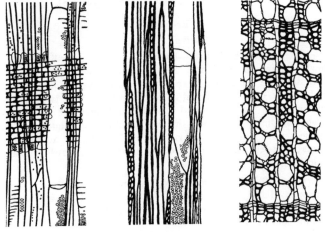

RADIAL   TANGENTIAL   CROSS

Sections of wood of Liriodendron tulipifera, x 69.

White Elm. American Elm. Water Elm

Ulmus americana L.

CHARACTERISTICS.—Bark ash-gray, deeply fissured into broad, scaly ridges; sapwood thick, yellowish; heartwood light brown; ring-porous; growth rings rather wide, distinctly marked by usually one row of large pores in the spring wood; pores of summer wood somewhat smaller, forming broad, mostly connected, tangential lines, which are strongly wavy; rays numerous, inconspicuous; vessels with spirals.

QUALITIES.—Fairly heavy, 34 pounds per cubic foot, seasoned; medium hard; fairly strong; warps and checks considerably; coarse-grained, with the fibers commonly interlaced; not durable in contact with the soil; difficult to split; tough and hard to work.

USES.—Wheel-stock, cooperage, heavy timbers, heavy agricultural implements, etc.

Tulip Poplar. Tulip-tree. White-wood

Liriodendron tulipifera L.

CHARACTERISTICS.—Bark ashy gray, thin and scaly on young trunks, with age becoming thick, brownish and deeply furrowed with rounded ridges; inner bark intensely bitter; sapwood thin, cream-white, often variegated or striped; heartwood variable, light yellow to green, or brownish, depending upon age and locality; growth rings relatively narrow to moderately wide, defined by a distinct light-colored line; pores visible only with magnifier, usually numerous, rather uniformly distributed throughout the ring; wood parenchyma confined to a narrow line terminating the growth ring; rays numerous, fine, but distinct to the unaided eye; vessels without spirals.

QUALITIES.—Light, 26 pounds per cubic foot, seasoned; soft; rather weak, brittle; straight-grained; easily worked; not durable in contact with the soil; comparatively tough; hard to split.

USES.—Construction work, interior finish, woodenware, shelves, drawer-bottoms, plywood for furniture, shingles, boat-building, and in fact wherever a soft, easily-worked wood is required.

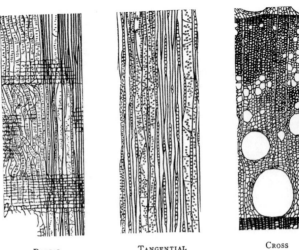

RADIAL   TANGENTIAL   CROSS

Sections of wood of Castanea dentata, x 45.

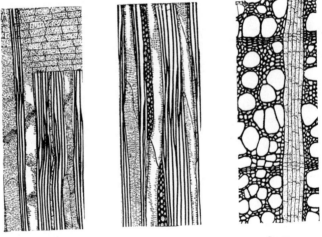

RADIAL   TANGENTIAL   CROSS

Sections of wood of Platanus occidentalis, x 108.

Chestnut

Castanea dentata (Marsh.) Borkh.

CHARACTERISTICS.—Bark thick, gray-brown, shallowly fissured into broad, flat ridges; heartwood gray-brown, yellow-brown or red-brown, with very thin, lighter colored sapwood; ring-porous; growth rings mostly moderate in width, but highly variable; pores in spring wood very numerous, large, mostly oval or elliptical, open or plugged with tyloses, forming a broad ring; pores of summer wood very small and numerous, arranged in irregular, branched, radial bands; wood parenchyma scattered among the pores, indistinct; rays all very fine, barely distinct with magnifier; vessels without spirals.

QUALITIES.—Light, 28 pounds per cubic foot, seasoned; soft; weak; straight- and very coarse-grained; easily split; liable to check and warp in drying; very durable in contact with the soil.

USES.—Cheap furniture, interior finish, railroad ties, telegraph poles, fence posts and rails, a source of tannin extract, etc.

Sycamore. Button-wood. Buttonball-tree

Platanus occidentalis L.

CHARACTERISTICS.—Bark thick, red-brown, broken into oblong, plate-like scales, separating higher up on the trunk into large thin plates which peel off, exposing the greenish or yellowish inner bark; sapwood thick, pale yellow; heartwood light red-brown; diffuse-porous; growth rings moderately wide to wide, terminating in narrow, light colored bands of summer wood; pores small, crowded, fairly uniform in size and distribution throughout the ring; wood parenchyma not visible, even with magnifier; rays nearly all broad, appearing in radial-section as conspicuous and attractive red-brown flakes; vessels without spirals.

QUALITIES.—Moderately heavy, 35 pounds per cubic foot, seasoned; fairly hard and compact, though not very strong; cross-grained, difficult to work; takes a high polish; stands up well when not exposed; warps badly when sawed into lumber.

USES.—Butchers' blocks, tobacco boxes, crating, cabinetwork, furniture, interior finish, fuel, etc.

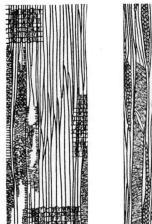
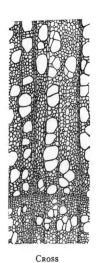

RADIAL   TANGENTIAL   CROSS

Sections of wood of Prunus serotina, x 63.

RADIAL   TANGENTIAL   CROSS

Sections of wood of Acer saccharum, x 105.

Black Cherry

Prunus serotina Ehrh.

CHARACTERISTICS.—Bark on young trunks red-brown, smooth, with conspicuous, whitish, horizontal lenticels, the outer layer peeling off in strips transversely, becoming thin, almost black, and broken into scaly plates with age; inner bark of twigs bitter; sapwood thin, yellow, in contrast to the rich, red-brown heartwood; diffuse-porous; growth rings moderately wide, fairly distinct; pores small, not visible to the unaided eye, evenly distributed, or gradually decreasing in size and number in the summer wood; rays fine, but very distinct; wood parenchyma not noticeable; vessels with spirals.

QUALITIES.—Moderately heavy, 36 pounds per cubic foot, seasoned; rather hard and strong; fine- and fairly straight-grained; easily worked; does not warp or split in seasoning.

USES.—One of the most valuable and popular of our native woods and valued from pioneer days for cabinetmaking, furniture and the interior finish of houses.

Sugar Maple. Hard Maple. Rock Maple

Acer saccharum Marsh.

CHARACTERISTICS.—Bark dark gray and deeply furrowed, often cleaving up at one edge in long, thick plates; sapwood thin, lighter colored than the light brown heartwood; diffuse-porous; growth rings narrow, but distinct; pores somewhat uniform in size, not crowded, inconspicuous; rays fine, but distinct; vessels with spirals.

QUALITIES.—Heavy, 43 pounds per cubic foot, seasoned; very hard; very strong; warps badly; close-grained, but the fibers sometimes twisted, waved or curly, producing "bird's eye" and "curly" effects; not durable when exposed; wears evenly; splits badly in nailing; hard to work.

USES.—Flooring, fuel, furniture, wagon-stock, carving, tool-handles, etc.

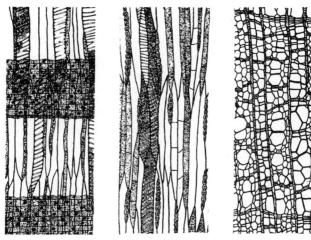

RADIAL   TANGENTIAL   CROSS

Sections of wood of Tilia americana, x 91.

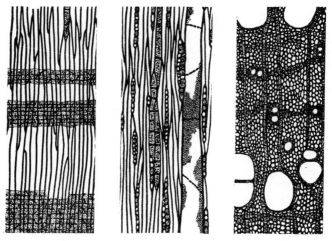

RADIAL   TANGENTIAL   CROSS

Sections of wood of Fraxinus americana, x 75.

Basswood. Linden

Tilia americana L.

CHARACTERISTICS.—Bark thick, dark gray or brownish, deeply furrowed into broad, scaly ridges; inner bark fibrous and tough; sapwood thick, light red-brown to nearly white, hardly distinguishable from the heartwood; diffuse-porous; growth rings rather narrow, but distinct; pores all the same size or nearly so, rather evenly distributed; rays numerous, obscure; wood parenchyma forming continuous or somewhat broken, tangential lines or bands, alternating with wood elements in a tier-like arrangement; vessels with spirals.

QUALITIES.—Light in weight, 28 pounds per cubic foot, seasoned; very soft; very weak; very straight- and close-grained; warps comparatively little; not durable in contact with the soil; somewhat tough to split and nails well; very easily worked.

USES.—Carriage and wagon bodies, woodenware, boxes, toys, numerous small articles, etc.

White Ash

Fraxinus americana L.

CHARACTERISTICS.—Bark gray, deeply furrowed into firm, narrow, flattened ridges; sapwood thick, whitish; heartwood brownish; ring-porous; growth rings rather narrow, distinctly marked by 3-5 rows of large pores in the spring wood; pores of the summer wood small and inconspicuous, joined by wood parenchyma to form short, broken, tangential lines, especially near the periphery of the growth ring; rays inconspicuous to microscopic; vessels without spirals.

QUALITIES.—Fairly heavy, 39 pounds per cubic foot, seasoned; rather hard; fairly strong; warps little; straight- and close-grained; not durable in contact with the soil; splits readily and nails badly; becomes brittle with age.

USES.—Farm implements, oars, handles, interior finish, cheap cabinet-work, carriage-stock, etc.

RADIAL   TANGENTIAL   CROSS

Sections of wood of Swietenia mahogani, x 60.
(Nicaraugua)

Mahogany

Swietenia mahogani Jacq.

CHARACTERISTICS.—The true mahogany is native to Central America, in a region extending from the extreme southern part of Florida to the West Indies and along the Gulf Coast from Tampico to the northern part of South America. Other mahoganies come from Africa and India, and there are many other woods which are sold as mahogany. Mahogany woods from different localities vary widely in their properties. Some are heavy and hard, while others are light and soft. Under the circumstances, exact description is impossible. The bark is rough, dark reddish brown, fissured into rather narrow, scaly ridges; sapwood pinkish, pale yellow to nearly colorless, thin in old trees; heartwood rich red-brown, the freshly sawed lumber turning red on the surface when exposed to the sun, and darkening with age; growth rings often indistinct; rays numerous, fine, but distinct; diffuse-porous, the pores large to small, uniform in size and distribution, often filled with dark red gum or whitish deposits; wood parenchyma conspicuous, in few widely separated tangential lines terminating the growth rings and also about the pores; vessels without spirals; wood often highly figured.

QUALITIES.—Light to heavy, 24-52 pounds per cubic foot, seasoned; soft to hard; strong; brittle; seasons well without serious shrinkage, checking or warping; not readily susceptible to atmospheric changes; very durable; holds glue; takes stains and can be polished; works readily.

USES.—Cabinetmaking, veneers, furniture, interior finish; prized by ship-builders.

A LIST OF WOODS ARRANGED IN THE ORDER OF THEIR WEIGHT FROM HEAVY TO LIGHT

1. Shagbark Hickory
2. Hornbeam. Ironwood
3. Flowering Dogwood
4. Osage Orange
5. Sweet Birch
6. White Oak
7. Locust. Black Locust
8. Hackberry
9. Blue Beech
10. Mahogany
11. Canada Plum
12. Haw. Thorn. Hawthorn
13. Yellow Oak. Black Oak
14. Coffeetree. Kentucky Coffeetree
15. Sugar Maple
16. Beech. White Beech
17. Honey Locust
18. Yellow Birch
19. White Ash
20. Red Oak
21. White Elm. American Elm
22. Black Gum. Pepperidge
23. Tamarack
24. Red Maple
25. Black Walnut
26. Red Mulberry
27. Black Cherry
28. Sycamore. Button-wood
29. Mountain Ash
30. Sassafras
31. Red Juniper. Red Cedar
32. Red Pine. Norway Pine
33. Largetooth Aspen
34. Black Spruce
35. Bald Cypress. Cypress
36. Ohio Buckeye
37. Basswood
38. Chestnut
39. Black Willow
40. Boxelder
41. Hemlock
42. Tulip Poplar. White-wood
43. Redwood
44. Hardy Catalpa
45. Butternut
46. White Spruce
47. Aspen
48. White Pine
49. Balsam Fir
50. Arborvitae. White Cedar.

GLOSSARY

With page references to explanatory figures

Abortion. Imperfect development or non-development of an organ or part.

Acorn. The fruit of the oak, consisting of a nut with its base enclosed in a cup of imbricated scales.

Acuminate. Gradually tapering to the apex. Page 12.

Acute. Terminating with a sharp angle. Page 12.

Alternate. Said of leaves, branches, buds, etc., scattered singly along the stem; not opposite.

Androgynous. Composed of both staminate and pistillate flowers.

Anterior. The front side of a flower, remote from the axis of inflorescence.

Anther. The part of a stamen which bears the pollen. Page 13.

Apetalous. Without petals.

Apex. The top, as the tip of a bud or the end of a leaf which is opposite the petiole.

Apiculate. Ending in a short-pointed tip.

Appressed. Lying close and flat against.

Arborescent. Attaining the size or character of a tree.

Aromatic. Fragrant; with an agreeable odor.

Axil. The upper one of the angles formed by the juncture of a leaf with a stem.

Axillary. Situated in an axil.

Bark. The outer covering of a trunk or branch.

Bast fibers. Attenuated, sharp-pointed, thick-walled cells, which give strength and protection to the tissues of the stem. Page 283.

Bearded. Bearing a long, bristle-like appendage, or furnished with long or stiff hairs.

Berry. A fruit which is fleshy throughout.

Bipinnate. Twice pinnate.

Blade. The expanded portion of a leaf, etc.

Bloom. A powdery or waxy substance easily rubbed off.

Bordered pit. A type of pit in which the cavity is partly enclosed by overhanging portions of the cell-wall, appearing in surface view as a bright spot or slit within a circle or ellipse. Page 283.

Borer. A beetle or other insect that bores, usually in the larval state, in wood.

Bract. A more or less modified leaf subtending a flower or belonging to an inflorescence.

Branch. A secondary division of a trunk.

Branchlet. A small branch.

Bud. An undeveloped stem or branch, with or without scales.

Bud-scales. Modified leaves covering a bud.

Bundle-scars. Dots on the surface of a leaf-scar, which are scars left by the vascular bundles which run through the petiole into the blade of the leaf. Page 16.

Bur. A spiny fruit.

Calyx. The outer part of a perianth, usually green in color. Page 13.

Cambium. A layer of cells between wood and bark, capable of producing new elements, by which the stem grows in diameter; it is this layer which is torn when bark is stripped from a living tree.

Campanulate. Bell-shaped.

Capsule. A dry fruit of more than one carpel which splits at maturity to release the seeds.

Carpel. A simple pistil, or one member of a compound pistil.

Catkin. A spike of unisexual flowers, each subtended by a bract, and usually deciduous in one piece.

Cell. The unit of structure of living things. Page 283.

Chambered. Said of pith which is interrupted by hollow spaces.

Ciliate. Fringed with hairs on the margin.

Cinereous. Ash-gray color.

Claw. The narrow, stalk-like base of a petal, sepal, etc.

Cleft. Cut about half-way to the middle.

Cluster. A group of two or more organs (flowers, fruit, etc.) on a plant at a node or end of a stem.

Compound. Composed of two or more similar parts united into a whole. *Compound leaf,* one divided into separate leaflets.

Compressed. Flattened laterally.

Concentric. One within another, with a common center.

Cone. A fruit with woody, overlapping scales.

Confluent. Blended or flowing into one; passing by degrees one into the other.

Conical. Cone-shaped, largest at the base and tapering to the apex.

Conifer. A tree of the pine family, so called from its bearing cones.

Coniferous. Cone-bearing; of, or pertaining to, the pine family.

Connective. The portion of a stamen which connects the two lobes of the anther.

Cordate. Heart-shaped. Page 12.

Coriaceous. Leather-like in texture.

Corky. Made of, or like cork.

Corolla. The inner part of a perianth, usually bright colored. Page 13.

Corymb. A flower-cluster in which the axis is shortened and the pedicels of the lower flowers lengthened, forming a flat-topped inflorescence, the marginal flowers blooming first. Page 14.

Corymbose. Arranged in corymbs.

Crenate. Dentate, with the teeth much rounded. Page 13.

Crenulate. Finely crenate.

Cross-. Said of a section cut at right angles to the long axis. The end cut of a tree trunk shows a cross-section of the annual layers of growth. Page 281.

Cross-grained. Having the grain gnarled and hard to cut.

Crown. The upper part of a tree, including the living branches with their foliage.

Cutting. A piece of the stem, root or leaf which, if cut off and placed in contact with the soil, will form new roots and buds, reproducing the parent plant.

Cyme. A broad and flattish inflorescence, the central flowers of which bloom first. Page 14.

Cymose. Arranged in cymes.

Deciduous. Not persistent; falling away, as the leaves of a tree in autumn.

Decurrent. Said of a leaf which extends down the stem below the point of fastening.

Decussate. Alternating in pairs at right angles.

Dehiscent. Opening by valves or slits.

Deltoid. Delta-shaped.

Dentate. Toothed, with the teeth usually pointed and directed outward. Page 13.

Depressed. Somewhat flattened from above.

Dichotomous. Branching regularly in pairs.

Diffuse-porous. Said of the wood of broad-leaved trees in which the pores are of practically uniform size throughout the growth ring, or decrease only slightly toward the outer portion of the summer wood. See *ring-porous.*

Digitate. Said of a compound leaf in which the leaflets are borne at the apex of the petiole; finger-shaped.

Dioecious. Unisexual, with staminate and pistillate flowers on different individuals.

Dispersal. The various ways by which seeds are scattered.

Dissected. Cut or divided into numerous segments.

Distribution. The geographical extent and limits of a species.

Divergent. Said of buds, cones, etc., which point away from the twig, or of pine needles, etc., which spread apart.

Dormant. A term applied to parts which are not in active life.

Dorsal. Pertaining to the back or outer surface of an organ.

Downy. Covered with fine hairs.

Drupe. A fleshy or pulpy fruit in which the inner portion is hard or stony.

Ellipsoid. An elliptical solid.

Elliptical. Oval or oblong with regularly rounded ends. Page 12.

Emarginate. Notched at the apex. Page 12.

Entire. Without divisions, lobes or teeth.

Escape. Any plant formerly cultivated that grows wild in fields.

Excrescences. Warty outgrowths or protuberances.

Exfoliate. To cleave off, as of the outer layers of bark.

Exposure. Situation.

Falcate. Scythe-shaped.

Fascicle. A compact cluster of leaves or flowers.

Fascicled. Arranged in fascicles.

Fastigiate. Said of branches which are erect and near together.

Feather-veined. Having veins extending from the midrib to the margin, feather-wise.

Fertile. Capable of bearing fruit.

Fertilization. The mingling of the contents of a male (pollen) and female (ovule) cell.

Filament. The part of a stamen which bears the anther. Page 13.

Filamentose or Filamentous. Composed of threads or filaments.

Flaky. With loose scales easily rubbed off (bark).

Fleshy. Succulent; juicy.

Flexuous. Zigzag; bending alternately in opposite directions.

Flora. The wild plants of a particular region or area.

Flower. An axis bearing stamens or pistils or both (calyx and corolla usually accompany these). Page 13.

Fluted. With rounded ridges.

Frond-like. Like the leaf of Ferns.

Fruit. The part of a plant which bears the seed.

Fungous. Relating to the *Fungi,* i.e., plant organisms of a lower order destitute of chlorophyll.

Fusiform. Thick, but tapering towards each end, like a spindle.

Germinate. To sprout, as of a seed.

Gibbous. Swollen on one side.

Glabrous. Neither rough, pubescent, nor hairy; smooth.

Gland. Secreting surface or structure; a protuberance having the appearance of such an organ.

Glandular. Bearing glands.

Glaucous. Covered or whitened with bloom.

Globose. Spherical or nearly so.

Globular. Nearly globose.

Grain or Graining. A general term used in reference to the arrangement or direction of the wood elements and to the relative width of the growth rings.

Gregarious. Growing in groups or colonies.

Growth ring. The layer of wood produced in a single growing season; in a cross-section of the stem, these layers appear as concentric rings of growth. Same as annual ring. Page 281

Habit. The general appearance of a plant, best seen from a distance.

Habitat. The place where a plant naturally grows, as in water clay soil, marsh, etc.

Hairy. With long hairs.

Halberd-shaped. Like an arrow-head, but with the basal lobes pointing outward nearly at right angles. Page 12.

Hardwood. A broad-leaved tree; the wood of such a tree.

Heartwood. The dead central portion of the trunk or large branch of a tree.

Herb. A plant with no persistent stem above ground.

Hirsute. Covered with rather coarse or stiff hairs.

Hoary. Gray-white with a fine, close pubescence.

Homogeneous. Uniform; composed of similar parts or elements.

Host. A plant which nourishes a parasite.

Hybrid. A cross between two nearly related species, formed by the action of the pollen of one upon the pistil of the other, yielding an intermediate form.

Hybridize. Forming a cross-breed of two species.

Imbricate. Overlapping, like the shingles on a roof.

Indehiscent. Not opening by valves or slits; remaining persistently closed.

Indigenous. Native and original to a region.

Inflorescence. The flowering part of a plant, and especially its arrangement.

Internode. The portion of a stem between two nodes.

Intolerant. Incapable of recovery after suppression.

Involucral. Pertaining to an involucre.

Involucre. A circle of bracts surrounding a flower or cluster of flowers.

Keeled. With a central ridge like the keel of a boat.

Laciniate. Cut into narrow, pointed lobes.

Lanceolate. Lance-shaped, broadest above the base and tapering to the apex, but several times longer than wide. Page 12.

Lateral. Situated on the side of a branch.

Lax. Loose.

Leaf. The green expansions borne by the branches of a tree, consisting of a blade with or without a petiole.

Leaflet. One of the small blades of a compound leaf.

Leaf-scar. The scar left on a twig by the falling of a leaf. Page 16.

Legume. A pod-like fruit composed of a solitary carpel and usually splitting open by both sutures (*Leguminosae*).

Lenticels. Corky growths on young bark which admit air to the interior of a twig or branch.

Linear. Long and narrow, with parallel edges (as pine needles) Page 12.

Lobe. Any division of an organ, especially if rounded.

Lobed. Provided with a lobe or lobes. Page 13.

Luster. Brilliancy or sheen; gloss.

Lustrous. Glossy; shining.

Medullary rays. Strips or strands of tissue in the stem extending from the pith toward the bark, appearing on the cross-section of the wood as radiating lines crossing the growth rings at right angles. Page 281.

Membranaceous. Thin and somewhat translucent.

Midrib. The central vein of a leaf or leaflet.

Monoecious. Unisexual, with staminate and pistillate flowers on the same individual.

Mucilaginous. Slimy; resembling or secreting mucilage or gum.

Mucronate. Tipped with a small, abrupt point. Page 12.

Naked. Lacking its usual covering, as without pubescence, or flowers lacking the perianth, or buds without scales.

Naturalized. Said of introduced plants which are reproducing by self-sown seeds.

Nectariferous. Producing nectar.

Node. The place upon a stem which normally bears a leaf or whorl of leaves.

Non-porous. Said of wood whose structure is homogeneous, without large pores.

Nut. A hard and indehiscent, 1-celled, 1-seeded fruit.

Nutlet. A diminutive nut.

Oblanceolate. Lanceolate, with the broadest part toward the apex. Page 12.

Oblique. Slanting, or with unequal sides.

Oblong. Longer than broad, with sides approximately parallel. Page 12.

Obovate. Ovate, with the broadest part toward the apex. Page 12.

Obovoid. An ovate solid with the broadest part toward the apex.

Obtuse. Blunt or rounded at the apex. Page 12.

Opaque. Dull; neither shining nor translucent.

Opposite. Said of leaves, branches, buds, etc., on opposite sides of a stem at a node.

Orbicular. Circular. Page 12.

Oval. Broadly elliptical. Page 12.

Ovary. The part of a pistil that contains the ovules. Page 13.

Ovate. Shaped like the longitudinal section of a hen's egg, with the broad end basal. Page 12.

Ovoid. Solid ovate or solid oval.

Ovulate. Bearing ovules.

Ovule. The part of a flower which after fertilization becomes the seed.

Palmate. Radiately lobed or divided; hand-shaped.

Panicle. A loose, irregularly compound inflorescence with pedicellate flowers. Page 14.

Paniculate. Arranged in panicles or resembling a panicle.

Papilionaceous. Butterfly-like, as in flowers of the *Leguminosae*.

Pedicel. The stalk of a single flower in a compound inflorescence.

Pedicellate. Borne on a pedicel.

Peduncle. A primary flower-stalk, supporting either a cluster or a solitary flower.

Pendent. Hanging downward.

Pendulous. More or less hanging or declined.

Perfect. Said of a flower with both stamens and pistil. Page 13.

Perianth. The calyx and corolla of a flower considered as a whole.

Periphery. Circumference.

Persistent. Long-continuous, as leaves through the winter, calyx on the fruit, etc.

Petal. One of the divisions of a corolla. Page 13.

Petiolate. Having a petiole.

Petiole. The stem or stalk of a leaf.

Petiolulate. Having a petiolule.

Petiolule. The stem or stalk of a leaflet.

Pilose. Hairy with long, soft hairs.

Pinnate. Compound, with the leaflets arranged along both sides of a common petiole.

Pistil. The seed-bearing organ of a flower, normally consisting of ovary, style and stigma. Page 13.

Pistillate. Provided with a pistil, but usually without stamens.

Pit. A term used in wood structure, referring to an unthickened spot or small, thin area in the cell-wall, providing for interchange of fluids between cells. Page 283.

Pith. The softer central part of a twig or stem. Pages 16, 281.

Pith flecks. The tunnels made by the larvae of an insect, appearing on the cross-section of certain woods as crescent-shaped, discolored patches, the presence of which may aid in the identification.

Plumose. Having fine hairs on each side, like the plume of a feather.

Pod. A dry and many-seeded, dehiscent fruit.

Pollen. The fecundating grains borne in the anther.

Polygamo-dioecious. Sometimes perfect, sometimes unisexual, both forms borne on different individuals.

Polygamo-monoecious. Sometimes perfect, sometimes unisexual, both forms borne on the same individual.

Polygamous. Sometimes perfect, sometimes unisexual, both forms borne on the same or on different individuals.

Pome. A fleshy fruit, as the apple.

Pores. A term applied to the vessels when seen in cross-section, appearing on the cross-section of wood of broad-leaved trees as holes or openings.

Porous. Having large pores visible to the unaided eye. See *ring-porous* and *diffuse-porous.*

Posterior. The back side of a flower, next to the axis of inflorescence.

Prickle. A small spine growing from the bark.

Procumbent. A term descriptive of the cells making up a medullary ray, when they are elongated in a radial direction, as seen in radial-section; lying on the ground or trailing, but without rooting at the nodes.

Protoplasm. The living matter of cells, into which all nourishment is taken and from which all parts are formed.

Puberulent. Minutely pubescent.

Puberulous. Minutely pubescent.

Pubescence. A covering of short, soft hairs.

Pubescent. Covered with short, soft hairs.

Punctate. Dotted with translucent or colored dots or pits.

Pyramidal. Shaped like a pyramid, with the broadest part near the base.

Pungent. Ending in a sharp point; acrid.

Raceme. A simple inflorescence of flowers on pedicels of equal length arranged on a common, elongated axis (rachis). Page 14.

Racemose. Resembling a raceme.

Rachis. The central axis of a spike or raceme of flowers or of a compound leaf.

Radial-. Said of a section cut lengthwise and which passes through the center or pith of a stem or tree trunk, i.e., parallel to a medullary ray. Page 281.

Rays. See *medullary rays;* a term used for brevity.

Receptacle. The more or less expanded portion of an axis which bears the organs of a flower.

Recurved. Curved downward or backward.

Reforestation. The process of putting a forest growth upon an area which had its forest growth removed recently.

Regeneration. Formation of new plants, tissues or parts to supply those which have been lost.

Remotely. Scattered; not close together.

Resin cells. Usually cylindrical or prismatic, thin-walled cells, provided with simple pits and filled with resin; usually invisible without the microscope, but in mass sometimes visible to the unaided eye.

Resin ducts. Long, narrow channels between the elements of the wood, filled with resin.

Reticulate. Netted.

Ring-porous. Said of the wood of broad-leaved trees in which the pores are comparatively large at the beginning of each growth ring and decrease in size more or less abruptly toward the summer wood, forming a distinct ring of large pores in the spring wood.

Rough. Harsh to the touch; pubescent.

Rugose. Wrinkled.

Rust. A fungous disease.

Samara. An indehiscent winged fruit.

Sapwood. The outer portion of a trunk or large branch of a tree between the heartwood and the bark, containing the only living elements of the wood. Page 281.

Scalariform. Having markings suggestive of a ladder.

Scales. Small modified leaves, usually thin and scarious, seen in buds and cones; the flakes into which the outer bark often divides.

Scaly. Provided with scales.

Scarious. Thin, dry, membranaceous; not green.

Sculptured. Having raised or grooved markings on the surface.

Scurfy. Covered with small bran-like scales.

Seed. The ripened ovule.

Segment. One of the parts of a structure that is cleft or divided.

Sepal. One of the divisions of a calyx. Page 13.

Seriate. A term usually applied to designate the width of the medullary rays, as seen in tangential-section, referring to the number of cells making up the width of the ray.

Serrate. Toothed, the teeth sharp and pointing forward. Page 13.

Sessile. Without a stalk.

Sheath. A thin enveloping part as of a leaf; any body enwrapping a stem.

Shrub. A bushy, woody growth, usually branched at or near the base, less than 15 feet in height.

Simple. Of one piece; not compound.

Sinuate. Strongly wavy. Page 13.

Sinuous. In form like the path of a snake.

Sinus. The cleft or space between two lobes.

Smooth. Smooth to the touch; not pubescent.

Spatulate. Wide and rounded at the apex, but gradually narrowed downward. Page 12.

Species. The aggregate of all those individuals which have the same constant and distinctive characters; the unit in classification. Page 10.

Sphagnous. Resembling or allied to the genus *Sphagnum,* a moss.

Spike. A simple inflorescence of sessile flowers arranged on a common, elongated axis (rachis) Page 14.

Spine. A sharp woody outgrowth from a stem.

Spirals. Spiral thickenings or markings on the inner walls of tracheids and vessels. Page 283.

Spray. The aggregate of smaller branches and branchlets.

Spring wood. That portion of a growth ring which is formed in the spring; the softer, more open wood on the inner side of the growth ring.

Stamen. The pollen-bearing organ of a flower, normally consisting of filament and anther. Page 13.

Staminate. Provided with stamens, but usually without pistils.

Staminodium. A sterile stamen.

Stellate. Star-shaped.

Sterile. Unproductive, as a flower without pistil, or a stamen without anther.

Stigma. The part of a pistil which receives the pollen. Page 13.

Stipules. Leaf-like appendages on either side of a leaf at the base of the petiole.

Stipule-scar. The scar left by the fall of a stipule. Page 15.

Striate. Marked with fine longitudinal stripes or ridges.

Strobile. A cone.

Style. The part of a pistil connecting ovary with stigma. Page 13.

Sub-. A prefix applied to many botanical terms, indicating somewhat or slightly.

Subtend. To lie under or opposite to.

Sucker. A shoot arising from a subterranean part of a plant.

Summer wood. That portion of a growth ring which is formed in the summer; the harder, denser wood on the outer side of the growth ring.

Superposed. Placed above, as one bud above another at a node.

Suture. A junction or line of dehiscence.

Tangential-. Said of a section cut lengthwise but which does not pass through the center or pith of a stem or tree trunk, i.e., at right angles to the medullary rays. Page 281.

Terete. Circular in cross-section.

Terminal. Situated at the end of a branch.

Ternate. In threes.

Tetrahedral. Having, or made up of, four faces (triangles).

Texture. A term referring to the relative size, quality or fineness of the elements as related to the structural properties of wood.

Thorn. A stiff, woody, sharp-pointed projection.

Tissue. The texture or material built up by the union of cells of similar origin and character.

Tolerant. Capable of enduring more or less heavy shade.

Tomentose. Densely pubescent with matted wool.

Toothed. With teeth or short projections.

Torus. The part of the axis of a flower which bears the floral organs.

Trachea. Same as *vessel*.

Tracheids. Elongated cells with pointed ends, characterized by bordered pits in their side-walls and sometimes by spiral thickenings on the inner walls. Page 283.

Transition. Change, as from spring wood to summer wood.

Transverse. Said of a wood section made at right angles with the axis of the stem; across the grain.

Tree. Usually defined as a plant with a woody stem, unbranched at or near the base, reaching a height of at least 15 feet.

Truncate. Ending abruptly, as if cut off at the end.

Trunk. The main stem of a tree.

Turbinate. Top-shaped.

Tyloses. Balloon-like ingrowths in vessels and ducts formed from neighboring parenchyma cells, which crowd through the wall-pits and, when abundant, are plainly visible to the unaided eye as a glistening, froth-like mass.

Umbel. A simple inflorescence of flowers on pedicels which radiate from the same point. Page 14.

Umbellate. Arranged in umbels.

Undulate. With a wavy margin or surface. Page 13.

Uniseriate. In a single row or series. See *seriate*.

Unisexual. Of one sex, either staminate or pistillate; not perfect.

-valved. Referring to the pieces into which a capsule splits.

Vascular bundle. A strand-like portion of the conducting system of a plant.

Veins. Threads of vascular tissue in a leaf, petal, or other flat organ.

Vessel. A tube-like duct, made continuous by the more or less complete absorption of the cross-walls of the cells of which it was originally composed, and characterized by pits or spiral thickenings or both. Their function is to facilitate the ascent of water in the stem. Page 283.

Villose or *Villous.* Covered with long, soft hairs.

Viscid. Glutinous: sticky.

Whorl. An arrangement of leaves or branches in a circle round an axis.

Wing. Any membranous or thin expansion bordering or surrounding an organ.

Wood. The hard part of a stem lying between the pith and the bark.

Wood elements. The cells or units making up the wood.

Wood parenchyma. A vertical series of more or less elongated cells placed end to end, the abundance and distribution of which, as seen in the cross-section of wood, is important in identification of the species. Page 283.

Woolly. Covered with long and matted or tangled hairs.

INDEX